THE

MW01114990

"Whosever therefore shall humble himself as this little child, the same is
the greatest in the kingdom of heaven."
Matthew 18:4

THE MAKING OF ETERNAL RELATIONSHIPS WITH YOUR CHILDREN

By: Lawrence A. Bradley, M.A. LMFT

ACKNOWLEDGEMENTS

I would like to offer a special thanks to everyone that helped with this project, especially my family that sacrificed much while I was writing. For the past year, I have averaged about 18 hours of being up, working to provide for my family and writing between those hours where I was not working for them. They have been the cause of my efforts and I wish to express my love for each of them.

I would also like to thank those that continued to show interest and encouraged me to keep writing. I have had many good neighbors and even the community to which I belong, pushing me to keep going.

To Vicki Walker, my sister, an incredibly talented individual, I would like to thank for her willingness to read the manuscript and provide helpful feedback; and to Gary Farnsworth who has assisted with some of the editing issues in spite of his own very busy schedule. To both of them I wish to acknowledge as great and trusted sounding boards.

Finally, to Rod Peterson for providing a wonderful picture for the book cover. I like the picture because you can see in the countenances of all of the children, regardless of age, a belief that they are important to the Master. I believe it captures the main theme of this book that children need and want to know of their importance, their acceptability and capability. We act in partnership with the Savior in providing and shaping such beliefs.

Artist Website: www.gethsemanefineart.com

A Quick Note to Every Reader

This book is integrative in nature, meaning that it references religious writings in support of the material being presented. For those that desire to more fully appreciate the author's message are invited to turn to Appendix A, "Navigating Scriptural References" for instructions on how to get the most out of this work.

In the Introduction of this book, I give a *valid* reason to explore the scriptural references, recognizing that many that will read this book are not religious and may have certain prejudices against material presented from a religious or spiritual basis. As I state in the Introduction, the purpose of my approach is not to "convert" but to examine what is being taught and how it helps children to live with understanding and purpose.

The family is central to the Creator's plan for the eternal destiny of His children. This is a tenet of faith for Latter Day Saints and in many others a rational conclusion. The foundation of society is the home. As such, it becomes our responsibility as parents to instill within our children the *beliefs* they need that will elicit the thoughts and behaviors leading to living productive, meaningful, and happy lives – as such, societies function better.

What our children become to be, so becomes the world. Better families begin with training a better generation. As we view world trends, the need for more effective parents is obvious. It is in the home where virtue is planted, the place where personal belief systems are developed that engender good character, and where healthy relationships are formed. A better tomorrow begins in each of our homes.

It has been my experience in training parents, that emotions can easily be elicited. There is no intent on the author's part to make anyone feel bad, yet the information provided herein will naturally create reflection. The intent and hope of the author is to illuminate how parents can be *more effective* in rearing their children. It is about starting today to do something different that will promote better relationships and happier children. Let us not become burdened with any past parenting mishaps; instead, let us take the energy of regret and turn it into the energy of creating families that desire to be with one another for eternity!

1

Table of Contents

Preface

Humbling ourselves as little children has everything to do with placing ourselves in a position to listen, learn and *believe*.

> We must "humble [our]selves and become as little children, ... submissive, meek, humble, patient, full of love, willing to submit to all things which the Lord seeth fit to inflict upon [us], even as a child doth submit to his father" (Mosiah 3:18–19).

Why a book about becoming like little children in order to parent our children? In the increasing knowledge that is filling the earth (Isaiah 11:9), the Lord has declared that the purpose of this increase was so that we can magnify our callings and mission (D&C 88:80). Elder James E. Faust provided the following:

> "Being a father or a mother is not only a great challenge; it is a divine *calling*..." (The Greatest Challenge, October General Conference, 1990)

God is preparing his people to fortify their families, so that we might come off conquerors in the increasing battle for the family. There are already many wounds afflicted, severe deep wounds to society's understanding of the nature and purpose of families. Our survival may require fundamental change in some of our approaches to parenting if we are going to experience healing and strength to get our families through the battle and into a place of safety.

Our desire to look at our parenting styles and interactions with our children may be influenced by recent scientific discoveries of anatomy and physiology. Our ability to now peer at physiological structures, such as cells and DNA; and watch how these structures respond to environmental influences informs us on how individual belief and behavior are shaped within our children.

The ongoing theme of this book is to have parents be highly aware that every interaction they are having with their children is influencing their child's personal belief system, which is being recorded in the source of ongoing genetic instructions used in the development and functioning of all living organisms. If encoded upon that genetic material are repeated messages that the child has worth, is acceptable, needed and capable, then that child will have developed a belief system that is filled with motivation, energy, and emotional stability. On the other hand, if our interactions send the message that our child is bad, incapable, a disappointment and only acceptable when they are doing what we want them to do, then that child will have developed a sense of shame and doubt, accompanied by emotional unrest, and energy directed toward proving worth, or worse, a lack of motivation to improve one's station.

Fundamentally, it is the child's personal assessment of self, the experienced identity which shapes the child's personal belief system. Whatever that belief system is, it is from that source that the child's thoughts and behaviors are organized.

Many, many parents experience the "twighlight zone" effect when they observe their child's behaviors, not understanding why their child has chosen a course that leads to unhappiness. As such parents delve deeper into understanding their child they are met with even further confusion as they discover that their child perceives themselves differently than the way the parent perceives him or her. How did this all happen? How did we get to this point? What do I do now? Each of these questions grows out of our desire to see our children not live a life filled with unnecessary pain and heartache. We also worry about the ongoing impact on our grandchildren if something doesn't change.

This book will explore the developing belief system of our children, what influences or shapes their identity, and what implications that has for our responsibility toward them. In the midst of providing an explanation of the most recent developments in human research, I will provide practical, everyday good parenting advice, which is found in many other books – as these have been demonstrated to provide needed resources in every family. As I do so, I will be doing one other thing – I will be tying those "everyday good parenting" resources into your child's developing belief system so that you can get into the habit of parenting more intentionally, recognizing that every parent-child interaction is influencing and shaping a child's sense of "I or Identity."

The education provided herein is to improve the well-being of not only our children, but for the family as a whole (D&C 88:118). As I had undertaken to review what experts are discovering about Epigenetics, Neuroplasticity, Neurogenesis and Quantum Science, I recognized quickly that what was being discovered aligned very well with what prophets and inspired leaders have been teaching for thousands of years. Scriptures came flooding into my mind, which became even more meaningful when I recognized the physiological impact that occurs based upon what someone comes to believe about themselves. The Lord, through his inspired servants, has been inviting us to believe specific truths about our identity, purpose and potential. It appears that those that do so make positive changes at many levels of their physiological systems.

As the reader spends some time becoming acquainted with the author's information, some may wrongly conclude that what I write about is just common sense. If what I write in this book is simply common sense, then why aren't more parents doing something about their parenting interventions? If this was just the average typical parenting advice then how come so many parents struggle creating the next generation of responsible and caring citizens? My suggestion is that the research and my interpretation of how that research can help us a s parents is very recent, but not so recent that we haven't already had incredible success in shaping cellular and DNA activity by paying high attention to environmental signaling.

Konstantine Eriksen explains:

> "Contrary to what many people are being led to believe, a lot of emphasis placed on genes determining human behavior is nothing but theory and doctrine..... We are free to make decisions that impact our lives and those of others. ... *Our beliefs can change our biology.* We have the power to heal ourselves, increase our feelings of self-worth and improve our emotional state." (The Science of Epigenetics – How Our Minds Can Reprogram Our Genes, Wake Up The World, March 26, 2012, http://wakeup-world.com/2012/03/26/the-science-of-epigenetics-how-our-minds-can-reprogram-our-genes/ ITALICS ADDED FOR EMPHASIS)

Epigenetic science reveals that you are an extension of your environment, which includes everything from your thoughts and *belief systems*, to toxic exposures (including repeated exposure to toxic thoughts); exposure to sunlight, exercise, and, of course, everything you choose to put onto and into your body. Epigenetics shatters the idea that you are a victim of your genes, and shows that you have tremendous power to shape and direct your physical and *mental health*.

The work of epigenetic researchers shows clearly that the "environmental signals" include and are profoundly affected by one's thoughts and emotions—both of which have been shown to directly affect DNA expression and therefore is a large focus of this book.

Many of us parent the way we were parented, or simply by what we think is best. Humility allows us to modify our current beliefs and our current behavior when we receive truthful information and act upon it. The forthcoming of so much information on how we form learning into belief, and how that belief alters physiological structures and the ongoing impact of all of that has on our identity, is incredibly timely as we prepare for the battle of our children's souls. If I were to borrow the psalmist's expression; *"This is the Lord's doing, it is marvelous in our eyes"* (Psalm 118:23).

As you move forward in this book, you will discover the physiological accruements associated with child-like humility. This quality of humility is what our Father in Heaven desires from each of us so that he can teach us; so that our learning will have the positive effects we desire as we fulfill our calling as parents.

Children come with believing hearts. Their vitality is evidence of their faith. These little ones appear to be the most susceptible to the feelings of the Spirit. They are faithful stewards and examples of choosing the right, a willingness to submit their will to a will that has their best interest at heart. They embody, so naturally the quality of love that accepts us for who we are and forgives us so readily when we have made mistakes. While reading this book, may we each become as little children, humbling ourselves

3

when we recognize our approach to parenting may need some adjustments. It is within our family experience where the ongoing process of perfection is realized. It is in the home where we can all grow and learn together. If humble, we may experience the view of prophets, which have declared:

> "The greatest work you will ever do will be within the walls of your own home" (Harold B. Lee, Strengthening the Home [1973]

Introduction

Life can be distracting. It presses on us and creates demands. It also provides us with dreams, which we may center in on – in hopes that we can live life in a way that we believe will bring us happiness. In the midst of the great race of life, many of us lose sight of what is essential; what matters the very most. We let things get in the way and sometimes allow wrong things to take highest priority.

Some of us don't even have an idea of what or if there is a purpose to life. We simply examine our surroundings and get involved in the competition for resources that perhaps will allow us to make memories, relax, and not be so stressed out.

While we press forward through life we seek for companionship, as at some level we instinctively recognize that someone else's thinking of us provides a benefit to our sense of importance. At the highest levels of this seeking are those that understand the central purpose of family; while at the lowest levels the pursuit to fulfill selfish desires, no matter what the cost to self or others, becomes the aim of daily living. The latter is an illusion to real intimacy. Either course, however, leads to the bringing of children into this world. Children act as game changers – whether we planned on having them or not. How do we know this?

We know this because even the most selfish amongst us bear the pain of hurt that results from failure to develop and influence those relationships that depend so heavily upon us – I speak specifically of our children. No matter what our approach to life is, no matter what drives us, no matter what informs us, when our children are not doing well and when our relationship with them is strained, we become unhappy and concerned. When so moved to improve that relationship, frustration becomes even greater if we experience resistance to our intention to have our children interact differently in the attempt to find that happiness we sense is somewhere to be found.

These uncomfortable feelings are trying to convey a message, the message of what matters most and what should be our highest priority. When one stops long enough to pay attention to these feelings, one has entered into a realm of higher learning, because these are spiritual promptings!

President David O. McKay's famous quote, "No other success can compensate for failure in the home" (Home: The Savior of Civilization, Conference Report, April, 1935), summarizes the haunting anguish felt by parents who know that their priorities and failings to be something, other than a terrific parent, have led to greater unhappiness in their children.

To His Galilean friends, and in turn to each of us, Jesus correctly identified our highest priority, said He:

"Except ye be converted, and become as little children, ye shall not enter into the kingdom of heaven."

"Whosever therefore shall humble himself as this little child, the same is the greatest in the kingdom of heaven."

"And whoso shall receive one such little child in my name receiveth me."

"*But whoso shall offend one of these little ones* which believe in me, it were better for him that a millstone were hanged about his neck, and that he were drowned in the depth of the sea." (Matthew 18:3-6; Italics for emphasis)

These words were in response to the question, "Who is the greatest in the kingdom of heaven?" whereupon Jesus selected a child that was standing nearby and placed this child before all those that would listen and understand (Matthew 18:1-2). One definition of "little ones" is children or those who have become as little children, by faithfully following the teachings of the Savior. To "offend one of these little ones" is to cause such to stumble because of false beliefs we administer or uphold by the way we interact with them. When through our interactions with our children we contribute to an unhealthy, untruthful self-identity, we have caused them to stumble.

We live in a day where children are not the highest priority and are constantly being offended by the way they are used, treated, trafficked, neglected, ignored, abandoned and abused. Too many parents mistakenly believe that children will just turn out to be whatever they were going to be and so little effort is expended in trying to shape outcomes. Many of today's parents raise children in survival mode, not knowing who their children really are. Such misinformation leaves modern parents with the goal of having their children experience happiness through what modern society says will bring happiness. Too many parents believe 'things' will appease their children and so in our day, more and more parents are substituting their time with things. A vast majority of them (meaning our children) are being provided a cell phone and other forms of technology, where increased use is leading to even greater isolation. As a result, a portion of our children are growing up with uncertainty about their purpose and potential. Their growing lack of socialization impacts a sense of their importance and interferes with establishing and maintaining relationships, which in turn decrease self-esteem and confidence in themselves. They are growing up with unhealthy personal belief systems that prevent them from finding joy in their existence, and meaning to what they do. With unhealthy and distorted core personal beliefs, children are struggling at greater rates of inattention, impulsivity, immoral and illegal acting out, anxiety, depression, mood dysregulation, social isolation, social ineptness, self-harm, prescription taking and suicide. These that should be the greatest in heaven are taking the lowest priority on earth.

If you are a parent that desires to have the best outcome for your children, but have run into so many dead-ends in trying to improve the situation, then this book is for you, because it gets to the core of the matter. It speaks of belief, the personally held beliefs of our children. It discusses how these beliefs develop and how we interact with our children to increase a positive, truthful belief system within them. While it is written in an integrative style, meaning that it draws upon references from scriptures, and other spiritual sources, it also provides a vast amount of research from the fields of psychology and other sciences. I believe that the process of integrating research and spiritual aspects provides the greatest resource for parents in understanding how to be effective parents and why what you do will have the outcomes you desire. The reason for such a stance is based in our dual nature (Job 32:8).

Knowledge is obtained through our own intellectual efforts, but it also comes by inspiration, including individual revelation or through correct priesthood lines. It is clear that we are expected to learn all that we can (D&C 130:18; 88:79; 118; 109:7, 14), but there are limits to our earthly learning. The scriptures clearly indicate that the things of God can be known only by the Spirit of God (1 Corinthians 2)

The Lord has counseled us to learn as much as we can pertaining to things both in heaven and in the earth (D&C 88:78-79). From a heavenly perspective, families are central to God's plan in bringing about His purposes. From an earthly perspective, there is a lot of research on human experience, including how to have very strong relationships with our children. With those of us that see things from an eternal perspective, we should be extra desirous to begin the process of learning how to develop and maintain healthy relationships with our children while in the mortal realm, so that we can treasure up in heaven those things that matter there (Matthew 6:19-21).

Outcome studies provide the basis upon which we make certain conclusions and decisions. This book is filled with outcome studies from various backgrounds, including:

1. Parental styles and their impact on children's attitudes
2. Secure attachment and the ability to regulate emotions
3. Understanding of child development and how mastering certain milestones work within the child in gaining healthy esteem
4. Learning and correspondent, developing belief systems
5. A parent's communication style and the child's willingness to take greater personal responsibility; and
6. Successful emotional communication as a means to create internalized motivation in our children.

The six areas just mentioned will all be covered in this book, but if we are only willing to look at secular, academic research and ignore spiritual or religious learning, we will experience what Paul described of our day, that we will be "Ever learning, and never able to come to the knowledge of the truth" (2 Timothy 3:7). Truth is not divisible.

Whether it comes through the laboratories of research, whether we happen to stumble upon it accidentally, or whether we receive it through the process of Divine revelation, truth provides the means to make sense of who we are and the environment we find ourselves in. We would do well to be careful to not dismiss any truth simply because of our prejudices.

In order to have you entertain the importance of considering both academic and spiritual sources in learning how to become more effective parents, another outcome study that I would point your attention to is the National Study of Youth and Religion, which was conducted at the University of North Carolina at Chapel Hill. While America has moved away from religiosity, and more and more parents are trying to raise their children secularly, with a few moral anecdotes thrown in, it is apparent that one religious sect is producing better than average outcomes for their children (Matthew 7:17,20). In a book, which summarized the findings of this study, Professor Kenda Creasy Dean stated:

> "In nearly every area, using a variety of measures, Mormon teenagers were consistently the most positive, the most healthy, the most hopeful, and the most self-aware teenagers in the study. Mormon young people also showed the highest degree of religious vitality and salience, the greatest degree of church teaching, *and the highest degree of congruence between belief and action.*" (Almost Christian: What the Faith of our Teenagers is Telling the American Church, Page 203)

No matter how you spin it, you can't ignore it – there is something generally about the homes of Latter Day Saints that provides the environment for their children to do better.

The last observation from the quote above, i.e., "the highest degree of congruence between belief and action," is hitting the nail on the head and is the framework for this book. Almost every area covered in this book, is tied to the development of a child's personal belief system, because what a child believes about him or herself is going to impact how the child functions throughout life. That is why we are having this discussion, and why the most important thing we can do, is be intentional about developing a healthy, truthful personal belief system within our children. What our children end up believing about themselves has serious, ongoing ramifications. How our children see themselves tends to be their destiny. I am unaware of any other parent book that makes this the focus of learning, i.e., how to become more effective and more influential in the positive outcomes of our children by influencing a healthy, personal belief system within them.

Mormon teens, in general do better because of what they believe about themselves. They tend to believe in themselves in such a way that allows them to steer clear of many issues that concern parents, as the study also concluded that Mormon teens outranked their peers in nearly every area of adhering to moral standards, including refraining from premarital sex, substance abuse, self-harm, and the like. Likewise it was demonstrated that Mormon adolescents were happier because their beliefs helped them to maintain a bigger picture than just "what can life provide me" type of attitude.

As with all outcome studies that show connections between beliefs, attitudes and styles of interaction with individual and family pro-functioning, it would be a mistake to ignore what it is that Mormon's believe and how they teach their children, seeing that they are doing something correctly. The point of such investigation is not to "convert" but to examine – so that modern day parents can understand what it is they may be missing in their approach.

So as stated previously, this book is intended for every parent, whether religious or not. It is intended for parents that desire to make their children a priority. It is for wise parents that understand they are responsible for rearing the next generation of parents, civic leaders, business men and women, professionals, teachers, policy makers and leaders. Even though this volume strongly references many Latter Day Saint beliefs and teachings, there should be no offense taken as what is taught is true, whether it comes from secular research or the mouths of inspired men and women. I don't believe that any parent will take offense to my selected references in support of the concepts being taught in this book.

Now, I have read many parenting books, but not all of them. From what I have read, I can clearly state that there is an ample amount of good advice out there to assist us as parents in becoming and being good, effective leaders of our children.

Some of the books I have read have been authored by Latter Day Saints and others by esteemed researchers and practitioners or ministers from other faiths. To each of them I express my gratitude to the insights I have gained, allowing me to alter a few of my own approaches, enjoying the positive outcomes by so doing.

As I have studied, taught and counseled other parents, I have done so through the prism of the gospel. As I have researched and read, I too have done so through that same prism. As just stated, I have adopted many of the good things taught by these individuals, but likewise I have seen the errors in some of the approaches (Moroni 7:13-18).

One of my greatest joys is when I see individuals, couples and families thrive because they discover correct principles and then work hard to implement them. The satisfactions expressed in the changes they experience are a witness to the importance of how correct principles positively impact our lives and our relationships. True principles, when followed faithfully, will inevitably lead to much better outcomes in our children.

The reason I feel inspired to write this book is to help parents increase their faith in revealed truth about family and the purpose of life and combine it with practical ways of interacting so that their confidence increases in Heavenly Father's plan for his children (Abraham 3:24-26; Moses 6:55). It has been my experience that many, many parents don't trust revealed truth and instead rely upon their own wisdom to raise their children, having the opposite result of what they were intending. Their wisdom forgets to take into account about how God designed us. Understanding and utilizing *human design* is crucial if we want to influence better outcomes. I don't know if I am being too simple minded, but it seems that if there is revealed truth regarding us as individuals and revealed truth about correct principles that guide our personal development and relationships then the closer we adhere to those truths, the better outcomes we can expect.

Our test of faith seems to be in believing the revelations, including that our children are related to God and that they each are able to have spiritual awakenings and live according to what the Holy Ghost teaches them (Jacob 4:8, 10; Proverbs 3:5-6). The question every faithful parent should repeatedly ask themselves is, "Does God ever vary from that which He has said" (Mosiah 2:22)? The correct answer to that question produces faith, the incorrect answer, fear and doubt.

In this book we are going to discuss relevant research on various topics related to family life and parenting. We are going to hear a lot of references to the brain to help us see how the scriptures and modern prophets are pointing us to important matters (2 Nephi 9:39). I want to make a clarification here so that when I speak of things that appear temporal, like the brain, I firmly believe the revelation which says that "all things were created spiritually before they were naturally upon the earth" (Moses 3:5-7). Parley P. Pratt commented:

> "The spirit of man consists of an organization of the elements of spiritual matter in the likeness and after the pattern of the fleshly tabernacle. It possesses, in fact, all the organs and parts exactly corresponding to the outward tabernacle" (Parley P. Pratt, Key to the Science of Theology, 79).

It appears to me that there is a distinct similarity as to how the natural brain works and how the spiritual brain works. I think this is an important concept to understand. We are told through the revelations to us that when we die, our spirit continues to have vitality (Luke 16:22-31), knowledge (D&C 130:18-19), memory (Alma 11:43), and similar attitudes (Mormon 9:14) as when it was connected to our body in mortality. In mortality, each of these functions is sustained through the physical workings of the brain. How are they then sustained when out of our body?

When we begin to understand how the natural brain works, it will not be too big of a leap to recognize that what and how we learn here in mortality is also shaping and developing our spiritual mind. However, I want to be very clear on this point, your spirit learns in a different way than does your intellect; as the scriptures point out:

> "There is a spirit in man: and the inspiration of the Almighty giveth them understanding." (Job 32:8) and the Spirit of Christ "giveth light to every man that cometh into the world." (D&C 84:46)

Just as our natural learning and experiences shapes the spiritual mind, so does our heed to these spiritual manifestations shape our natural mind. There seems to be an important connection so that our corruption can take on incorruption in a way that we may enjoy mortality and immortality to the fullest (Mosiah 16:10-11; 1 Corinthians 15:53; Alma 41:3-5).

Now comes the wake-up call! Who is responsible for orchestrating the positive outcomes of children and what should those outcomes look like (D&C 68:25; 93:38-40; Mosiah 4:14-15; Deuteronomy 4:8-9)?

Elder H. Verlan Anderson, referencing these verses said,

> "When our Heavenly Father sends one of his spirit children into a home, it is as if he says to the parents: "John, Mary, here is my most priceless possession—the soul of a little child. As you can see, he is helpless and completely dependent upon you even for life itself. You are now given the privilege of molding his life as you think best. Please teach him that I am his Father and that Jesus is his Savior and that we want him and you to return and live with us when mortality is over. Remember that I am always available to guide you in rearing this child of ours if you will but seek my help. I hope you will do so often. Your Heavenly Father."
> (Bringing Up Your Children in Light and Truth, October Conference, 1991)

Just previous to this statement, Elder Anderson also taught, "The early teaching of children by parents offers the solution to many of the problems, which otherwise may afflict our lives." Elder Anderson's insightful teaching is congruent with the growing research on the impact of the parent's interaction with their children between the ages of birth and six years old. These years are critical in developing a child's template of self or identity. I want to emphasize this point so that there is no misunderstanding. Research indicates that parents are the most influential aspect in wiring a child's brain for success or failure (The Biology of Belief: Unleashing the Power of Consciousness, Matter, and Miracles, Bruce Lipton, Ph.D., 2005).

In both the genetic expressions we pass on to our children, which influences cellular activity and feedback to our mind; and how a parent interacts with a child will either develop wiring that leads to a sense of personal capability, a sense of fitting in and

11

being acceptable, as well as developing a healthy view of one's own body or its opposite; the child coming to feel inadequate, not being loveable and a distorted view of his or her body. These are the three distinct areas that must be developed correctly, if one is to enjoy the inherent agency we each possess to its fullest potential.

Distorted beliefs about oneself, about worth, about capability, about being lovable and acceptable and about our body image directly impact our belief that we actually have choice. If one has learned to believe that they are inadequate, or somehow don't fit in, or that they are not good enough, will likely result in a cycle of defeating *reactions* that merely reinforce the distorted held beliefs. *Reactions* are a result of unawareness and when we fail to have perspective, it is difficult to fully employ the gift of agency. As parents, we are in the business of training our child's belief system. Words, moral lessons, uplifting stories, time spent together, encouragement, kind and patient correction are important aspects of this training. But teaching has much more to it than providing instruction. If we fail to utilize all of *human design*, then we will be less effective in helping develop the healthy belief systems we desire. The *power of observation*, meaning the observing parents do for their children about their children's experience, is a necessary part of good parenting, which very few parents do. This book will teach very clearly about *human design* so that there is no mistaking why we are doing what we are doing when wanting to be effective parents.

When working with parents, I will sometimes ask, "What do you want your child to believe about him or herself?" Every time parents answer with very positive desires. I then ask them what they think they must do in order to get that desired outcome. This is a point where many parents begin to fumble because parents do not understand *human design* and how to utilize it for the very outcomes they are hoping for.

Elder Bruce R. McConkie, in his book, A New Witness of the Articles of Faith made these insightful points, which lead to a growing understanding of where purposeful parenting focuses:

1) Belief is antecedent to performance – (Remember, we are training their belief system)
2) Belief is the beginning of spiritual (internal/emotional) discovery and progression.
3) Belief is a gift bestowed upon all mankind (including your children).
4) Beliefs are born of thoughts, they are then expressed in words; and finally are manifest in one's actions.
5) Every normal and accountable person believes something.

With this revealed information about us as humans, and knowing that parents have the single most impactful influence on the development of a belief system in their children, how do we influence the beliefs we are hoping to instill? If I were to ask that question in my parenting workshops, what answers might I receive? – Many and varied; and probably mostly good, because it is true that we are doing so many different things interactionally to develop a positive sense of self in our children. But why does, what we do, actually have the outcomes they do, positively or negatively? This is one of the purposes of this book, is to shed light on how we learn and how we influence positive belief systems based upon that understanding.

But the book is also about tying gospel truths and teachings into this thing we do called "parenting." Let me say, human beings are complex and that complexity is what has one parent saying, "Oh that would never work with my child." There is no textbook, concrete system of parenting. Parenting is more of an *art form*, and necessarily so for the reason just mentioned – the personality differences and other variations that are obviously inherent in each of us. But with that aside, every human shares a design and if we understand that design, and go with it, then our parenting is going to be more effective, no matter what our child's propensities may be. There are many gospel teachings that support positive human interactions, which are pointed out in this book.

I grew up with a sister that had incredible, inherent artistic abilities. She was creative and to me seemed that she could do anything as it related to the expression of that gift. However, if I were to ask her about her accomplishments I am sure that she would tell me how she had to learn and develop techniques, theories, concepts, skills and other aspects that improved upon her inherent ability. I am sure that there were times where she may have been working on one area of creative expression and then had to pull from another area in order to have the outcome she was looking for. Her knowledge and understanding of so many areas is what allowed her to remain *unstuck* in her desire to complete a creative work. So it is with parenting. When I hear a parent say, "Oh that would never work with my child," I have a parent that has only prepared themselves in a limited way to parent. There are so many theories, so much research, an enormous amount of skill sets, techniques and concepts within the field of family relationships and parenting that we should rarely get stuck in our calling and responsibility of parenting. The more we learn the more we are able to utilize this information in assisting our Father in Heaven in completing His creative work for the children He has entrusted to us. Like my sister, we can do our work in an artistic way or form and never be found saying, "Oh that will never work!"

Part of human design necessarily includes the spirit of the individual. If our parenting is going to have the best results, we must, absolutely must take this truth into account. As it relates to things that are spiritual, remember, every child that we call our own is also a child of God and there is a spirit in each one that is connected to the Almighty (Job 32:8). He knows our children better than we do and He wants to work in partnership with us to raise our children to discover and believe truth, especially the truth about their divine nature and potential.

When our children receive a testimony of their true identity, a witness born of the Holy Ghost (Moroni 10:3-5; Hebrews 12:9), the newly acquired understanding provides increasing light through the path of mortal experience.

Individuals that face mortality everyday, believing the truths transmitted by the power of the Holy Ghost appear to do better and do not experience as much in the way of doubt, fear, anxiety, depression, and difficulties regulating. Such individuals, having experienced strengthening sustenance by abiding in truth, continue to live in a manner that invites the supportive process of spiritual understanding and receive the ongoing witness that they are on the path that leads to personal satisfaction and eternal life.

When our bearings become corrected, we have a unique way of looking at life. Our experiences are not limited by the unique time in which they occur. Instead, we are able to view every experience in terms of eternal existence. Therefore, we more consistently rely on our Father in Heaven, drawing closer to Him, being guided by His Spirit, keeping earthly experience in perspective. This perspective, this way of living, we refer to as spirituality.

We live in a day where we have the best resources available to us to help us become confident and effective parents. We have the words of past prophets and leaders, we have the words of living prophets and leaders, we have manuals, and research studies; we have clinicians and experts, we have all around us good examples of parenting, and most of all, we have access to the holiest means of communication through prayer and revelation, wherein the Holy Ghost does and will give utterance (2 Nephi 32:4-5; 33:2) in our concerns for our children.

As you move forward in this book, I would like you to do so with some questions in your mind:

1. Do I see my child the way Heavenly Father and Jesus Christ see my child?
2. Do I trust the design they have been created with?
3. Do my children know that I recognize their inherent worth?
4. Do my children know that I trust and believe in them?
5. Do I see and appreciate their individuality, their strengths and believe in their utmost potential.
6. Am I a good role model in the very things I want them to believe about themselves?
7. Do they know how I feel about them?

These questions are purposeful because they raise our awareness about what good parenting does. If our children experience our *observation* of them in these positive ways, they shall be very obedient (Abraham 4:31), not because we are demanding it of them but because through our influence they will come to know and believe in what they were created for (Abraham 4:27), and through our positive messages of our faith in them, they are blessed to increase faith in themselves (Abraham 4:28) and faith in their Savior.

As we continue to have a growing partnership with the Lord, our children will feel of that influence and recognize the joy that accompanies the influence of the Spirit. This prepares our children to recognize that same spiritual influence in their own lives. As our children feel the undeniable, penetrating intellectual and emotional responses to the Spirit's communications, those personal spiritual experiences will not only increase personal understanding; not only provide strength to live purposefully, but will literally act as an anchor to their soul, so that they will not be tossed to and fro by the waves of worldliness and distorted beliefs.

Elder L. Tom Perry, when a new parent, recalls what President David O. McKay taught concerning the role of parents:

> "At the time I was a new parent, President David O. McKay presided over the Church. His counsel was clear and direct regarding our responsibilities to our children. He taught us the most precious gift a man and woman can receive is a child of God, and that the raising of a child is basically, fundamentally, and most exclusively a *spiritual* process." (Train Up A Child, General Conference, April 1983)

If what President McKay taught is true, then our partnering with heavenly inspiration is vital if we seek to improve our ability to act as ministers to our children.

J.E. McCulloch's famous quote, reiterated by President David O' McKay, "No other success can compensate for failure in the home," may have been viewed slightly differently by these men. For Mr. McCulloch, it may have been the preserving of Christian tradition and its impact on society as a whole, but from President McKay, it was an understanding that the eternities require families working together for the salvation of the entire family unit (Moses 1:39). With this understanding, there is a natural ordering of priorities; there is going to be a mental classification of those things that matter most (Alma 34:32-34).

Ultimately, our greatest joy, our greatest achievement, our greatest triumph, and our greatest love will be experienced in the family that is sealed together by the Holy Spirit of Promise (D&C 132:19), and has made it safely back home. That sealing and binding (Matthew 16:19) begins by what we believe about ourselves and our children. The Gospel of Our Lord reveals to us the truth about ourselves, it is as things really are (Jacob 4:13). Therefore, let us be faithful and have hope in the revelations and bring ourselves to act in accordance with revealed truth, until we become what we were created to become (D&C 132:20; Mosiah 3:19). The *potential* is in each of us, and when parents understand the role they have been given in this sacred partnership, they become sober in their duties to teach, encourage and act in such a way with their off-spring that provides a platform of trust, so that their children can form a belief system that leads to eternal life. Whether trust develops or not is highly dependent upon the personal attributes of the parents. It is our attributes that form our character and it is our character that is being sensed by our children. If our children have a correct sense of our character, depending upon that character, either power comes to their mind to exercise faith or doubt and fear will become their companion.

It is my prayer that we learn how to lead our children to eternal life and to do this in a manner that is not rigid, judgmental, selfish, perfectionistic, critical and controlling. Such strategies will ultimately have our children not believe much except that they are worthless, can never be good enough, and are an ongoing disappointment. Instead, the strategies, concepts, examples, principles and stories throughout this book are meant to show us how to be with our children so that they do come to believe in themselves in congruence with our revealed nature and potential; giving them power to act according to their belief.

Setting the Stage

In order for any of us to understand what this book is really trying to accomplish, we must first talk about where we have been and where we are now, in context of how we learn and the formulation of our self-concept. It is not my purpose here in the beginning to talk in agonizing detail about this topic, as later in the book we will discuss *learning* in greater depth. However, in order for the reader to begin connecting dots from topic to topic, it is important to review to some degree of what is occurring during our interactions with our children.

A child's identity begins to form based upon the child's perception of how their parents view them. If a parent sends the message of value and importance in their interactions with their children, their children will come to have an identity of value and importance. On the other hand, if a child perceives that they don't matter much, due to their parent's interaction with them, then they will more likely form an identity laced with a personal belief of insignificance. Therefore, one of my drum-beating themes is that parents absolutely play a critical and significant role in helping their children develop a personal belief system. A personal belief system is what the child believes about him or herself, a template from which the child perceives self – and how that belief assists in meeting life's challenges, or contrariwise, disrupts the child's empowerment to overcome and make healthy adjustments throughout life. A *healthy* personal belief system, or template, has an added bonus in that it activates moral and spiritual reasoning, both of which are necessary in order to grow in faith.

Though I express strong opinions about this theme, it is not for the purpose of inducing guilt or pointing fingers at parents. It is for the purpose of increasing awareness in parents so they quit parenting by the seat of their pants and become really engaged in *the art of effective parenting*. The research indicates that adept, conscious parenting will increase the chances that our children will develop a healthy personal belief system and turn out the way we want them to. I said, "increase the chances," not guarantee the outcome. If the gospel is true, then so is its doctrine and the doctrine of agency (D&C 101:78) is always involved in this process of nurturing, teaching, inviting; interactive dance we do with our kids. Remember, when Heavenly Father began providing spiritual bodies for His premortal children (Hebrews 12:9), He was and still is the Perfect Parent, but even He refused to tamper with His children's agency (Alma 29:4).

Agency is the power to consider our thoughts and which ones we entertain and act upon. There is opposition in all things, therefore there are opposing thoughts to truth always available to consider (2 Nephi 2:27). Agency acts on what thoughts we allow to become more powerful. We are the gatekeepers of our minds and if we allow wholesome, uplifting, truthful, empowering thoughts to be the welcomed guests of our intelligence, then we become the product of those types of thoughts. On the other hand, if we decide to entertain unwholesome, depressing, error filled, and strength

sapping thoughts in the room of our mind, then we lose power over our lives (2 Nephi 2:26-27)
.

In our pre-mortal existence, it appears that ideas and belief systems were introduced and made available to us that opposed the truth taught by our Heavenly Parents. Elder Bruce R. McConkie elaborated on the impact and outcome of premortal experience and choice:

> "We do know that we are His children, created in His image, endowed with power and ability to become like Him. We know He gave us our agency and ordained the laws by obedience to which we can obtain eternal life. We know we had friends and associates there. We know that we were schooled and trained and taught in the most perfect educational system ever devised, and that *by obedience to His eternal laws* (obedience implies choice) we developed infinite varieties and degrees of talents."

> "And hence comes the doctrine of foreordination.... Melchizedek came into this world with such faith and spiritual capacity that 'when a child he feared God, and stopped the mouths of lions, and quenched the violence of fire.' Cain on the other hand, like Lucifer, was a liar from the beginning... " (God Foreordains His Prophets and His People, April 1974)

We all know the outcome of that First Estate (D&C 29:36; Revelation 12:4; Jude 1:6). The outcome of those that did not keep their First Estate was and is *not* a reflection of Heavenly Father's parenting! It is a reflection of which thoughts were entertained and acted on the most by that third part of the host of heaven.

Now here in mortality, for those of us that kept our First Estate, the continuation of choosing our course direction is occurring on a daily basis, minute-by-minute. As in the pre-mortal existence, factors of influence in mortality also play a role in the outcomes of us as humans, including our pre-mortal development of faith and spirituality, experiences we encounter living in mortality, the culture of our family and/or country, media's onslaught of worldly pleasures, our choice of relationships, and our biological inheritances. With so much interference, developing an A-Game is essential if we are going to counter the false beliefs that can be formed by some of these other powers.

Let's get back to the "then and now" of learning and the development of self-concept. I went to school in the 80's, and as we studied learning and issues related to personality, the dogma was that things were pretty static. Genetic determinism was the secular doctrine being promoted. We were taught that we are born with the brain we are born with and if there happened to be any deficits, cognitively, emotionally, or otherwise, there was not a lot we could do to change the brain. Interventions were more behaviorally driven, meaning that we could teach individuals behaviors (operant and classical conditioning) that would increase management of the deficit, but not really resolve it. After all, "you are born with only so many brain cells; your intelligence is a fixed quotient, and you are who you are." That was the message of not so long ago. This attitude and directive about human existence was founded in Newtonian physics, a very linear, cause and effect type of system. Just as a side-note, many physicians continue to support this system as evidenced by their intervention methods, not with behavior management, but with medicine management. Either approach is evidence of how the old system still has its roots firmly planted.

As a psychology student and as a Latter Day Saint (believing the revelations given to us), I had a difficult time reconciling this "fixed" state in light of the principle or doctrine of agency, which if used correctly, would allow us to grow unto the measure of our creation (Ephesians 4:13). I didn't think that *behavior management* alone was going to be sufficient to provide the increase that would be necessary to attain to my potential.

A spiritual corollary to this concept is the experience Adam had when he was expelled from the Garden of Eden. Adam was given a commandment to offer sacrifice, yet there was no clear understanding as to what purpose the sacrifice ritual served. Adam was simply going through the motions – the behavior alone did not provide for much else. It wasn't until after many days when a heavenly messenger appeared and asked Adam, why he was offering sacrifices; and Adam's response was, "I know not," that Adam was informed and made *aware* of the spiritual and eternal significance of what he was doing (Moses 5:6-7). This increased *awareness* forever changed how he looked at his ritual behavior and this increased *awareness* informed his personal belief. As a result, Adam, his wife Eve, and anyone else that wanted to, could now begin to exercise faith in the Atonement of the Lord, Our Savior, Jesus Christ. Faith in the Lord Jesus Christ; and His gift of the Atonement provides the power to be exalted; again the ritual behavior alone being inadequate in itself to effect the desired outcome.

Saving faith is *spiritual belief* and spiritual belief is an organization of our thoughts that have been acted upon by the influence and power of the Holy Ghost (1 Corinthians 2:9-14). This divine influence acts to shape our personal belief system as it reminds us of our true identity and purpose.

With *belief* come direction, purpose and hope. Obedient actions interact with belief by bringing us to truth and amplifying the importance of truth after it has been discovered. Obedient "behavior" is an essential element of fulfilling the measure of our creation, but it must be connected to belief in order to empower and fulfill its divine purpose. Obedience, when coupled or associated with truth, develops neural pathways that act as resonators of established truth, and in essence develops a mind that becomes like the Source of All Truth (1 Corinthians 2:16).

To those who are honest in the feelings transmitted by the power of the Holy Ghost view life through the lens of spiritually transmitted data. Such data has us act in and evaluate life accordingly. As the Apostle expressed:

> "We look not at the things which are seen, but at the things which are not seen: for the things which are seen are temporal; but the things which are not seen are eternal." (2 Cor. 4:18.)

> "For they that are after the flesh do mind the things of the flesh; but they that are after the Spirit the things of the Spirit. For to be carnally minded is death; but to be spiritually minded is life and peace." (Rom. 8:5–6.)

Therefore, to be spiritually minded is to view and evaluate our experiences in terms of the enlarged perspective of eternity.

In Adam's reply "I know not, save the Lord commanded me" to the heavenly messenger's question of why he was behaving and performing as he was, is a principle of great importance to our parenting approaches and your ability to act in faith of what I am going to invite you to do. In this book you are going to read about specific approaches, which may seem alien to you. Most of us, to some degree or another, learn our parenting techniques from our own parents, having never developed or even considered developing other resources that influence better outcomes in our children's personal belief systems. You may question why I encourage teaching while correcting; or consequences not being viewed as punishment, but as teaching moments, or refraining from anger when your child has chosen to oppose a family rule or your specific instruction; or simply ignoring some of your children's behaviors. Your questioning of some of the approaches will "feel counterintuitive or unnatural" because of the styles you have already developed or your misinterpretation of gospel teaching. Your understanding of why I teach what I teach will progressively increase as you approach the end of the book.

I will be teaching you about human design throughout the text. Understanding human design is essential if you are going to be effective in your parenting. It is going to take several chapters to teach how we are designed, so if in your mind you are apt to reply, "I know not," in response to what I am asking you to do, realize that once your understanding of human design is developed, your increased awareness will allow you to act in greater faith and be more intentional in what you are doing to influence your child's belief system.

A lot of parents just want me to tell them what to do in every situation that arises. Many of them don't care about the why; they are simply focused on the immediate obedience of the child and the comfort of their own existence. Of course I am going to teach you such techniques that will result in quickly improved behavior, but long-lasting change *requires the appropriate development of the child's personal belief system*, establishing a positive *implicit memory* (i.e., cellularly stored learning), that induces our children to make more automatic choices and behaviors leading to happiness and positive outcomes.

This returns us to another concern I had while earning my degree. Aside from the limiting approach of behavior management, I was also being taught that "choice" was illusionary, as so many things were being driven genetically, of which I had no power over. But that was not my experience. All I had to do was *view* my own life experience and recognize that the *power of choice* had allowed me to change, or to learn, or to grow. At a very simple level, throughout my college years, I had the choice to do my homework, study and show up for classes or not. I chose to do what I believed would allow me to pass all of those classes, and guess what — I graduated. After all, neither of my parents graduated college and so there would have been no specific genetic information passed on to me that said I will graduate college. To me, there was no specific genetic marker that pre-determined any of that. More importantly, throughout my life I had recognized that I was able to *observe* my thoughts, my emotions, and my behaviors and that somehow *the innate ability to observe is what produced the reality of choice.*

Much of this "fixed" mentality is still being promoted today. All one has to do is look at the Diagnostic Statistical Manual (DSM), and read about every diagnosis and disorder listed therein as having a biological component to it. Addiction; ADHD; Mood Disorders, and the like are analyzed and through that analysis, the statistics demonstrate higher correlations of conditions in individuals with their family of origin and ancestry. I have heard so many times, parents of addicted teens, tell their children, "Well you need to be careful because alcoholism runs in the family." The reasoning or logic of such people is a misunderstood belief that there must be a genetic component to these mental health issues and therefore the intervention is once again, *behavior modification or management.*

Well, truth be told, genetics do play a role in how we experience life, but not in the "fixed" state theory still being evangelized by evolutionists and Newtonian physicists. So, let's look at what we know today to understand what is really going on with learning, developing self-concept, and the role genetics play in this whole process.

The idea that we are the *observer* of our thoughts, our emotions and behaviors and not merely victims to their presence, helps us to recognize that there appears to be some life-giving intelligence that has the capacity to *act upon* the biology (Mosiah 4:30). You and I both know people that seem to be "driven by their emotions" and struggle with feeling at ease. They appear to be concerned with the past and the future, rather than slowing down long enough to pay attention to the present. Such individuals believe that if they just think enough, they can prepare themselves for the worst case scenario, thus alleviating themselves of their intrusive feelings. What they find in its stead is increased, ongoing anxiety and depression. The issue is not that they are incapable of thinking well, or having good feelings, or even choosing more helpful behaviors, the issue is that they *believe incorrect things about themselves*, using their emotions as evidence of that incorrect belief. Now their task, as they see it, is to eliminate the *noticeable*, uncomfortable, negative feelings and so they rev-up the reactionary engine increasing the noise inside of their heads, and become overwhelmed with the rapidly moving negative thoughts and emotions. These become all-consuming. Literally, they are being *acted upon* by a well trained brain of anxiety, rather than *acting on* their anxiety by becoming a better *observer* of what they believe about themselves (2 Nephi 2:14). This information is tapping into an understanding of different types of learning, implicit vs. explicit memory. When we are *acted upon*, we are experiencing our unhealthy implicit memory, when we *act upon* we are experiencing our healthy implicit memory, combined with aspects of our explicit memory. We will discuss learning and memory in more depth throughout the book, but again, this section is beginning to introduce some of the concepts that you will be learning about in order to become more effective parents.

Lehi points out that the ability *to act,* and the power to not be acted upon, requires first a knowledge of "good and evil" (2 Nephi 2:26). Other words we might use are "light and darkness," or "truth and error." I don't want the reader to miss what was just stated. The power to act requires an understanding of absolutes and absolute truths. In order for someone to grasp the importance of these polar concepts requires enough experience to recognize that absolutes do exist. For those that would like to take a dramatic leap into facilitating positive change, I invite a serious inquiry into and acceptance of the Originator of Truth and Light (Matthew 11:28-30). Lehi's reasoning on this matter helps us understand that if we are going to make sense of our existence, we need to believe the truth about our existence. When we accept the truth as being real, then we naturally accept the reality of our being a member of God's family and that He is real (2 Nephi 2:11-14). With our bearings being set correctly, we have the opportunity to experience increased hope and greater relief from the distorted, error-filled way we believe about ourselves:

> "Wherefore, whoso believeth in God might with surety hope for a better world," the scriptures teach, "which hope cometh of faith [and] maketh an anchor to the souls of men, which would make them sure and steadfast" (Ether 12:4)

Many times, people grow up with very poor examples of parenting. Their negative interactions with the adults in their life can create significant obstacles in future functioning, especially as it relates to positive self-concept and healthy relationships. God, who has revealed that He is our father, can become a way for such individuals to have that healthy parent-child relationship, which was missing in their mortal family. Heavenly Father possesses all of the attributes and power necessary to develop healthy, positive personal belief systems within us. Likewise, He knows what is best for each of us and desires to interact with us in a way that produces our willingness to trust Him and gain for ourselves those things that will bring peace, happiness and fulfillment in our lives.

Written between the lines of what was just said is the truth about our existence. We have parents that have provided for us a physical body. But we also have a Heavenly Parent that provided for us our spirit (Ecclesiastes 12:7). Scientific, reductionist dogma, *removes the core truth* of our dual nature. Without truth, we are exposed to greater struggles, likely looking for relief in behavior management techniques, such as externalization; perfectionism or perhaps medicinal interventions. When we come to believe that we are made in the image of God and all that implies, that concept alone can act as a great anti-anxiety agent or anti-depressant! The relief, not being found in the form of a pill, but in the form of a thought, a truthful thought, which increases positive energy and assists in better emotional regulation.

Let me see if I can expand on what we are talking about in regards to learning and developing personal belief. Part of our design, when it comes to learning, is to make as many things as automatic as possible. This *automaticy principle* is a great benefit to us, as it allows us to manage daily life without having to concentrate on everything we do. The automatic tendencies form due to the Law of Associative Memory, wherein our repetitive behaviors, for example, become wired together, forming neural pathways so strongly linked, that the behavior becomes practically effortless. If you have ever heard of the saying, "what fires together wires together" is a description of what the brain is doing during our learning process. The amygdyla is largely responsible for the development of implicit memory, i.e., that which becomes automatic and subconscious.

An example of this may be learning how to ride a bike. In the beginning, the behavior is new and therefore the brain is just beginning to develop associated neural pathways for that activity. As one continues to repeat the behavior of riding a bike, it appears that less effort has to be expended in doing so. In fact, after time, we hardly even think about what we have to do in order to ride a bike – we just jump on and go. We are able to do so because of the long term associations of neural fibers that fired together over and over again. Once the brain has developed these long-term associations, not only do tasks or activities become easier, they also go to a place of subconsciousness. The *subconscious is a place where we don't attend to with a lot of awareness* anymore.

So, let me repeat, the things we do over and over again, creates long term neural circuitry and stored within that circuitry is our implicit learning. Within that learning are strong associations, so feelings, ideas, the meanings we put on events, people, places, odors, sounds; any and all of these can be linked together in our learning. For example, a combat soldier having spent two years in active duty in Iraq would have experienced a lot of stress as he fulfilled his duty. All of the sounds, smells, thoughts, and fears would be associated with the experience of his stress. However, all of these indicators are being stored in the subconscious or implicit memory. So let's flash forward five years and this same individual is sound asleep, safely in his own home, has been out of active duty for those five years, and at 2 am, a helicopter flies over his home. What is that helicopter noise associated with and what might it trigger? If learning occurs as described, then the helicopter sound is associated with stress. What does this individual do? That's right; he immediately *reacts* as if he is back in the stressful situation. This is not conscious awareness and intentional use of one's agency – this is merely *reactionary* response developed from long term associations. As you can see, this has serious implications for how and what our children learn about themselves, based upon their own associations learned in the home environment.

In order to avoid becoming too complicated, learning is stored as memory. There are different types of memory, but let me speak generally of two types, *explicit* and *implicit* memory. Explicit memory is what allows us to recall facts, figures, and other rote information, both semantic and autobiographical. Explicit memory is largely accomplished through the hippocampus functions. It is related more to data extraction or autobiographical recall. Data type of memory was stored through conscious and somewhat repetitive effort, but not at the level required for implicit learning and memory. Things in explicit memory may not always be at the forefront of consciousness, but the details are stored in a way that recall is relatively easy. For example, what day were you born? What is your social security number? Where did you go to elementary school? Who was the 16th President of the United States? What is the formula for solving a hypotenuse triangle? How do you rebuild a carburetor? Your answers to any of those questions demonstrate explicit memory.

Implicit memory on the other hand are the things that get stored without full conscious awareness and don't require much, if any, conscious effort to utilize. As stated before, the amygdyla plays an important function in this type of learning. Riding a bicycle is an example of implicit memory, but so also is chronic negative interactions with our parents. Other things tied to implicit memory are the meanings we attached to the learning and the emotional responses experienced during the learning. Additional factors in forming implicit memory are the circumstances under which such learning took place. Was the circumstance viewed as threatening or did we experience something negative during the learning? As you can tell, implicit memory seems much more multifaceted. This type of memory creates "reactivity" to wiring that took place under the conditions of our early years, or highly charged emotional experiences – the personally held beliefs (templates) that we developed due to our parent's style of interaction, for example, or other significant events during our lifetime. Some researchers have indicated that over ninety percent of our daily functioning is being driven by implicit memory. This information provides understanding that many parent's negative approach to raising their children is likely being driven through their own implicit memory, which memory is often triggered by their child's behavior.

Since the purpose of this book is to detail how parenting influences our children's personal belief systems or templates, let me list a few things that parents do that may lead to a child being filled with a shame-based template or shame-based implicit memory:

1. When a parent's interaction is perceived by the child to be hostile
2. When a parent fails to recognize and speak well of a child's positive behavior
3. If discipline seems too harsh, (i.e. guilt beatings, rigidness, isolation, deficit model consequences, etc.)
4. A too over-protective parent (helicopter)
5. If the child perceives that acceptance and love are conditional
6. When parental emotions are utilized as weapons and tactical control
7. When discipline becomes associated with who the child is rather than the behavior the child exhibited
8. When a child is consistently humiliated in public
9. Withdrawal of the parent (not being interested enough to know the child and respond to his or her emotional needs)
10. Abandonment
11. A controlling parent
12. When the parent fails to adequately communicate at an emotional level, (i.e., having successful emotional communication)

Though not an exhaustive list, these all have a tendency to shape an inner experience in the child of not being worthwhile, needed or wanted, incapable and personally undesirable. This inner experience then develops into a template of shame, by which the child continues to perceive the world through, even carrying into adulthood. Worthlessness becomes the child's bearings; it becomes the child's core belief.

Recall, the things we do over and over again, develop implicit memory. A child that experiences chronic poor parenting as listed above, has said to him or herself, over and over again, "I AM NOT VALUABLE," "I AM NOT WORTH KNOWING," "I AM NOT LOVEABLE," "I AM NOT CAPABLE," "I AM STUPID," "I AM BAD," and so on, and so on, ad nauseum! The problem is, that they have said these things so many times, that they are stored in the subconscious, meaning that the child's core belief and the constant things he or she has said (or continues to say), are not in their full-awareness. *This is their implicit memory!*

As this child continues to go through life, the core belief interferes with coding future information correctly that may otherwise lead to resolving the distortion. Instead, the individual interprets experiences as merely reinforcements of their negatively held core belief, likely leading to perpetual struggles well into adulthood. Evidence of this is when someone compliments or praises an individual that struggles with the template or core belief of shame – such individuals quickly dismiss such praise as, insincere, manipulative or uninformed. This is the power of subconscious programming of templates. Negative programming also has devastating effects on our health, genes, and personal effectiveness.

Let me sidetrack for just a moment to bring you up to date on what the research is showing on how our implicit memory acts on our genetic mapping. More recent genetic studies clearly demonstrate that genetic expression can be directed by our thoughts, not simply by some pre-programmed biological blueprint. DNA is found encoded in every cell of the body and how those cells function, meaning how the DNA is told to behave, is largely based upon the effects of our thoughts. We will discuss these processes in greater detail later, but please consider the following brief description of the *biology behind belief*.

An organelle in the brain is the hypothalamus. The hypothalamus acts like a switch point in the process of cognitive/emotional functioning. It attempts to discern what the mind is thinking in order to know what to do to move the thoughts forward to the rest of the human organism. The hypothalamus is a factory that assembles simple amino acids (proteins) into polypeptide chains (protein synthesis), based upon what it hears (senses) the frontal lobe is thinking (Note: There are other areas of the brain and body that feed into these thought development processes, but I don't want to get too complicated, since it is well established that the frontal lobe acts in capacity of executive functioning).

These polypeptide chains are synthesized to create responses at the cellular level, based upon what the hypothalamus believed it was being told. Literally, the thought becomes embedded within the protein structure that now acts as a carrier of information for the cells of the body. An example of this is when a man or woman sees someone that is attractive. Almost immediately, thoughts of lust (attraction) can be formulated, which sends a signal to the hypothalamus to create "lust polypeptides" and these are then expelled into the bloodstream and transported to every cell in the body. When the "lust polypeptide" docks with a receptor on the cell membrane; like a key, the cell begins to perform or becomes activated based upon the encoding of the polypeptide. Our limbic system interprets the cellular activity as an emotion, which then reinforces the whole electromagnetic/chemical process. However, a person that has been taught that lust is a sin (Matthew 5:28; 3 Nephi 12:28); especially if it is being experienced with someone other than one's spouse, may counter that original thought with a moralistic (different) thought, creating a *different* cycle of i.e., "he or she is God's child and deserves respect as a whole complete person, not just as an object" polypeptide synthesis, thus returning the individual to their previous emotional state. This process is rapid, less than 2 milliseconds – actually, faster than the speed of light!

For those that repeatedly send the same signals to their cells based upon the same thoughts one consistently and continually has, the genetic component stores this information as "physical memories" of the individual's learning experience. If these become a persistent, repetitive pattern of associations, the more influential the thoughts and feelings that pertain to that association become. As Joe Dispenza points out:

> "If you get angry on a daily basis, if you get frustrated on a daily basis, if you suffer on a daily basis, if you give reasons for the victimization in your life you are rewiring or reintegrating that neural network on a daily basis and that neural net now has a long term relationship with all of those nerve cells that give us an identity" (Joe Dispenza, What the Bleep)

So cemented these become that we no longer challenge the reality of that network, but instead it becomes an automatic reaction – and recall, if it has reached the level of automaticy, it becomes a subconscious filing, making it more difficult to reach. How awful it would be to walk around with a subconscious identity of incapability, or social outcast, or any other inferior complex. The severity of negative, untruthful thinking on our physiology, as well as mental stability is staggering. What is emerging from the research is astonishing, where now it is being said, *if you truly understood the power of thoughts, you would work really hard to avoid negative thinking.*

What this says about DNA is that it is filled with potential, but remains kind of dormant until it is told through electromagnetic/chemical informing what it is to do. This is the power of thoughts; our thoughts unfold the potential of our DNA based upon what we tell it to become.

This however is not an endorsement of the "positive thinking" crowds that go around speaking and writing about psyching yourself-up with religious fervor. This is about "truthful thinking" which is the based in our relationship with the Almighty and the potential implied in that relationship. I hope to make a clear distinction on those two concepts. Positive thinking must be congruous with our design and purpose if it is to be effective, and therefore it must be connected to the Source of our life and the truth as it has been revealed by Him:

This is the process of becoming a new creature, of shedding the carnal and natural man and becoming spiritually minded (Romans 8:6; 2 Nephi 9:39).

I don't think it would surprise you to know that many that engage in the process of pop-optimism, and pop-positive thinking, do so in order to combat their own low self-concept. Grandiosity – "I am the best," "There is no one better than me," "Brag, brag, brag, ad infinitum," is the signal that someone is covering up how they really feel about themselves. In fact, many studies demonstrate that such individuals end up even feeling less optimistic. I believe the reason is because they have not yet discovered the truth about themselves, because they have not yet tapped into the source of truthful thinking, therefore they measure their worth through worldly standards – likely falling short of what the world says a person of worth is and having the resulting belief and emotion that "I don't really measure up."

I hope that the reader is having a light-bulb experience within their mind right now. Because what the new research is demonstrating is the complex process of Neuroplasticty, Neurogenesis, and Epigenetics. Unlike what I was taught back in the 1980's, the brain is no longer seen as static and genetically driven. The brain today is observed to be renewable (Neurogenesis), malleable and formable (Neuroplasticity), and that our thoughts, not strictly an emergent property of our genes, are what signal how our genes should express themselves (Epigenetics).

Just a quick thought on genetics being passed down to our progeny. Cells, and the DNA which they house, are programmable. If I live my life in a depressed mode, I do so because of what I believe about myself. My attitude and lack of personal responsibility for my current condition will create "depressed" polypeptide chains, which inform my cells how to express the DNA within it. My thoughts, my attitudes, my beliefs, and my behaviors about life being unfair, or that I don't matter, or that I am not worth as much as others, become encoded upon my DNA.

If I possess such genetic and cellular functioning at the time of creating another life, I pass onto that child the likelihood of having depressed genetic expressions. That is one way how I influence the next generation to continue the curses of the fathers.

Being spiritually minded is not being depressed minded. We literally pass either blessings or cursings to the next generation based upon our own personal belief system, our faithfulness or faithlessness to what is true. The power is in us to become masters of our fate (through grace), and the influence of generations yet unborn. Beliefs heavily influence biology!

President McKay defined spirituality as "the consciousness of victory over self, and of communion with the infinite. Spirituality," he said, "impels one to conquer difficulties and acquire more and more strength. To feel one's unfolding and truth expanding the soul is one of life's sublimest experiences" (David O. McKay, comp. Llewelyn R. McKay, Salt Lake City: Deseret Book Co., 1971, p. 99).

President McKay's insightful comment aligns with what the science is saying today – obviously, inspiration's power manifested in the Lord's servant!

The developing belief system of the child is heavily influenced by parent-child interactions. Parents have an overwhelming influence on the mental and physical (genetic) attributes of the children they raise. Dan Siegel states:

> "For the growing brain of a young child, the social world supplies the most important experiences influencing the expression of genes, which

determines how neurons connect to one another in creating the neuronal pathways which give rise to mental activity, and *identity*." (The Developing Mind, Siegel, 1999)

How much easier would it be to be nurtured from the beginning of our mortal experience (a continuation of our pre-mortal nurturing) by parents that are clear in what their responsibilities are, assisting us in developing truthful, personal belief systems so that we can reach our genetic potential (Genesis 1:27)? How much better to become a parent that parents from a place of understanding and hope, being intentional in our interactions with our children, to influence developing personal belief systems, that lead children toward living life more abundantly, with purpose, joy and hope? This is the calling of parents; it is the most vital, eternal work of which we are engaged.

Our children need a nurturing environment that activates genes that develop healthy belief systems. Parents act as genetic engineers throughout their child's life, not just as contributors at conception. From a child's perspective, how does a child's subconscious (implicit memory/personal belief system/template/mental model) know what it knows and how has it learned it? By now, it should be coming clear how we learn and how our interaction with our children interacts and influences how our children perceive themselves. The basis for this influence is two-fold. All humans are extremely sensitive to "signaling." We receive signals from both our inherited genetic material and the messages imbedded in our environmental experience. Much more of this will be discussed in greater detail later.

In relation to the messages received through environmental experience, the first few years are the most vital in transmitting correct learning to our children. The home environment, consisting of attitudes, sounds, language, tones, spiritual expressions, our personal character, etc., all act as strong signals to developing children. The home is not required to prepare the child for his or her career path during these first few years, but it should be expert in teaching true identity as a child of God. It is from healthy, truthful identities that the seeds of later choices are planted.

While many of us do a wonderful job of parenting, even the very best, if left to their own devices would struggle. We need the help and support of Heaven. We are going to do much better when we provide truth to our children; and when we point them to the Source of their spiritual nourishment:

> "Abide in me, and I in you. As the branch cannot bear fruit of itself, except it abide in the vine, no more can ye, except ye abide in me. I am the vine, ye are the branches: He that abideth in me, and I in him, the same bringeth forth much fruit: for without me ye can do nothing. If ye abide in me, and my words (words are expressed thoughts) abide in you, ye shall ask what ye will, and it shall be done unto you. Herein is my

Father glorified, that ye bear much fruit; so shall ye be my disciples." (John 15:3-5, 7-8)

Since Christ is the Way, the Truth and the Life (John 14:6), our acting in accordance with His teachings is going to provide better outcomes. Spiritual power is harnessed through this discipleship, the power to hear, discern, heed and endure well. Whatever challenges we face in mortality, the best way to understand how to interact in the midst of such experiences will be through devoted discipleship.

Many times, we as parents just hope that the restored gospel will sink deep into our children's understanding and that they will believe the truth that has been revealed about them. I am reminded of the description found in the book of Moses, of Adam and Eve and the joy that filled their heart when they discovered the truth of the gospel plan. Their immediate desire and by way of commandment, "made all of these things known unto their sons and daughters" (Moses 5:10-12). The next verse indicates that Adam and Eve, however, faced some opposition to their invitation.

And Satan came among them, saying: "I am also a son of God; and he commanded them saying, BELIEVE IT NOT........" (Moses 5:13, Capitalization for emphasis). This to me is the whole crux of the matter, BELIEF. Getting our children to believe in the truth of their existence is a process, yet it should ever be a part of our influencing. Children that have spiritual assurances develop healthier, personal belief systems, which give rise to activated motivational circuitry that supplies power to healthy behavioral choices.

It is difficult to say what the conditions were back then that led to many of Adam and Eve's posterity's resistance and opposition to believe their parents. It is obvious that Adam and Eve received an understanding of the gospel later in their lives, after they had already had so many children — therefore the gospel would have been a change in the children's previous understanding. What doesn't seem to be so different about Adam and Eve's children and ours, is that both are raised in a world where carnality, sensuality, and devilishness are strongly promoted (Moses 5:13). The pleasures associated with this way of living can have a very strong pull on any of us.

It has been estimated that our children today view 40,000 plus commercials annually. Those commercials are filled with carnality, sensuality and devilishness, and so are the many television shows being watched between those commercials. Add in today's music, and other indicator's of moral decline and it becomes alarming on how much our children are being bombarded with messages that go contrary to revealed truth. Remember, what we expose our minds to the most, creates the development of strong belief systems, positively or negatively. But as parents act as gatekeepers of what influences they allow in their homes, and as parents live lives consistent with having the influence of the Holy Ghost, like Adam and Eve, there will be a good portion of our posterity that will live righteously (Moses 6:23) even in the midst of so much opposition.

And that is all this entire book is doing; is inviting parents to understand how belief is developed and encouraging parents to become partners with the Divine, so that our children have the best chance to develop personal belief systems that will have them thrive and feel joy and optimism.

While we want our children to feel accomplished in meeting the demands of mortality, true success will be measured in these words, "Well done thou good and faithful servant thou hast been faithful over a few things. I will make thee ruler over many things: enter thou into the joy of thy Lord" (Matthew 25:21). Those words can only be spoken to people of belief (faith) in the truth of their existence.

So now the stage has been set. Whether we like it or not, our personal way of being (i.e. our character, our attitude, and our own personal belief system), our parenting skill sets, and our spiritual development are all going to act as an influence (either for good or for bad) on our children. In the next chapter, we are going to address the huge influence we have on our kids, just by being who we are, or who we can become. Our personal way of being is and will continue to act upon the learning and development of our children's personal belief systems. We act as ongoing genetic engineers throughout the time of our influence with them.

So, what do you want your child to believe about him or herself? What 'template' would you like them to operate from throughout their life? What implicit memory do you want them to experience? What internal mental model do you want driving their everyday experience?

A template provides a pattern by which something is created. Heavenly Father is so aware of the importance of healthy templates that He provided a place where we can go on a regular basis, in order to remind ourselves of who we are, why we are here, and what we may become. It is a place where we get our bearings, where we are reminded of the great truth of our existence. As we regularly attend, the learning that takes place is consistently reinforced and the neuro-pathways associated with that learning become stronger and stronger. When the Holy Ghost acts upon that learning, it changes the very expression of our DNA, allowing us to change the nature of our being (Alma 5:12).

Interestingly, and likely not without coincidence, we call this place a "TEMPLE." TEMPLE and TEMPLATE are the same word. A TEMPLATE is where we get our bearings; it informs us of how to get repeated, successful outcomes. The TEMPLE is where we are reminded of our bearings, it tells us of the three-part act we are all involved in and it provides the pattern by which we can have personal successful outcomes. It should become the core belief or template we operate from. May we have a desire to shape healthy templates in our children, understanding that our mere presence is a constant source of that development, but just as important is the responsibility for us to teach our children to understand doctrines that lead to faith in the Source of their being and a desire to follow in his footsteps (D&C 68:25-32).

The Need For Confident Parents

In order to assist in developing this truthful template within our children, I believe that Heavenly Father wants each of His children to have the best possible chance in this life to find and experience joy (2 Nephi 2:25). How a child begins his or her life plays a pivotal role in that attainment. I believe that Heavenly Father wants parents to prepare themselves to receive the children that He will send them.

I believe that the best possible start for children is to have two parents that are bound by love and *covenant*, that have themselves learned how to be faithful, positive, and optimistic; that have learned to work hard to maintain economic stability and self-sufficiency; and have attained good relationship skill sets, all of which contribute to minimizing stress in the home.

I believe that parents who believe in the plan of happiness (Alma 42; Moses 6:62), and have gained their own spiritual assurance, that live lives in harmony with this revealed plan, demonstrating the fruits of such spiritual manifestations (Galatians 5:22, D&C 11:13), are in pole position to effect positive core beliefs, including spiritual saving beliefs, within their children.

These conditions are highlighted by a personal experience I will share, as well as what the research clearly says:

Dustin was 15 years old when I began to work with him. He had been sent to a youth residential program by his adoptive parents, due to some escalating behaviors, including sexual misconduct, fire setting, and a complete lack of personal responsibility. When he first arrived, Dustin would sleep or play during class time. During free time or physical education, Dustin would be found separate from his peers, usually making something with sticks or perhaps playing with insects.

When I did some history on Dustin, I found out that he had been abandoned in a car, in the upper deserts of Southern California when he was 15 months old. Fortunately for Dustin (and likely evidence of a tender mercy), an aware highway patrolman noticed sunlight reflecting off of some metal in the far distance. Upon closer examination, the police officer found that the metal was an old car and inside that car was a 15 month old child, with hardly any life in him. When Dustin was checked out at the hospital, it was discovered that he was filled with parasites and that his organs were in the process of shutting down – a failure to thrive condition.

I wonder what it is Dustin believed about himself by this point in his life, and what he believed about his environment. Many of us would not even bother with such inquiry, believing that children of this age are not capable of forming any real estimation of self or of one's environment. But all of the research indicates otherwise; that even while in embryo, children are interpreting their environment and are already developing implicit memory (physical-cellular memory), which is shaping the child's personal belief.

Eric Erickson, Ph.D., a developmental social scientist, indicated that there are very important developmental tasks that each of us must master, if we are going to build positive belief systems. He further indicated that these tasks have certain time frames when they begin to emerge, *signaling* when we should begin mastering the tasks. Failure to master these tasks, when *signaled*, will lead to complications in our later development.

From embryonic development until approximately eighteen months old, we are trying to master the *task of trust*. By eighteen months, we should have already come to the realization that our environment is predictable and safe. We come to this assessment by having an environment and parents that provide the maximum amount of comfort, with the least amount of inconsistency. We should have abundantly experienced having our needs met consistently, being raised in a stress-free manner, having had thousands of positive interactions with our caretakers, and having been highly attuned to. If a child is fortunate to have had all of this, then he or she is going to naturally develop trust in them self, in their environment, and in their parents. If trust is not developed, then shame and doubt, along with mistrust will become the child's companion.

In a later chapter, we will discuss these task mastery items and provide greater detail on what we do to assist our children in accomplishing these developmental markers. In relation to Dustin and the question I asked about what he believed about himself up to this point in his life, I believe it is safe to say that he did not believe the world was a safe, stress-free place; nor that the big people in his life cared about him. With so much uncertainty, and with parents (biological) that sent the message that Dustin was not important enough to know, it is an easy conclusion that Dustin had already developed a strong sense of individual unimportance and doubt about how to gain security for himself and for his place in the world. Such conditions create physiological reactions within the child's system, including the heightened production of cortisol and adrenaline, leading to feelings and activation of survival responses. These two chemicals create negative responses at the cellular level and a person that experiences chronic exposure to these chemicals begins to crumble emotionally, especially when it is the constant experience from the get go. Is it any surprise that at age fifteen, Dustin is having so many difficulties in his life and is practically lethargic in taking any ownership?

And now he is with me and it is very important on how I interact with him. I have to be very intentional on what I do. Knowing that Dustin has not yet mastered trust, this is where I must begin, and for the next 7-8 months, I interacted in a way with Dustin that allowed for trust to form. 7-8 months you say? Yes, if it takes a newborn 18 months, it is very reasonable that a lengthy time period would be required, no matter what the age.

(**Side-note:** That should be a lesson for couples where infidelity and other forms of betrayal have occurred. Time is a necessary element in recovery of trust. So when the unfaithful becomes angered because he or she believes that their spouse should be more quick to forgive and forget, and begin trusting again, please understand that such requests go against human design)

What did Dustin experience with me? What did he come to know about me? What in turn did he come to know about himself, due to my heightened awareness of my interaction with him? That is right, the very thing that we hope our infants experience by the time they are 18 months old, the development of trust. Dustin experienced someone that never activated his survival mode. I never became frustrated with Dustin, I never questioned his capability, I didn't compare him to others or ever sent a message that there was something wrong with him. I played with him. I attuned to his needs and emotions and provided the correct interaction that sent the message of importance. I was consistent with him, I never lied to him, I made time for him, and I empowered him by inviting him to take greater responsibility for his life. Dustin began to believe in himself, because I believed in him. He began to see himself as important because I saw him as important. He began to put effort in his own life because he was replacing old belief systems of no worth with belief systems of profound worth. As he put forth effort he experienced better outcomes, all leading to whole new positive experiences that led to increased trust in himself. The point of all of this is not to say I am wonderful, the point of all of this is to have you consider the importance of your influence in your children's lives by *who you are* and *how you interact* with them. Both will play a role in the development of their personal belief system.

In the Lectures on Faith, Joseph Smith taught that in order for someone to exercise faith in God, and by so doing secure to him or herself the blessings of happiness and eternal life they must first possess a correct idea of God's character, perfections and attributes. Character is associated with moral qualities of an individual and is exhibited by a high awareness of their importance and by consistently aligning one's actions with those professed qualities. Important characteristics, attributes and perfections of God include being completely honest, knowing all things, being all powerful, filled with perfect, pure love and being benevolent. As our Eternal Parent, we detect God's character and by our correct assessment of His character are then empowered to act in the guidance He provides us.

While as earthly parents we have not yet *perfected* these necessary characteristics in us, still, we have the capacity to possess and live such moral qualities to the extent that our children can exercise faith in the guidance we provide them. Our character is a significant element of our successful parenting. It is our good character that allows us to be effective, remarkable parents. Our character *underwrites* our parenting. One of the best ways our character is known by our children is in the capacity we have to attune to their own internal states and to demonstrate how much we care about what they think and how they feel; to be able to detect and assess their personal belief systems and interact in such a way that promotes truthful, positive templates.

The consistent, caring reaching out quality that promotes faith in our children has an opposite. Many parents have not yet developed the character of reaching out, but instead are still struggling with the effects of their own upbringing and therefore are found to be constantly looking inward. Because of their own uncertainties, they struggle with their identity, their own personal belief system, and the distorted core belief and template of being unworthy, ineffective and unimportant. In that struggle, such parents become self-absorbed and selfish, putting their own wants and needs ahead of their children's – sending the same exact message they received in their own childhood and thus continuing to the next generation a house of disorder, instead of a house of faith. Parents that do not know themselves, tend to have difficulty attuning to their children and knowing them. Usually such parents are more focused on obedience to rules rather than relationships, compulsions rather than moderation; and cleanliness rather than interaction.

As stated earlier, character matters in this calling of parenthood. Our character is *who* we are, our deepest held convictions; our way of being. Our character determines whether our children can exercise faith in us and in extension what we teach them. If our character is severely flawed, our children will doubt our ability to guide them safely and in turn begin to doubt themselves. We teach what we are – and that's about all. Master teachers have master character!

Here is the one thing that children know instinctively, that of themselves, they do not possess the knowledge and skills to direct their own life – they know they need to rely on some adult to help them acquire the information and skill-sets that will keep them from harm and allow them to feel good about themselves. Here is another thing children know instinctively, whether or not their parents have what it takes to be trusted in their role as parents. It has been my experience that children that qualify as Oppositional Defiant, many times have parents that have produced doubt in their child's mind! Therefore, let us look closely at our character and in the flaws that we discover, let us not become discouraged, but let us look to He who was and is perfect, and let us learn from Him how to take our weaknesses and turn them into strengths (Ether 12:27). He is the great exemplar (John 13:15)! Such an effort will not go unnoticed by the Lord. He will assist us in becoming more like Him (3 Nephi 27:27). The closer we emulate the character of Jesus, the more effective our parenting becomes – you cannot separate character from the act of faith.

God's invitation to each of us parents is to:

> "Therefore, let (the light of your good character) shine before (your children), that they may see your good works, and then glorify your

Father who is in heaven." (3 Nephi 12:16; substituted words for enforcement of the idea in parenthesis)

Improving one's character requires first to recognize and acknowledge those aspects that need improving or strengthening. The promise to all is:

"....Because thou hast seen thy weakness, thou shalt be made strong." (Ether 12:37)

Elder Neal A. Maxwell observed,

"It is not an easy thing... to be shown one's weakness... Nevertheless, this is part of coming to Christ, and it is a vital, if painful, part of God's plan of happiness." (Hope Through the Atonement of Jesus Christ, Ensign, Nov. 1998)

As we allow God to polish the brassiness of our weaknesses, the brilliant reflection of goodness will be the end product. What seemed dull and perhaps less than impressive; will one day be made priceless and glorious beyond compare. That type of glory will cause our children to take notice, and simultaneously create a desire to do the same.

Gratitude is a catalyst to all Christ-like attributes. A thankful heart is the parent of all virtues. Again, we are promised that if we will receive all things with thankfulness that we will be made glorious (D&C 78:19). Hence we have the first clue on developing a character of glory – be thankful and live your life in gratitude!

Christ's character allowed Him to proceed in fulfilling His mission unto the children of men. His meekness and humility prepared Him to suffer and sacrifice for the blessing of each of us. Likewise, His character provided for much joy and gratitude for His associations and for those that desired an abundant life because they looked to Him, believed Him, and then followed Him. His character allowed Him to see beyond His own inconveniences and discomforts (Matthew 8:20), so that others could be attended to and blessed. Christ was able to do all that He did, because of what He believed about Himself. We are ever grateful because of His character and confidence in whom He is.

Our calling and mission is to be foremost teachers, caretakers, and examples for our children. This is no small matter and our earthly accounting will likely be weighed heavily in the discharge of this duty. Though our children come with their own pre-mortal training, personality and inherent strengths, their mortal experience still requires that they develop faith in their true nature; and a personal belief system that promotes faith in Christ and His Atonement, displayed in acceptable motivation and good works worthy of celestial inheritance.

To provide the very best start for achieving these desired outcomes, our children need confident parents of good character. As we have discussed the importance of good character in promoting faith in our children, becoming confident parents also requires acquisition of knowledge about human design, it insists on the discovery and acquisition of principles that mediate human relationships, and most importantly, it mandates that we ourselves have developed healthy, truthful, positive personal belief systems.

Good families don't just happen! Good families have as a foundation, confident parents that understand and live an optimistic lifestyle and teach their children to do the same. Confident parenting elicits within children a sense of security, of worth, and faith in their individual potential. The confident parent creates within their children a positive sense of esteem in his or her abilities, providing protection against severe struggles such as anxiety, depression, eating disorders, sexual promiscuity, lack of motivation, lack of achievement, and poor interpersonal relationships.

Confident parenting is directly related to the parent's motivation to learn. It is enhanced by acquiring family skill-sets and becoming consistent in them. It comes from the recognition that we have an obligation to teach our children and in the understanding that we can begin creating the family we desire beginning today. Confident parenting must start with ourselves becoming appropriately disciplined and modeling an optimistic lifestyle for our children. Qualities such as a strong work ethic, being consistent, honest and kind; demonstrating service and being patient are all positive qualities of a good character. It is also essential that we model for our children the importance of self-responsibility, by ourselves taking personal responsibility in all aspects of our lives.

Some parents struggle with parenting because they have had poor examples themselves, and though that may be the case, we should never permit it to be an excuse to keep the status quo. If you recognize that your parenting example was a poor one, take that as a challenge to want to do better than the previous generation.

I once had a client at a residential program, a young man of 17 years old. His mother was an alcoholic and this young man suffered tremendously while growing up because of the many poor decisions his mother made. At the time of his program stay, it was his grandmother that had custody, because his mother "hooked up" with another guy and left her son behind.

When we were doing some history on his family, I gave an assignment to this young man to trace as far back as he could the issues related to alcoholism in his family. He was able to trace the prevalence of alcohol and drugs back to 1895, to his great, great, great, grandparents. Generational alcoholism was simply part of the family culture. This was an eye-opening experience for this young man, and his grandmother!

His grandmother thought she had functioned well as an adult and parent, and could not understand how both her daughters struggled so much with addiction. With a lot of work in opening both my client's and his grandmother's eyes to the devastating impact of addiction and a recognition that this disease had been so engrained within their family line, the young man's grandmother made a commitment to stop drinking and do everything in her power to support her grandson's approach to recovery and sobriety. This commitment came after an extraordinary statement from this young man during an open interview with other parents that had come to learn more about the program he was in.

There were several young people on a panel that were sitting in front of about 65-70 parents. This was an open panel, meaning that parents could ask anything they wanted and the panel could say whatever in response. One parent asked my young client, "What have you learned about yourself and how will that change your life when you graduate from the program." This young man began to choke-up as he replied,

> "I have learned that I grew up in a family that never thought about the impact of alcohol and drugs. They just viewed it as a way of life. My therapist had me do an interesting assignment in which I discovered that alcoholism has been in my family from at least the late 1800's. But now in 2012, I recognize that I can change all of that. I can stop all of the madness now by continuing my sobriety, and help my children see the importance of staying away from alcohol and drugs. I literally have the opportunity to stop alcoholism in my family line and I am going to do just that. That is the legacy I want to leave my family!"

This young man recognized that he did not have to repeat what was set as an example for him for generations prior to his existence. His grandmother also recognized that her own example contributed to her daughters' struggles and she made the decision to do something different. That is what confident parenting does, it chooses to make children a priority and do everything in its power to influence children to become better.

James Brewer once said:

> "Lucky parents who have fine children usually have lucky children who have fine parents."

If there is anything, whether it is a deficiency of those items mentioned above, or any issues that interfere with you being a better parent, I encourage you to check your pride and get busy in overcoming those issues, which negatively impact your children, and yourself! If you struggle with anxiety, depression, anger, irresponsibility, laziness, feelings of 'I don't care,' or whatever, please understand that your children will likely learn the same ways that you handle things. Your anxiety becomes their way of handling life, your depression becomes their way of handling struggles, your anger becomes their way in dealing with relationships, your entitlement becomes their sense of being owed things; your withdrawal from life and relationships due to unhealthy esteem, becomes their solution to handling unhealthy esteem, and so forth. Become the very best parent you can become, so that your children will learn to do the same.

The previous chapter provided the basis for change. It is real! I have had many adult clients go through the process of increasing their awareness of their implicit memory and by so doing, effectively changing out the distortions associated with unhealthy symptoms (i.e., anxiety, depression, mood dysregulation, suicidal tendencies, unhealthy esteem, etc.) and replacing it with implicit memories filled with truthful self-perceptions. The change is miraculous and improves not only self-concept, but also one's relationships. When one learns the truth about themselves, they then can act in faith. They shake off the chains of anxiety, depression, and other negative emotional reactions because they have replaced self-defeating beliefs that lead to poor functioning, with truthful, positive beliefs that lead to hope and other positive feelings.

Samantha was a client that had come seeking help with her anxiety. By seemingly every measurable external indicator, Samantha would be the envy of so many others. She was fit, she was attractive, she was highly intelligent, had a good marriage and children that were doing relatively well. She also had established herself as a highly sought after office manager, due to her people and organizational skills. She was known for taking professional practices and creating strong cash-flows, where before there had been financial struggles.

However, Samantha recognized that she *took a lot of things personal* and that it caused her to doubt her importance and effectiveness. I recall one example she gave of a hand towel that hung in her bathroom. Samantha had made sure that the towel was folded in such a way that would allow it to not interfere with another device close by. She reported that her husband, after using the restroom, would replace the towel but that it would be folded differently. She explained that she believed her husband was displeased with the way she had folded the towel and that his displeasure was upsetting to her.

Another problem Samantha struggled with was her appearance. She said that she would be late for dates with her husband, getting her kids to school or other appointments, because she would find herself changing her clothes several times, tending to find flaws with how her clothes made her look.

Lastly, Samantha really took her children's lack of personal responsibility for keeping their rooms and other areas of the home neat personally. She believed that she was an ineffective mother and that her children did not care for her because of this ongoing conflict in her home. Samantha reported that it resulted in either a lot of nagging or her eventually giving up and going to do it herself.

As with so many, Samantha built her self-esteem the wrong way, nor did she have any understanding of how to build it correctly. Her self-concept was tied up in what she had been telling herself for years of what it meant to be a good, acceptable woman, spouse, mother and any other humanly role she would take on. And so the dismantling began and it wasn't long before she recognized that her ups and downs about self-perception were based in her evaluation of what it meant to be worth something. She was literally tying how a hand towel was folded, how she perceived her clothes made her look, and how well her children kept the house to her worth as a human being.

Such 'tying' led to many incorrect thoughts of, "I am not good enough," or "I'm disgusting," or "I'm powerless," or the big one, "I only matter if I'm doing the right thing." The "right thing" was built into her based upon the messages she received from her parents and her religious culture. Unfortunately, she failed to balance what she was doing with what had been revealed about her nature. In essence, all of the negative beliefs she held were contrary to what had been revealed about her worth, her relationship with Heavenly Father, and her purpose and potential.

Within four months, Samantha had completely rebuilt her understanding of self-worth and appropriately built her self-esteem. She finally made the decision to believe what had been revealed about her and reject the things she had been saying to herself. Like magic, the distress of taking things so personally had gone away. She recognized that her husband and children were more relaxed and that her children had begun taking greater responsibility for their stuff, in large measure because Samantha had relaxed. By so doing she could now turn herself outwards, attuning to her husband and children in more empowering ways, connecting with them and sending the message of their importance based upon who they were instead of what they did. She no longer was consumed with being tuned inward, having to constantly analyze and judge, and figure out why she felt poorly of herself. Her implicit memory was now set correctly, which allowed her to feel secure and happy with whom she really is.

As a side-note to this story about Samantha, one day I was in a local retail establishment, when a gentleman approached me and asked me if I knew who he was? I said, "I'm sorry, but I do not." He replied, "I am Samantha's husband, and I don't know what you did, but I want to thank you. Our family has completely changed. It has been wonderful!"

Now one last thing I want to add to Samantha's story. Samantha described her children as also having some anxiety. I want to speak to this subject because it highlights another aspect of being a confident parent.

When someone comes in to receive help with anxiety, the first question I ask is, "In your estimation, which of your parents exhibited the greatest amount of anxiety?" I have yet for a client to be stumped – they answer immediately – either "mom" or "dad!" When I asked Samantha, she quickly replied, her mom. Anxiety is heavily influenced by environment. If a parent is anxious then so will be at least one of his or her children. The literal truth is that the parent's anxiety wires the child's brain with anxiety. This is in addition to whatever genetic expression has been passed on from the parent. This is a child learning how to regulate from the parent's mode of regulating. This is important stuff and leads to an important question. Do you want your children to experience an ongoing doubt and fear of his or her standing or of their circumstances, because of your own unwillingness to resolve the anxiety in your own life? Of course not!

But remember, the wiring for anxiety is occurring because of one's deepest thoughts and held beliefs. The persistent thoughts that lead to core beliefs and templates also act on the DNA of each cell.

In a research project of anxiety, experts recognized that within the same species of rats, some appeared quite calm, while others shook like a leaf. Researchers wanted to know what created the difference. In time, these scientists located the gene where either calmness or anxiousness was being expressed. Yes, that's right – it was the very same gene, only it was expressing itself differently within the rats. As the researchers looked for answers, they recognized that the calm rat pups had mothers that licked their pups and allowed their pups to remain close for longer periods of time. Just the opposite was found in the rat pups that exhibited higher levels of stress and anxiety. Their mothers were not as good (quantity and quality) in their nurturing. They seemed to push their pups away or did not spend much (if any) time licking them.

Researchers then took some of the anxious pups and placed them with the more nurturing mother rats. In a short amount of time, these anxious pups began to take on the traits of calmness. As researchers looked at the genes of these transformed pups, they recognized that the gene expression had been switched. This tells us that environment plays heavily on genetic expression. What our environment tells us we should believe, or in other words, the messages we receive and interpret in our environment create thoughts and beliefs about ourselves that literally act on our DNA expression. This is called Epigenetics, meaning "above our genes." Literally, the science of Epigenetics is declaring that our thoughts act as the rulers (above) of our genes.

What I want to reemphasize here is that however *our* DNA expression is set, when we have children – we will potentially pass on to our children the same genetic expressions. This is an unseen reason of becoming charactered and confident parents. If our genes are filled (expressing themselves) with hope, and strength, and calmness, and deep spiritual understanding, then these are the genetic strains our children will inherit.

The pathway to developing more positive genetic expressions is included in this revelation to us, "Look unto me in every thought, doubt not, fear not" (D&C 6:36).

In his research on Spontaneous Remissions (diseases just disappearing), Dr. Joe Dispenza, discovered that there were four common elements found among individuals that experienced these miraculous recoveries. The *first* was that each individual believed that a higher order of intelligence lived within him or her. Latter Day Saints would likely view such a belief in this manner:

> "The light which is in all things, which giveth life to all things, which is the law by which all things are governed, even the power of God, who sitteth upon his throne, who is in the bosom of eternity, who is in the midst of all things" (D&C 88:13)

> "And he (meaning Christ) is before all things, and by him all things consist" (Colossians 1:17)

As the Bible Dictionary explains:

> "The light of Christ is divine energy, power, or influence that proceeds from God through Christ and gives life and light to all things"

This power of intelligence animates our trillions of daily chemical reactions within the body, without thought. This light, which lighteth every man... (John 1:9; D&C 93:9), is expressing itself through us, it *orders* all things, and *directs* all things, and *governs* all things, and *regenerates* all things. Each descriptive word just used identifies the processes of biological survival we experience every second of our life. In the midst of all of this life giving power is the gift of agency – the gift to believe or disbelieve what has been revealed about us. As we disregard the truth, our physiology becomes impacted negatively. As we accept the truth, our minds and bodies express themselves in healthier ways (Isaiah 40:31).

It is interesting to note that our thoughts contain energy that give off light when we are being reflective about our thoughts. When we capture our thoughts and consider them, more energy or light is produced. These electromagnetic/chemical reactions produce a cascade of responses throughout the body. As described in the previous chapter, our thoughts are the catalyst to protein synthesis and protein synthesis is the molecular tool that tell our cells what to do. The ability to capture our thoughts provides the mechanism that allows us to empower healthy, truthful thoughts or disempower unhealthy, untruthful thoughts.

For those that experience the undesired effects of negative feelings, i.e. anxiety and such, also have higher levels of cortisol within their system. Cortisol is experienced as stress and its effects on every organ and tissue of the body is "deadly." It is highly toxic!

Cortisol is the antecedent to disease, memory loss, organ failure, and emotional unrest. However, its maintenance is governed by our thoughts.

When individuals began to look unto this Life Giving Power with every thought and replaced doubt and fear with faith and courage – this had a powerful impact on their health (D&C 6:36).

The *second* common element of individuals that experienced spontaneous remissions was a recognition that positive thoughts send signals to the cells to be more resistant to the enzymes and other chemical properties that are part of disease.

When my mother was in the hospital in April of 2005, my father called me and said that if I wanted to see my mother before she passed away that I better come see her soon. My father informed me that based upon the lab reports, my mother's cellular/blood composition was indicating that she would unlikely be able to live much longer.

When I arrived at the hospital and entered her room, my mother was kind of between heaven and earth it seemed like. She would gain enough energy to speak for awhile, but then seemed to doze-off for periods of time. I felt fortunate that day, as it had been a long time since I had the opportunity to have my mother all to myself. After her and I were alone, my mother said to me, "Larry, I know it must be hard for you to see me this way. I know that you wished you could have had more time with me, but my body appears to be worn out and can no longer sustain itself." I replied, "Mom, seeing you this way does not bother me. I have an eternal perspective that you helped develop within me. Our time apart will be but for a moment and I know that we will see each other again and be able to hold one another." My mother smiled. But then I added, "Mom, I think you ought to go out with your boots on!" This was a reference to a movie that had recently come out on video, called "Second Hand Lions." Michael Cain was a favorite actor of my mom and so I said to her, "Mom, we need to laugh and make this visit positive." I then told her about the movie and said that I would be right back. On my way out of the hospital, I asked a nurse if she would roll a T.V. with a DVD Player into my mother's room. When I returned, my mom and I watched that movie. She laughed and laughed that lovely, spontaneous, joyous laugh that I loved. I said my goodbye's and kissed my mother gently on the forehead and thanked her for all that she had done for me and then left. I drove to the airport later that night to catch a flight back to Los Angeles.

The next day I received a call from my dad. I was expecting him to tell me that my mother had passed. Instead I heard, "Son, the doctors can't explain it, but overnight your mother's vitals and labs had come back to within the normal range. I am bringing her home"

As I reflect back now on that moment, and knowing what we know now, it is likely that my mothers positive, happy thoughts and emotions played a significant role in that

44

temporary remission. She lived another six months. She's probably mad at me for making her go another six months of this life! She was ready to go to the other side. I guess I'll have to deal with that later.

The *third* element that was found common among spontaneous remission individuals was the decision to take control of not only all of their thoughts, but also their actions. New thoughts and new actions appeared to provide more and more insight to these individuals. Things that they had never considered and the various connections they were making with mind and body were exhilarating. Thoughts of what they really wanted to become or achieve replaced their daily routine of rising, working, eating and retiring to bed, just to do it all over again the next day.

The key to this third element was doing it persistently (reinventing, recreating life purpose, etc.) until it had become their familiar way of being. Or in other words, they had created a whole new implicit memory based upon truth and reality. Their emotional state soared and reinforced these new thoughts and new ways of being.

The *fourth* element was their commitment to meditation and reflection. Meditation and reflection are known as pondering, but purposeful pondering is what leads to renewal and heightened awareness. Another word that reflects this fourth element is *observing*.

Joseph Smith's pondering of the scripture he read in James led to a powerful awareness, which was accompanied by the overshadowing of the Holy Ghost. For a moment, the experience of the First Vision left him drained, but in time these repeated ponderings and manifestations of the Holy Ghost strengthened him and provided confidence to be in the presence of the Lord and other heavenly messengers.

When we ponder and receive important eternal truths, we do so by the power of the Holy Ghost. When we ponder about our progression and thoughtfully enter into ordinances worthily, we are renewed in both body and spirit (D&C 84:33).

Nephi, in instructing us in the connection between pondering truth and being influenced by the Holy Ghost said this:

> "And now, behold my beloved brethren, I suppose that ye ponder somewhat in your hearts concerning that which ye should do, after ye have entered in by the way.... Do ye not remember that I said unto that after ye had received the Holy Ghost... feast (read and ponder) upon the words of Christ; for behold , the words of Christ will tell you all things what ye should do. Wherefore, now after I have spoken these words, if ye cannot understand them it will be because ye ask not, neither do ye knock... For behold, again I say unto you that if ye will enter in by the

way, and receive the Holy Ghost, it will show unto you all things what ye should do" (2 Nephi 32: 1-4).

Nephi is observing for us the very process of change. It is the appropriate and empowering connection of real faith accompanied by works. Nephi, when pondering his father's words he spoke concerning the vision of the tree of life, was "caught away in the Spirit of the Lord" (1 Nephi 1:11), and he appeared to lose track of time and space. That is what real pondering does – it has us so focused on the truth being taught, that we become somewhat oblivious to our day-to-day surroundings and when we return to daily consciousness, we feel empowered to choose better, to be better, and to see the world in a better way.

The effect of *not* following this four-step process is well summarized in Alma 12:14:

> "For our words will condemn us, yea, all our works will condemn us; we shall not be found spotless; and our thoughts will also condemn us; and in this awful state we shall not dare to look up to our God; and we would fain be glad if we could command the rocks and the mountains to fall upon us to hide us from his presence."

When our lives are completed, whatever its story, will be a product of our thoughts! We will become what we think about the most!

So let me summarize, charactered and confident parents influence their children like none other. Children learn something about themselves by what we reflect back to them. Parents that have developed characteristics of kindness, patience, sincere interest in another, great knowledge, honesty, a good work ethic, who have overcome their own doubts and fears, are able to provide a healthy sense of importance in their children; these types of parents also pass on genetic expressions that are more positive, truthful and realistic.

Our children *need* charactered and confident parents. Such parents create strong families. Strong families contribute to strong communities. Strong communities contribute to stronger education systems, stronger economic systems, and stronger support systems. A nation's wealth, strength, and effectiveness are only as good as its families. If the majority of families or a growing majority of families are broken, then a nation becomes broken – period (Deuteronomy 4:5-9; 28).

In a study done by Judith Wallerstein and Joan Berlin Kelly (Surviving the Breakup: How Children and Parents Cope with Divorce, 1980) described what I have experienced first hand in the counseling office – that broken homes have long-term effects on mental and emotional stability of all parties, but especially upon children. The study demonstrated one eye-opening statistic that I want to highlight. Nearly 50% of the children followed in this long-term study, upon reaching adulthood, demonstrated a much higher rate of worry, underachievement, self-deprecating thoughts and unstable mood regulation. Especially apparent was underlying agitation that frequently amplified into excessive anger. It isn't difficult to surmise the impact of such self-negative attributes will have on the relationships these victims of divorce will enter into. This becomes the amplification effect, the exponential growth of broken families.

In a later chapter, I will review many social statistics, that are alarming and that can only be attributed to the decline of strong families, which is attributable to the decline of developing positive belief systems within our children.

Conceptualizing Parenting – The Big Picture

At the end of the book's introduction, I had stated that my desire was that parents would learn how to lead their children to eternal life (1 Nephi 8:12). In order for our children to choose such a course requires an understanding of saving principles and concepts. They have to come and believe what is being taught in order to act upon the doctrines of salvation.

Elder Paul H. Dunn addressing this issue said:

> "I suppose it seems all of us are in need of good counsel. Quite often parents and many young people ask the question, "How do you teach the gospel so that it's meaningful and applicable?" Do you know, my brothers and sisters, that learning any concept or principle or changing any behavior pattern requires five important steps?"

> "*First,* you have to expose a person. *Second* is the law of repetition. *Third* is to give understanding, the why. People of all ages want to know the whys of the gospel, not just the rules. This is the most important aspect of teaching because the *Fourth* step, that of conviction, and the F*ifth,* application, *cannot occur until we understand.*"

> "Too often our answers to young people's inquiries are "Well, because the scriptures say so" or "That is what the leaders tell us." Young people want to know why the scriptures say so and why the leaders are so concerned." (Teach The Why, October 1981)

While we are excited to share the gospel with our children (Moses 5:12), several of us experience setbacks due to our perceived inadequacies as parents. Most of us know that the delivery of the gospel message is not merely couched in preaching, explaining and exhorting. The quality of our relationship with our children bears a significant weight in the "hearing of the word" (Romans 10:17) and the development of faith within them. But such is true of anything we are trying to teach our children.

Questions and thoughts of:

- Why won't my children see the happiness the gospel brings?
- How come my children won't do their chores the way they're supposed to?
- If they would just obey, then they would be happy.
- How many times do they have to be told to choose the right?
- Why won't they study the scriptures themselves?
- Why do my children pick on each other relentlessly?

- Why is family night such a bear?
- How come my children feel the need to lie to me so much?
- I don't understand why my child is so resistant in going to church.
- I am so tired of the argument my child has with everything I ask him or her to do.
- Why won't my child just be more responsible for his or her schoolwork?
- How come my child's advisor has a bigger influence on him or her instead of me?

are normal, everyday experiences of family life and parental worry. Some of us however completely reach our wits end and feel like we are stuck in being able to provide any more thought or resources to start getting different outcomes. This section of the book is intended on helping parents assess the status of their parenting and if it does not seem to be getting the results one wants, where to turn to, to improve its quality and impact.

A good friend of mine introduced the Parenting Pyramid to me when we worked together at an adolescent addiction recovery center. Its simplicity and direction teaches parents what to do, what to consider, when they believe their children are leaning toward resistance to parental direction.

The first section of the pyramid has us look at our role when helping our children navigate life's opportunities and their choices related thereto. All children will make mistakes along the way, so the pyramid begins by highlighting one of our major interactions – that of correction.

Usually, when parents begin to sense the importance of their influence and responsibility toward their children, they act earnestly in delivering life saving principles with the intention that belief, saving belief will develop. When, as is so normal of the developmental process, our children demonstrate behavior contrary to the information we are providing, we typically react with fear and begin becoming *angry* at "unacceptable" behaviors being displayed. We may believe that our negative intervention is effective, because we recognize an outward appearance of subjection to what we want them to do as a result of our anger.

However, I believe when we stop long enough to analyze our angry reactions, more than likely, rather than being an effective tool to get our children to behave is instead our implicit memory's reaction to not having control and the meaning we attach to not being able to be in control.

When we are teaching principles, it is important to understand what a principle is and what space it has the ability to hold in our children's lives. A principle is a natural law; therefore it operates whether or not we are aware of it. When we are not aware of it or have not seriously considered the impact it may have on our lives, that principle occupies and maintains an external space. As parents, we are introducing the same principles over and over again (law of repetition), in order to have our children become acquainted with the principle in hopes that the child will experiment upon it (Alma 32:27). Upon doing so, a child will have a positive experience as is designed by our Father in Heaven. He is the one that has revealed these principles for our learning and benefit and he wants us to abide by those principles that both order and prepare us for Celestial Inheritance (D&C 88: 11-22). Naturally then, our obedience is going to be accompanied by impressions from the Holy Ghost through the medium of the Light of Christ, so that we will desire the good (Moses 6:55; D&C 29:39). When a child recognizes the benefit of a principle and begins to interact with it for his or her own good, the principle no longer occupies an external space, but has become internalized and has received some measure of value for the child. That is exactly what an internalized principle is – a value – that now acts as a guiding influence to receive more and more light (D&C 50:24-25).

In a moment I am going to address some of Elder Dunn's comments, because he hits on some things that are absolutely accurate and the reason why they are is because they tie in to our human design of how we learn. First, however, I believe that our children's desire to follow what they are being taught and to have reason to even consider doing so is largely related to our approach to parenting. The vast majority of parents are reactive in their attitudes, words and behaviors when dealing with raising kids. My desire is to have parents see that reactive parenting simply reinforces habitual interactions that compound over the years into less than desirable outcomes, both in our children's choices, as well as the quality of relationship we have with them. It is time to consider a paradigm shift when it comes to correcting our children. Correction is not about punishment, correction is about teaching.

Before, I referenced Elder Bruce R. McConkie's teaching on "belief" being antecedent to everything else we do. I know by now you have heard me harp on this concept several times. As we are talking about teaching and correcting, we are talking about a significant part of the process in developing our child's personal belief system.

In a talk, entitled, *Little Children*, Elder Boyd K. Packer added his witness to the power of belief, said he:

> "Our behavior is not totally controlled by natural impulses. *Behavior begins with belief as well."*

Elder Packer then hit a home run and woke-up the saints with this powerful insight:

> "True doctrine, understood, changes attitudes and behavior."

> "The study of the doctrines of the gospel will improve behavior quicker than a study of behavior will improve behavior. Preoccupation with

unworthy behavior can lead to unworthy behavior. That is why we stress so forcefully the study of the doctrines of the gospel." (October, 1986)

This book is trying to help parents become more responsive, more conscious and intentional to what they are doing to increase their influence on having their children develop the faith and fortitude to live by truth, with the promise that the quality of their relationships with their children will be strong and binding. To assist parents in discerning what leads to *reactive parenting* as opposed to *responsive parenting* is partially found in the type of questions parents ask themselves during the parenting process. There are two types of questions that parents ask themselves and which type of question asked most often determines the quality of parenting.

The first types of questions are reactionary:

1) What do I do, now that something has gone wrong?
2) What do I do to stop my children from engaging in self-defeating behavior?
3) What do I do when my child refuses personal responsibility and his or her life is falling apart?

The second types are responsive and proactive:

1) "What can I do to help things go right?"
2) "How do I teach my child to respect him or herself?"
3) "How do I teach my child to take greater responsibility and become self-motivated?"

Quality parenting insists on parents living consciously, rather than being reactive to our subconscious (implicit memory). If we are focused on being proactive and responsive we will more likely have the outcomes we are looking for.

CORRECTION

All parents provide correction as a means to have children adjust their behavior. Reactionary parents are found to focus and be more aware of negative behaviors in their children. When such behaviors emerge, the reactionary parent begins to intervene in order to get their child to conform. Parents that live consciously and responsively look at correction from a broader perspective, recognizing that commenting more on the desired behaviors, rather than just speaking about unwanted behaviors, is going to encourage their children to choose the desired behaviors more frequently.

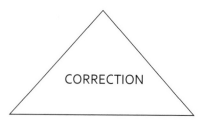

Reactionary approaches are more likely to be negative interactions, while proactive approaches are much more often positive interactions.

TEACHING

Elder Dunn made the connection between rule giving and teaching the why of rule giving. While we are in the business of correcting our children, it is critical that we involve ourselves in teaching at the same time. Our design requires that linkages and associations be taking place if we are going to learn anything. In fact, the simplest definition of learning is when two neurons connect! Therefore, if we are not teaching while we are correcting, our correcting is going to be far less effective, because neuronal connectivity is essential for building resources.

I heard this story in church and though I searched the internet to try and locate its source, I had no luck in doing so. But the premise of the story goes like this:

> One day, a young three old girl asked her mother if she could go out front and play. The mother thought for a moment and knowing that she was going to be washing some dishes in the kitchen and would be able to check on her daughter from the window, replied, "Of course dear, but remember, don't play by the curb."

> It wasn't long before the mother looked up from her washing to see that her young daughter was out playing by the curb. Immediately, the mother banged on the kitchen window to get her daughter's attention. As her daughter looked toward the kitchen window, she could see her mother waving her arm to come closer to the house, while mom was saying in a very concerned voice, "I told you not to play next to the curb." The child responded to mother's message and moved in closer to the house.

> In a few minutes, mother looked out the window, only to find that her daughter had once again positioned herself close to the curb while playing with her things. Mother began to feel both concern for her child's safety and anger that her daughter would go against the direction she

had provided. This mother went to the front door, opened it and from the porch raised her voice, calling her daughter and again stating with a stern voice, while waving her arm, "I told you – NOT TO PLAY BY THE CURB!" As before, the young girl gathered her things and moved closer to the house. Believing that her daughter understood, the mother closed the front door and resumed what she was doing in the kitchen.

To this mother's dismay, it wasn't but five minutes when she looked out and again saw her daughter next to the curb. Mother became enraged and marched out to where her daughter was, grabbing her by the arm and with a very negative look, matched by a negative tone in her voice asked, "How many times do I have to tell you not to play next to the curb?" In reply to the difficult situation, the young girl asked, "Mom, what's a curb?"

This story illustrates the importance of teaching while correcting. When we work to connect what we want with why we want it, then we have created a reason for our rules. That reason has a more impactful ability in having the child take greater responsibility for behaving. Our children's internal attribution originates from whatever rationale we supply during the correction. In the above story, not only did this young girl not know what a curb was, the mother spent no time in supplying a reason for mother's request. I believe there would be less correcting if we as parents did more teaching.

Additionally, it is important to understand that truth can have an incredible impact on our behavior, as Elder Boyd K. Packer pointed out earlier. Doctrinal truths are transmitted by the power of the Holy Ghost. When the Holy Ghost is involved in learning, the neural circuitry is enhanced and learning becomes more meaningful.

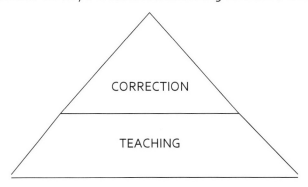

The effectiveness of our correction will always depend on the effectiveness of our teaching. Teaching is what builds moral reasoning. Parents who provide clear, consistent boundaries

whose reasons for existence are always explained generally produce children that develop choices that take into consideration factors other than just self.

PARENT-CHILD RELATIONSHIP

Many of us teach our children as a regular practice and still struggle with our children not choosing the better part. If this is the case then it would be beneficial to look at your relationship with your child. On a scale between 1 and 10, 10 being excellent and 1 being lousy, where would you place that number? Then go and ask your child the same question and compare the two answers. So many time parents are shocked and dismayed at the different perception their children have regarding the relationship in contrast to their own.

In a later chapter we will discuss five things that undermine the parent-child relationship. We will also highlight parenting styles as they relate to parent-child relationships. However, for the purposes of this chapter, I would like to speak to one very concerning aspect that likely creates the greatest challenge to having and maintaining a healthy parent-child relationship, and that is the quality of the husband-wife relationship.

Marriage, while intended on increasing happiness between two individuals, does not find its limits imposed just on the wed couple. It would be unwise to think that marriage does not reach far beyond the immediate couple. The joy of relationship extends purposefully to the children of this sacred institution and onto further generations. Likewise, if this relationship is fraught with difficulty, this too bears sway on the generations that follow.

Too often, husbands and wives teach their children to doubt true doctrine because of the relationship they have with one another. Our children are observing us, and if we don't have and promote a secure, loving, unselfish, sacrificing relationship with our spouse, many times they develop disdain for one or both of the parents. This attitude will likely interfere with our relationship with our children.

President Hugh B. Brown once said, "[we] cannot effectively teach what we do not profoundly believe. ... Our lives and our teachings must not be at variance." (*Eternal Quest,* Bookcraft, 1956, pp. 179, 181.)

Hypocrisy is easily detected by our children, whether that is in our behaviors in relation to gospel standards; or in our lack of Christ-like character as we interact with our spouse. Issues related to arguing, belittling, speaking negatively of, acting as if we are single by living parallel lives, not demonstrating a united front, not being supportive of each other and not demonstrating civility toward each other all lead to poorer relationships with our children.

Some parents that are reading this are already divorced, or are perhaps absent from their children's lives. I have sat with too many divorced parents that are quick to state, "Don't you think it is better that our children experience divorce rather than the negative environment they were experiencing when we were together?" Most don't like to hear my reply, "Don't you think it would have been better if the parents learned how to live decently with one another and their children, rather than divorce?"

My point is divorce, absenteeism and other forms of rejection speak loudly in the ears and hearts of children. That type of hurt is devastating and will likely have long term effects on the quality of our children's relationships and lives. If we are already divorced, please do all in your power to get along with your ex husband or wife. If you have been absent from your child's life, repent and demonstrate your love and interest in your child. These things matter and by improving our relationship with your spouse or ex-spouse, will have long-term benefits in your relationship with your children.

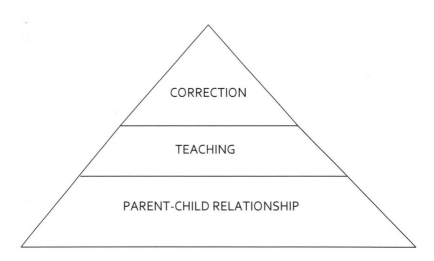

No matter how much time we spend teaching our children, they are unlikely to learn much from us if they don't like or respect us. The quality of our correction and teaching will depend upon the quality of our relationship with our children.

HUSBAND-WIFE RELATIONSHIP

As this is not a book about marriage, I don't want to spend a lot of energy and effort on detailing what makes husband-wife relationships ideal, but I want to emphasize a well known reality among therapists, counselors and family researchers worldwide. The most important subsystem of any family is the husband-wife relationship. The better this subset functions, the better the entire family functions.

When parents are in harmony, the children are happy and secure and grow up to be happy and secure themselves. There is no greater gift parents can give their children than their own harmonious relationship and all of the positive aspects that flow therefrom.

It goes without much reasoning that happy, effective couples do something different than unhappy, ineffective couples. The Family: A Proclamation To The World, outlines several principles and virtues that lead to successful relationships between husbands and wives:

> "Successful marriages... are established and maintained on principles of faith, prayer, repentance, forgiveness, respect, love compassion, work, and wholesome recreational activities."

From my experience as a family therapist, the happiest and healthiest couples are those that view their relationship as a treasure. These couples turn toward each other and place each other's interests consistently above their own. It is almost like a dance of reciprocal support. It appears that that their approach to their relationship receives its energy from having an eternal perspective of the significance inherent in the relationship.

While still enjoying their family of origin relationships, both spouses recognize the ancient counsel of "leaving father and mother" with the intent on having their family become what they intend on it becoming. Such wise couples bring into their newly established kingdom the honorable and healthy traditions from which they were derived, but also take into accounting those practices that either need to be improved upon or forsaken.

The decision of what to include or exclude is based in the ordained path of eternal partnership. That which leads to holiness, refinement, goodness, joy, and lives bound together in unity and harmony are the traditions and beliefs which wise couples allot for.

God has ordained marriage as both a gift and blessing to us. The strengthening and righteous operation of our marriage is a gift and blessing from us to Him. In that gift, we have the solemn responsibility to love, admire, and serve our spouse with all of our heart. By doing so, we earn the privilege of reciprocal fulfillment. The effects of this gift serve as an important structural feature for all other aspects of the family.

My own marriage ceremony has had a lasting impression on my view of an important principle that leads to successful and happy marriages. Interestingly, what I learned on that day is actually supported through modern research as an attribute common among successful marriages.

At the conclusion of the ceremony, the officiator had us look into a mirror hanging on the wall in front of us. On the other wall directly behind us was another mirror, which results in seeing the couple into perpetuity. That obviously symbolizes a doctrinal aspect of our faith, that the nature of the union is eternal, but what also occurs when looking into the mirror is the realization that beyond the initial reflection, the only person you can see is your spouse. I believe that symbolizes an important feature of successful marriages. When we look at the interest of the relationship, if we would each first look to the other, looking to how we can support them, how we can make their life more comfortable, how we can send the message of their importance in our lives, and how much we think of them, such an approach has always shown to be the most promising approach to marriages becoming what they were intended to become – everlastingly intact and eternal in their nature. Such is the quality and product of charity between couples.

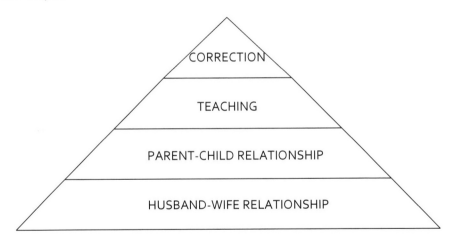

Of all subsets in a family system, the most important is that of husband and wife. How that subset is functioning will have the greatest importance and impact on family functioning. If the husband and wife subset do not support one another, if they are not aligned with what and how things are taught and administered in the home, if they display mostly self-interest, the children detect all of this and will likely grow to both resent the relationship and manipulate it for their own self-interest. It also creates an

impression about marriage relationships in general, which may set your children up for unnecessary relationship choices and struggles later. There is no way that children don't get dragged into and become negatively impacted when the marital relationship is not healthy.

OUR PERSONAL WAY OF BEING

When I entered 6th grade, I started playing tackle football. That first year, there was another player on my team by the name of Doug Hoden. Doug seemed more confident than me when it came to competitiveness, and it seemed that he was always out to prove that he was better than everyone else. If another player got the best of him or did a drill better, he would become boisterous, even threatening.

That same year I transferred to a new school and I soon discovered that Doug attended the same school. What could have been interpreted as athletic competitiveness at football practice soon became recognized as a character defect and in turn, I seemed to become the target of so much of his hostility. I don't know why I seemed to be such an easy target for him, but I found him growing increasingly difficult.

One day, his younger brother Dean invited me over to his house to help build some rockets. That is when I discovered that the Hoden's did not have a mother that lived with them. I don't know what the circumstances were that led to their mother not being there, but it became apparent, even for a 6th grader, that the Hoden's dad was a bit rough around the edges. Mr. Hoden kept pornography lying around, easily accessible to his boys. He was mean and critical. He raised his voice in anger more than he talked in conversational tones. He appeared to be constantly agitated and had a beer frequently in his hand. As I observed Mr. Hoden, I also recognized his children's reaction to his bad behavior. If his children did not do something to his liking, including doing things quick enough, it was not uncommon to see Mr. Hoden strike his children, or call them names, referring to them in girl-like terms.

This may seem like an extreme example of how individual functioning impacts the family, but it is representative of an understanding that at the foundation of every family is our own personal way of being. A lot of what I saw in and experienced in Doug was obviously a product of what was present in his father and likely having an absent mother. It goes without saying that our personal way of being is the foundation for the Parenting Pyramid and sets the tone for each of the levels above.

In the gospel, we are informed that all mankind is in a fallen state (world) and in that fallen state, as we begin to grow, "sin conceiveth in our hearts" ((Moses 6:55), and man becomes to some degree or another, carnal, sensual, and devilish by nature. As a result, God provided a probationary period where we could faithfully look to Him in helping us overcome the natural man (Alma 42:10); changing our carnal state, to a state of righteousness (Mosiah 27:25-26) with the understanding that such efforts would have us fulfill the invitation of becoming like our Savior (3 Nephi 27:27). Such change will not happen until we become converted. Elder Dallin H. Oaks provided the following understanding:

> "Now is the time for each of us to work toward our personal conversion, toward becoming what our Heavenly Father desires us to become. As we do so, we should remember that our family relationships—even more than our Church callings—are the setting in which the most important part of that development can occur. The conversion we must achieve requires us to be a good husband and father or a good wife and mother. Being a successful Church leader is not enough. Exaltation is an eternal family experience, and it is our mortal family experiences that are best suited to prepare us for it." (October General Conference, 2000)

I don't think most parents set out or intend to negatively impact their family. I think that most parents are well-intentioned; desiring that their families be happy and supportive of one another. I believe that most parents look at their responsibility seriously and go about trying to teach or show their offspring how to prepare for life by teaching life skills, personal responsibility, principles that lead to happiness, and a work ethic. Yet, even the best of intentions and desires can and are affected by the weaknesses and limitations found in every parent.

The point simply being, and please understand this, if we present more with the characteristics of the "natural man," we are likely to have a more difficult go of being an effective parent. On the other hand as we grow "unto the measure of the stature of the fullness of Christ" (Ephesians 4:13) in other words, as we think more like Christ, behave more like Christ, believe as He believes and share his perception and attitude, the better we become personally, and by default, we become better parents.

While God gives unto us weaknesses, He also expects us to humble ourselves and rely on His revelations to us, and the Divine help he reserves for all that do humble themselves before Him, in overcoming our weaknesses and turning them into strengths (Ether 12:27). And so I plead with you as I did earlier, everyone deserves the best you – yourself, your spouse and your children. If you know that you are struggling with anything that has not yet been resolved, go take care of it.

If our style of parenting includes rigidness, condescending judgment, selfishness, keeping secrets (D&C 121:37), demands of perfection, or we are critical and controlling, these are all indicators that our personal development is lacking.

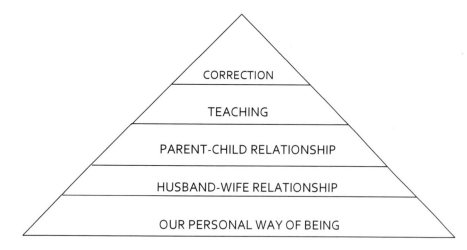

The Pyramid teaches us to focus on helping things go right. By focusing first on our way of being, working on improving the quality of the relationship between the husband and wife, demonstrating a keen interest in our children and focusing on teaching them correct principles, will all lead to more productive outcomes when we are faced with correcting our children.

If we begin to sense that our correction is not bringing about the desired outcomes, we can look to any of the underlying sections in the pyramid to find the answer to our difficulty. I want to say something very important here, so please pay attention. Children naturally do better with a father and a mother present and interested in their lives. Today, the majority of children (70%) will live in either a single parent or blended family. Whether parents are still married, separated, or are remarried – exes and new (step) parents would do their children well if they would put aside their pettiness and demonstrate goodness toward each other.

Of course, the quality of the husband-wife relationship is directly impacted by each partner's personal way of being, and so, as stated before, it is VERY IMPORTANT that if we struggle with our own personal, unresolved issues, these will directly impact our children. If you have issues related to addiction, trauma, low self-esteem, shame, character defects, etc. please get the help to overcome these. By doing so you will no longer live in fear, anger or shame and you will automatically become a better parent. Your children deserve your very best and so does your spouse!

So, in summary, the first levels of the pyramid are all concerned with helping things go right. The effectiveness of what we do depends on everything that lies below it. The solution to a problem in one part of the pyramid lies below that part of the pyramid.

Where should your focus be if your child is struggling? Focus on working on the three deepest levels of the pyramid. The surface or upper levels then tend to become more effective.

The Power of Correct Principles

The universe is filled with truth. There are laws by which all things are governed. Our discovery of these laws is just that, a discovery of something that already exists, not something new or that we created. These laws are immutable and provide order so that we can exercise faith that leads to happiness (D&C 130:20-21). Law is simply the application of truth!

Therefore, whether we are aware of these truths or not, has no bearing on their existence or the outcome associated therewith. Think about this in relation to our daily choices. If we were to review in our mind all the things we do everyday, we would recognize our total dependency on law (truth) if we intend on accomplishing anything we purpose. If we choose to deny or act in a way that goes against universal truth, such denial and opposition will not change or have any bearing upon that truth. In fact, denial and opposition will simply lead to evidence that these truths exist.

An example of this is the notion that we are free, wherein many suppose that they then have license to choose to do anything, with the insistence that there should be no negative consequences to that freedom of choice. For the wise, true freedom is found in obeying truth (law), living with the imposed limitations of truth (law), because doing otherwise leads to lack of freedom.

The freedom to choose a life of addiction, for example, entraps a person who is no longer in control. The freedom to choose a life filled with antisocial behaviors produces years of incarceration, where movement is restricted to an 8 by 12 foot floor plan. The freedom to worship the creation instead of the Creator is met with continuous dead ends and the eternal limits imposed by our lack of divine development. The law (truth) associated with freedom will always require the assessment of others in the equation, and a highly developed moral sense. True freedom is based not in selfishness, or self-seeking interest, but in the *principle* of selflessness.

In helping our minds become reinforced on this view of truth, W. Radcliffe said:

> "There is no progress in fundamental truth. We may grow in knowledge of its meaning, and the modes of its application, but its great principles will forever be the same." (A Dictionary of Thoughts, Tyrone Edwards, F.B. Dickerson Co., 1908, Pg 588)

The two views of freedom spoken of *do not* represent two types of freedom. There is only one true freedom. Those that lose their freedom based upon the wrong view are living evidence to consequences that come from breaking eternal law or truth — not an exception to it. In support of the concept that truth is absolute and applying this truth to our homes, President James E. Faust taught:

"To have successful homes, values must be taught, and there must be rules, there must be standards, and there must be absolutes. Many societies give parents very little support in teaching and honoring moral values. A number of cultures are becoming essentially valueless, and many of the younger people in those societies are becoming moral cynics." (The Greatest Challenge in the Word – Good Parenting, General Conference, October, 1990)

As I have pondered on the pervasive influence of truth, I have always been impressed with one of the revelations given through the Prophet Joseph Smith, as it is very much supported by what we know today regarding galaxies and demonstrates the reality of laws that govern their existence, said the Lord;

"And again, verily I say unto you, he hath given a law unto all things, by which they move in their times and seasons;"

"And their courses are fixed, even the courses of the heavens and the earth, which comprehend the earth and all the planets."

"And they give light to each other in their times and in their seasons, in their minutes, in their hours, in their days, in their weeks, in their months, in their years..."

"The earth rolls upon her wings, and the sun giveth her light by day, and the moon giveth her light by night, and the stars also give their light, as they roll upon their wings in their glory, in the midst of the power of God...."

"Behold, all these are kingdoms, and any man who hath seen any or the least of these hath seen God moving in his majesty and power." (D&C 88:42-45, 47)

I point toward this revelation as it brings to the forefront the truth of our universe – it is governed by law; would we think that our earthly experience would be governed by anything less? Other types of universal truth and law are those associated with nature, which all of us are to some degree or another familiar with, is that of electricity and gravity. I point to these two powers so that I might build upon the ideas that I am trying to convey in this chapter.

First of all, if I asked anyone to wet their fingers and then place them into an electrical outlet, very few would ever do so, because they have likely already experienced the outcome of that scenario. It only takes one good shock to prevent us from making such a clumsy choice again. Likewise, if I gave anyone a choice to jump off of a 100 story

63

building or a 1 story building, I can fairly well predict what the majority would choose. That wise choice is directly related to an understanding of the law and power of gravity.

Recognition of these two powers illustrates an important dimension of discovering truth and the laws that govern it. Truth is not dependent alone upon our eye sensory perception of it. In both the case of electricity and gravity, no one has ever seen either, yet no one would ever deny the power of these existing laws. Our growing knowledge of both of these natural laws has been on the basis of trial and error, experimentation, and other types of observation. As a result, we have learned how to use these great powers to our advantage. We would not have been able to do so if such powers did not have laws (truths) associated with them. Because of our discovery of how both laws operate in our lives, we have been able to harness the energy of both to produce heat, light, better travel methods, and many advanced technological improvements. When all is said and done then, truths and their laws are discoverable through our continued interaction with them and our careful, accurate interpretation based upon evidence.

We have been highlighting natural physical laws, though we have briefly mentioned the laws associated with *freedom*. When speaking in terms of laws that govern human interaction, another word we utilize is the word *principle*. Freedom is just *one* example of a principle.

A good working definition of a principle is a basic doctrine, truth or law. With some consideration, as with all law, some principles are vitally more important. Those that are associated with human joy should garner our greatest attention.

> "'Principles which have been revealed,' President Wilford Woodruff said, 'for the salvation and exaltation of the children of men ... are principles you cannot annihilate. They are principles that no combination of men can destroy. They are principles that can never die. ... They are beyond the reach of man to handle or to destroy.' [In Journal of Discourses, 22:342; italics added.]" (in Conference Report, Oct. 1993, 29; or Ensign, Nov. 1993, 22).

Principles are *natural human laws*. Like the natural physical laws we have spoken of, principles are too discoverable and when we determine or evaluate that these principles are beneficial, we operate within their limits to bring about better relationships with ourselves and with others.

When we are born and are helpless to understand ourselves or our world, we rely on parents to teach us principles, both by example and by precept, so that we can learn to manage ourselves. Principles occupy an *external* space to us until we discover them. As we begin experimenting with principles, we are likely to recognize their benefit to living more happily and so we begin to exercise conscious intention to behave or comply with the principle. If we recognize through our repeated experimentation that the principle is reliable we *internalize* it and it becomes a *value*. **THIS PROCESS IS THE BASIS OF SELF-MOTIVATION.**

These values are also associated with our character. When someone adopts the principle of "kindness," for example, we may refer to that person's character in this way, "He is such a kind person." It is the individual's adoption of the principle becoming internalized and then changing the nature or character of that individual. We recognize the person's values because of his character. In another chapter, I will discuss how we as parents engage with this process to have principles become internalized so that our children will build the engine of self-motivation.

Many times I remind parents that there is a real world out there, a world that our children are largely protected from because of the home environment. Our duty as parents is to prepare our children for that real world so that by the time they are ready to leave the nest, there will not be this great culture shock. Children will not be properly prepared if we have provided everything for them, have not allowed them to experience consequences long enough to teach, and have failed in educating them in principles. Responsibility for teaching human principles rests upon parents.

Effective parenting requires an awareness and understanding of principles, because there is real *power* in correct principles. True and correct principles act as a *navigation system* to discover our potential and capacity; as well as act as a *sure anchor* in experiencing peace and happiness. Joseph Smith understood this concept having universal application to progression when he clearly stated:

> "The Lord has revealed certain principles from the heavens by which we are to live in these latter days.... and the principles which He has revealed I have taught to the people and they are trying to live according to them, and they control themselves." (Brigham Young, Deseret News: Semi-Weekly, June 7, 1870, p. 3.)

Many have falsely accused Joseph Smith of some sort of brainwashing or some other power he had over other's choices, as it was recognized that so many were willing to follow him, desiring to do whatever Joseph asked of them. In response to this accusation, Joseph simply replied:

> "In relation to the power over the minds of mankind which I hold, I would say, it is in consequence of the power of truth in the doctrines which I have been an instrument in the hands of God of presenting unto them, and not because of any compulsion on my part. ... I ask, did I ever exercise any compulsion over any man? Did I not give him the liberty of disbelieving any doctrine I have preached, if he saw fit? Why do not my enemies strike a blow at the doctrine? They cannot do it: it is truth, and I defy all men to upset it." (History of the Church, 6:273; from a discourse

given by Joseph Smith on Mar. 24, 1844, in Nauvoo, Illinois; reported by Wilford Woodruff)

Because Joseph understood that truth is eternal and unchangeable, he never worried about whether the saints would continue faithful after his departure from this life. From a journal entry, Joseph recorded the following:

> "A brother who works in the St. Louis Gazette office ... wanted to know by what principle I got so much power. ... I told him I obtained power on the principles of truth and virtue, which would last when I was dead and gone." (History of the Church, 6:343; from a Joseph Smith journal entry, Apr. 25, 1844, Nauvoo, Illinois)

Both of these replies should settle any question in our minds as parents as to the importance and power of true principles, or the notion that effective teaching of truth will not inspire our children to govern themselves. For me the picture is clear – our Heavenly Father has designed us to discern correct principles and then through the power of intellect and emotion, move our behavior and nature in subjection to these principles because of the sheer joy of becoming (See: Dallin H. Oaks, The Challenge to Become, Conference Report, October 2000)

Henry Van Dyke wrote:

> "Four things a man must learn to do,
> If he would make a record true,
> To think without confusion clearly,
> To love his fellowman sincerely,
> To act from honest motives purely,
> To trust in God and heaven securely." (Four Things, An American Anthology, Edmund C. Stedman, 1787-1900)

In each of these lines is found *a* principle that if understood and utilized, would lead us to living an abundant life. But we live in a day where such principles are viewed by many as outdated and foolish; and many will continue to have such a view until they are found kneeling and confessing (Philippians 2:10-11; Mosiah 27:31). Elder Neal A. Maxwell testified of the importance of true principles when he taught:

> "You will also see that the living of one protective principle of the gospel is better than a thousand compensatory governmental programs—which programs are, so often, like 'straightening deck chairs on the Titanic'." (November Ensign, 1974)

This book has already spoken of many principles, and many will continue to be introduced, but for the purposes of this chapter, I would like to highlight just a few so as to assist parents in understanding very fundamental principles that will save them many wasted hours of exhaustion, and keep their eye on the ball, so to speak.

The first principle I would like to address is that of human agency and will. In doing so, I would like you to get a pad of paper and begin writing down everything you would like to have control over. Have fun with this list. If you are making $35,000 a year, simply write, "I would like to make $250,000 a year." If you wish you had more time, maybe you would write, "I would like to be able to control the rotation of the earth to create more daylight." Just keep going and write a list as long as you can think of.
Now that you have completed your dream list, I would like you to go back and cross out any items you recognize you don't really have control over. What do you notice is left?

So Principle #1 is: The only thing I really have any control over is myself – How I think, how I perceive things, how I regulate, how I behave and engage in limitless situations, and how I respond to others. This is what I affectionately refer to as the PRIMARY ISSUE. No matter what the circumstances thrown my direction, no matter how insulting or annoying someone is, no matter how tired I feel and no matter how many times I have had to repeat myself, still, the PRIMARY ISSUE is always centered on how you and I respond. Our response is the most vital part of our teaching correct principles.

Some examples of this concept may look like this – When we are filled with anxiety and demonstrate nervousness in response to stress, our children will learn the same way of handling stress; If we choose to consistently lose our temper when our children frustrate us, our children will likely turn it into shame and doubt; If we become good listeners, our children will feel important and wanted, etc.

Principle #2 is: What can't I control – For the purpose of this chapter I simply want to insert the idea that you have ZERO control over your children. Oh I know that it appears that we at times do control our children, especially when they are very little and we can pick them up and move them to another location, or maybe outsmart them. However, the will of the child always belongs to the child, so even though we can physically restrain or move a child, the will of the child and his or her associated thoughts still belong to them exclusively.

The restored gospel of Jesus Christ provides us with information that is largely absent from the world, namely that agency is a vital part of Heavenly Father's plan for our progression and fulfillment of our creation. How we interact with our children's agency will have long term outcomes on what our children will end up believing about themselves, as well as the quality of our relationship with them.

Agency and a person's will are sacred gifts that are endowments from our Father in Heaven (Helaman 14:30; Alma 12:31). We have been given guidance to these sacred gifts as well as warnings if we try and tamper with someone else's will. Let us briefly review this principle:

> "Agency is the ability and privilege God gives us to choose and act for ourselves. Agency is essential in the plan of salvation. Without agency, we would not be able to learn or progress or follow the Savior. With it, we are "free to choose liberty and eternal life, through the Great Mediator of all men, or to choose captivity and death, according to the captivity and power of the devil" (2 Nephi 2:27, as quoted from lds.org)

In influencing our children's agency, our approach will be the backdrop as to our children's ability to listen. If we are going to be effective, our lessons will be better received when we approach our children in an atmosphere of love and encouragement. When imposing limitations or setting rules, our tenderness in doing so will be associated with the moments we teach. As we invite our children to govern themselves, they are more likely to do so when they recognize that our approach is one of invitation not force. Our taking time to explain the reasons for our decisions will create the associations our children need to develop their own moral reasoning.

The process of any reasoning, including moral reasoning, is a process of repetition. Our consistent messages develop the integration of neural circuits where belief is not only stored, but strengthened. The brain is designed to pick up on patterns. Our continuing efforts to teach cause and effect increases recognition of these valued patterns in the brain. However, if our consistency is associated with control, fear, or rejection our children will likely miss what we are trying to teach, as they are paying more attention to the negative interaction. This is the great trial of parenthood, believing in our children enough to trust that they will do things of their own accord without our having to impose control on them. Parents that don't believe in their child's ability to learn are those that do abuse the power of parenthood.

If we are the type of parent that says "No" more than we say "Yes," or we resort to yelling, cutting-off, threatening, or pulling rank as a regular way of interacting with our children, such interactions continue to send messages of incapability and unacceptance. This style of parenting is always linked with hostile tones and attitudes that betray holy attributes of persuasion (See D&C 121:41-42). Whether we are right or not in our judgment of a particular situation, speaking this way to our children will lead to a loss of hope in them to follow our counsel.

We may succeed at times in getting them to obey us, but we are likely developing resentment in them where obedience will eventually decrease, especially when they are not in our presence. Our role is not to intimidate or belittle our children. Our role is to teach them. Learning comes when our children understand the connection between actions and outcomes. Many times we inhibit learning when we become perceived as a threat rather than an ally. When we become so linked, many decisions our children will make will be based in an emotional rejection of our authority rather than a rational acceptance of principles.

Tyrannical leadership, including tyrannical parenting is the opposite of Celestial leadership and parenting. The "you do it because I told you to do it" style of leadership is translated as unreasonable because it ignores human design. Our design includes the recognition of personal choice along with the need to feel capable and acceptable. When parents speak down to their children, rather than engage them with a desire to understand their child's experience, communication becomes blocked and influence wanes.

In essence, trying to exercise control over our children is a huge waste of time. It also becomes a quest for exhaustion and likely will lead to declining confidence in ourselves. So reviewing the first two principles I am insistent that parents understand, is to focus on the Primary Issue and refrain from trying to control your children.

We waste time and energy with incorrect thinking! Poor parenting involves a belief that we can control our children. We cannot and if we attempt to, it only builds resentment. Again, it is a huge waste of time.

Instead of trying to control our children, Principle #3 informs us of what we can spend our energy doing – *Influencing our children*. Human design gives us the ability to shape behavior, effect change, develop a moral compass, and train a belief system in our children *if* we learn and apply the principles associated with family systems and human design. This principle of influence is what the poet was referring to when he wrote:

> "Train up a child in the way he should go, and when he is old, he will not depart from it." (Proverbs 22:6)

This book is going to be filled with information, thoughts, stories and principles that will demonstrate a thorough understanding of how we influence the outcomes we are looking for. When it comes to the energy and effort we put forth in our relationships with our children, the only two areas we should consistently focus on is the Primary Issue and on *helping* things go right.

In large measure, helping things go right is about training a positive, healthy belief system and teaching our children how to govern themselves. Children who have learned to govern themselves take responsibility for their lives, including their thoughts, feelings, behaviors and choices. Such children demonstrate the capacity to be in control of their emotions, not the other way around.

I cannot tell you how many times I have sat with tearful parents, who after discovering the truths I highlight in this book, feel like they have failed their children. Most of these parents are already parenting adolescents and it is in these adolescent years where their poor parenting begins to manifest in not so subtle ways.

At times, it may appear to be more difficult in changing practices after our children have grown into their teenage years. It is then when we realize how much easier it would have been if we would have parented differently during the early years, but the cause is not lost. As soon as we begin to practice proper relational skills that improve our bond and connection with our children, provide inspired leadership, and trust in the Lord's design, we begin to experience recovery in our influence with our children.

Before I introduce the next seven principles, I would like you to recall what I mentioned in the chapter titled, 'The Need for Confident Parents.' I had stated that children develop either faith or doubt in us as parents in large measure based upon our character. The next seven principles are directly related to that concept because there are certain things that are fundamentally required if we are going to live together in a good way. In essence, these principles are what our children need to see in us if they are going to produce faith in their minds to listen and follow our direction. These concepts *underwrite* our parenting.

Principle #4: Our Making and Keeping of Promises – How important are the marriage vows, commitments, promises and covenants to our children? This is an important question to reflect on. Are the promises we made with God and our spouse extended to our children? Are they, meaning our children, in any way relying on the promises we made to God and each other in our marriage? In my estimation, the answer to that is a great big yes! There is something inherently held by our children and that is they see the intact family as a place of importance, and even though they may not be able to articulate how trust is an important element of relationships, yet when we break our promises made to God and our spouse, that dishonesty tears at the fabric of the children's heart as well.

The blessings associated with our promises, vows and covenants are transcendent. There is much more involved than just the husband and wife relationship. The very fact that children "born under the covenant" are recipients of the promises made to Abraham, tells us that our promises to God and each other flow to our children as well. Even if we fail to live up to our covenants, our children's faithfulness will keep their blessings intact.

What may be altered, however, is how our children respond to the belief system we have taught in light of our breaking of covenants. Obviously some do better than others; and the truthfulness of the gospel and our children's testimony of it can act as a buffer to our poor example, but still there is an impact upon them.

In April Conference, 1975, President Spencer W. Kimball spoke about the impact of principles with regard to marriage, he stated:

"We note the great increase in divorces. We disavow them. We sorrow with them, realizing that if there are justifiable ones, the justifiable ones are few. Generally, divorce is spelled S-E-L-F-I-S-H-N-E-S-S on the part of one party, generally both. It is ugly and generally most destructive for the people concerned, in their loss, their sorrow, their loneliness and frustration, particularly with the many children who are greatly deprived. It is easy to rationalize and justify the divorce. Our study reveals the fact that all too often it is because of their immoralities and their idolatrous worship of the god of lust."

"It is hard indeed to justify in one small city not far from us 272 divorces in the same time that 341 marriage licenses were given."

"When men and women are selfless and devoted to their companions, they will have returned more nearly to the image of marriage described by the Lord when he said, 'Therefore shall a man leave his father and his mother, and shall cleave unto his wife, and they shall be one flesh.' (Moses 3:24.)"

"When men are true to their covenants made with their wives and are loyal and selfless, divorces will take a downward trend. Paul gave the injunctions, 'Husbands, love your wives, even as Christ also loved the church, and gave himself for it. ... So ought men to love their wives as their own bodies. He that loveth his wife loveth himself. For no man ever yet hated his own flesh.' (Eph. 5:25, 28–29.)"

"And when women forget their pettiness and selfishness and submit themselves to their own righteous husbands as unto the Lord, and when they are subject to their husbands as the Church is expected to be subject unto Christ, then will the divorce rate reduce, and families will grow, and children will be happy, laughing children. God created male and female with special talents, powers, responsibilities, and with the ability to perform their special tasks." (Why Call Me Lord, Lord and Do Not The Things I Say, April Conference, 1975)

Every child I have worked with that comes from a home of divorce has felt betrayal and uncertainty. The impact creates doubt in the mind of the child as to the reliability of any human being. All of us do better when we know that we can rely on something or someone. When uncertainty creeps into our mind, we many times begin to replace faith with control, as a result of the increasing doubt we experience. Such tactical maneuvering is intended to prevent further hurt and doubt, but such coping interferes with happy relationships.

Jim married Dana, who had come from a home of divorce. Dana was only six years old when her parents broke their promises to each other and parted their ways. Dana's father remarried three times, even adopting one of his later wife's children, but had little and very infrequent visits with Dana and her siblings. Dana's mother too remarried twice. The first step-father crossed serious boundaries with Dana, which compounded all of the other issues she was working to reconcile due to the break-up of the family. Her second step-father was an alcoholic and created some difficult, emotional situations as a result.

Jim, though a good man experienced difficulty in making good money consistently. This frequently triggered safety and security issues that Dana struggled with her entire life. When Dana experienced this heightened stress, she would re-live all of the implicit memory associated with the initial break in her trust, including fears, doubt, anxiety, control and anger. These episodes marked serious downturns in their family functioning and Dana spent her time trying to resolve the uncomfortable feelings related to the stress by blaming her husband, withdrawing from him, becoming angry and controlling.

This story is not so atypical. Research indicates that children of divorce struggle in numerous ways, and the vast majority experience profound effects in their own marriage as a result. Coupled with the serious issues of continued trust breaking with her two step-fathers, Dana would crumble emotionally, even well into her adulthood, whenever she experienced heightened stress. All of Dana's negative attitudes and poor coping behaviors, resulting from her early trust breaches, only kept the insecurity tightly locked in place.

Likely one of the beliefs that Dana adopted was that relationships were going to bring disappointment. This mindset did not predict her relationships – it merely became a self-fulfilling prophecy for her. It became apparent, when speaking with Dana that she doubted whether Jim, or for that matter any person, loved her. In her mind, gestures of love were not sincere and so she continually prepared herself for the next time someone would leave her or hurt her. To compensate for this, Dana placed high importance on things or activities, as these tended to reduce stress by distracting her from internal, uncomfortable feelings associated with fear of being hurt in relationships.

Bottom line is this, regardless of what reason we afford ourselves when we break our promises, promises not kept deeply wound the human soul, and even more so of children who already recognize their lack of competency. We must be promise-keepers, we must be counted as one that is trustworthy; we must be reliable in order to increase our influence with our children. We must be a living witness of what the Covenant represents – that of a dependable relationship with Deity that will never fail or falter and forever unite us as one.

Principle #5: Consistency – Honesty is closely associated with the concept of keeping promises. Our consistent honesty provides the basis by which our children can make sense of their world. They rely on the idea that they can believe what they are being told. We must possess the attribute of consistent honesty, including being consistently dependable, consistently accountable, consistently showing good judgment and consistently being recognized as a person of their word. This is what develops trust within our children.

When I set-up my first office, I went to an office store and looked at their displays of desks, bookshelves, chairs, credenzas and other items that I desired. The displays were attractive and seemingly stable. I purchased several pieces and when I went to receiving. Instead of fully put-together furniture, I received boxes. Inside the boxes were all of the pieces of the furniture I desired – but it was going to require my effort to get it to look like what I saw on the showroom floor.

As I got to my office, unloading the heavy boxes into their respective rooms, I opened the boxes to find sometimes 50 pieces or more for an individual section of the set. In this state, it might be hard for someone to picture what the product was designed to look like. But as I got busy, *consistently* following the step-by-step instructions, I soon had sitting in my office the same system that was on display at the office store. I was happy with the result.

Looking at the end result and looking at the individual pieces strewn out on the office floor provided two different emotional responses. The system, when seen in its individual parts, was very ordinary in its appearance and seemingly unattractive; on the other hand, when completed, provided a handsome piece and addition to the overall appearance of the room.

Each time I *consistently* followed the instructions, each time I put a screw or a nail in their correctly corresponding holes, each time I connected the pieces as they were designed, I was building the intended purpose of the pieces. No one event in that process was impressive or memorable. But just as the *consistent* following of the instructions led to a handsome set of office furniture, so our *consistency* in what it means to be honest can lead to significant outcomes in our children's ability to live happy lives.

Consistency is a key principle as we lay the foundation of our children's ability to develop belief.

Principle #6: Children rely on the idea that we know more than they do – There is a description given children that have assumed the position of power in their homes, which is called becoming *parentified*. A *parentified* child is one that recognizes that their parent is lacking understanding about how to handle life and relationships in a good way. In order to prevent more disappointment, disruption and other painful

73

experiences, the child assumes the role of the parent and begins to direct the parent in what to do. Interestingly, is that such parents, willingly relinquish their role to their child.

Other times parents will describe their frustration when they tell their children "no" to something, only to have the child elicit the reasons for the parent's objection and then begin the process of reasoning that leads the parent submitting to the greater reasoning of the child. As a result, the child begins to doubt the parent's wisdom and ability to provide direction. The structure and government of these families become fragile, as the parent's self-doubt begins to manifest.

Other obvious scenarios where children doubt their parent's ability to provide correct information are in areas of ongoing domestic violence, addiction, relying on government programs for years, without practicing greater responsibility for self-care, and ongoing legal issues. How scary it must be for a young child to face his or her future, knowing that they cannot rely on and practice faith in their parent's knowledge. From such scenarios, doubt in their parent's wisdom becomes the only reasonable outcome.

Hopefully you can see the importance of this principle and how it operates in our ability to provide influence with our children. Relying on the idea that someone has enough information to provide reasonable direction is a necessary component of our children's ability to live well. Our children rely on the idea that we do possess enough information to guide them correctly and make reasonable decisions to reduce unneeded stress.

Principle #7: Relying on the idea that someone has enough power to provide, protect and lift – Children instinctively recognize their inability to care for themselves completely. It is the suggestion to their mind that we possess the power to provide, keep them safe and give them the principles that lead to their further development, which leads to emotional stability.

It is very difficult to develop the faith necessary to live carefree if we don't experience consistency in having our needs met. It is in the carefree state that normal human experience and development enjoy maximum benefit. It breaks our heart when we hear of children who experience severe degrees of neglect and inconsistencies. Such children become wired for survival or even worse, powerlessness. Their whole neurological system is shaped in such a way as to be very reactive to social encounters and learning and other forms of human development are severely hampered. Obviously I am speaking of an extreme on the spectrum of the human need scale, but even lesser degrees of physical and emotional distress decrease our children's ability to rely on us.

Principle #8: The Attribute of Justice – What good are parents if they are not engaged in teaching their children laws by which happy lives form and exist. A parent that is not so engaged, a parent that does not have any expectations of their children may as well be a parent that does not exist. Children *rely* on the idea that parents have a sense of what is proper and right and act fairly in relation thereto. Parents will lose their influence if they show favoritism or demonstrate hypocrisy, making absolutes relative.

As with the other principles discussed thus far, predictable outcomes are important to provide a sense of stability; i.e., cause and effect. Having a sense of what is proper and right, because we understand the difference between truth and error, provides an experience for our children wherein we act as guides – allowing them to explore – while we provide important safeguards. Some parents demonstrate otherwise, constantly making choices that bring hurt and distress into the lives of their children, as if they had no sense of laws and the demands of justice.

Parents should also have an idea that fairness does not mean perfect equality. Fairness takes into consideration factors such as age, temperament and what is trying to be taught. Too many children complain that parents are not fair. In their mind, fairness is defined as getting what they want in comparison to what they see others receive. Fairness, in the sense of what we are speaking is defined as the ability to exact judgment based upon a reasonable estimation of precipitating events and other vital data, including the demand of absolutes.

Most parents that have multiple children recognize that some are more apt to follow rules and expectations, while others seem to skirt or find reasons to go against family guidelines. The typical result is that such children (meaning the latter) experience much more negative interaction with their parents – leading to an idea that the other siblings are favored. As you learn about human design and focus on developing a positive, truthful belief system in your children, you will learn how to handle such children without negativity thereby avoiding any sense that some children are favored over others.

In the process of guiding your children to understand what is proper and right, remember that we too are responsible for living in accordance with truth and error. Truth is not relative and children are highly attuned to our expectations of them in living in accordance to it and our living contrariwise. They will have a difficult time following our words if they see with their eyes a double standard.

President James E. Faust counseled:

> "When parents try to teach their children to avoid danger, it is no answer for parents to say to their children, "We are experienced and wise in the ways of the world, and we can get closer to the edge of the cliff than you." Parental hypocrisy can make children cynical and unbelieving of what they are taught in the home. For instance, when parents attend movies they forbid their children to see, parental credibility is diminished. If children are expected to be honest, parents must be

honest. If children are expected to be virtuous, parents must be virtuous. If you expect your children to be honorable, you must be honorable." (General Conference, October, 1990)

Principle #9: The Attribute of Mercy – Relying on the idea that our parents, developed through their own experience, are longsuffering, forgiving, and possess unconditional love that will provide temperance to the attribute of Justice.

In preparing our children for the real world and the world beyond, it is imperative that we demonstrate the effects of mercy so that hope may be our children's constant companion; even in the midst of the pain they feel when they go against that which is proper and right. There is a balm sufficient to the pain of wrong choosing when we as parents consistently demonstrate acceptance of our children while we teach how unacceptable their behavior may have been. Unfortunately, so many parents fail to send the message of personal acceptance while in the midst of meting out consequences.

President Gordon B. Hinckley spoke about such men and women when he said:

"There are so many in our day who are unwilling to forgive and forget. Children cry and wives weep because fathers and husbands continue to bring up little shortcomings that are really of no importance. And there also are many women who would make a mountain out of every little offending molehill of word or deed." (General Conference, October, 2005)

God's mercy is enacted when one demonstrates understanding and sorrow for their choices. As Alma so well taught, "mercy claimeth the penitent" (Alma 42:23).

Jay Evensen, a writer for the Deseret Morning News, wrote about the lives of Victoria Ruvolo and Ryan Cushing and how the attribute of mercy found in Ms. Ruvolo provided a better hope for Ryan Cushing, wrote he:

"How would you feel toward a teenager who decided to toss a 20-pound frozen turkey from a speeding car headlong into the windshield of the car you were driving? How would you feel after enduring six hours of surgery using metal plates and other hardware to piece your face together, and after learning you still face years of therapy before returning to normal—and that you ought to feel lucky you didn't die or suffer permanent brain damage?"

"And how would you feel after learning that your assailant and his buddies had the turkey in the first place because they had stolen a credit card and gone on a senseless shopping spree, just for kicks? ..."

"This is the kind of hideous crime that propels politicians to office on promises of getting tough on crime. It's the kind of thing that prompts legislators to climb all over each other in a struggle to be the first to introduce a bill that would add enhanced penalties for the use of frozen fowl in the commission of a crime."

"The New York Times quoted the district attorney as saying this is the sort of crime for which victims feel no punishment is harsh enough. 'Death doesn't even satisfy them,' he said."

"Which is what makes what really happened so unusual. The victim, Victoria Ruvolo, a 44-year-old former manager of a collections agency, was more interested in salvaging the life of her 19-year-old assailant, Ryan Cushing, than in exacting any sort of revenge. She pestered prosecutors for information about him, his life, how he was raised, etc. Then she insisted on offering him a plea deal. Cushing could serve six months in the county jail and be on probation for 5 years if he pleaded guilty to second-degree assault."

"Had he been convicted of first-degree assault—the charge most fitting for the crime—he could have served 25 years in prison, finally thrown back into society as a middle-aged man with no skills or prospects."

"But this is only half the story. The rest of it, what happened the day this all played out in court, is the truly remarkable part."

"According to an account in the New York Post, Cushing carefully and tentatively made his way to where Ruvolo sat in the courtroom and tearfully whispered an apology. 'I'm so sorry for what I did to you.'"

"Ruvolo then stood, and the victim and her assailant embraced, weeping. She stroked his head and patted his back as he sobbed, and witnesses, including a Times reporter, heard her say, 'It's OK. I just want you to make your life the best it can be.' According to accounts, hardened prosecutors, and even reporters, were choking back tears" ("Forgiveness Has Power to Change Future," Deseret Morning News, Aug. 21, 2005, p. AA3).

How many of us as parents, for far less weightier wrongdoings of our children, feel the need to exact the last ounce of justice "so that our children will learn?" I have met so many parents that continually parent from the deficit model, i.e. taking away everything, including beds and bedroom doors, grounding children for excessive periods of time – isolating them from everyone and everything, and creating harsher and harsher punishments, believing that by so doing their children will eventually be broken and begin to do things correctly. In reality, the message of deficit model parenting is that acceptance is conditioned upon obedience, which turns the whole scenario into a battle for control! Even when the Lord instituted the Law of Moses, a far stricter code of requirements, its design and purpose was to increase faith, not demoralize its subjects (Galatians 3:24). When faith became appropriately developed, the law no longer had "life," it becoming dead because it had fulfilled its purpose (2 Nephi 25:23-25; Galatians 3:19).

When children do not believe that they are good enough for their parents, they begin to harden their feelings, because parents have not demonstrated the importance of the child's feelings. Remember, every person that is born into this world has a special gift, called the light of Christ (John 1:9). This gift is designed partly so that all accountable humans will discern between right and wrong (Moroni 7:16, 18). This gift becomes strengthened when parents fulfill their calling in teaching their children principles, thus increasing moral reasoning. In essence, our children become more sensitive to the feelings associated with their choices. When we recognize that our children feel sorrowful, it becomes our duty to teach the blessings of mercy.

While mercy cannot rob justice (Alma 42:25; Galatians 6:7), it does have claim on the penitent and we as parents would do well if we would nourish our children's feelings of regret, sorrow and embarrassment for wrong choices, by being empathetic to such demonstrations and by taking into consideration these feelings in deciding what consequences need to be extended.

If we as parents are void of the attribute of mercy, our children will have difficulty understanding their own nature and purpose. It robs children of hope. Mercy fans the fire of hope and a better way of living. It also provides the merciful blessing of having mercy extended to us in greater measure (Matthew 5:7). President Hinckley encouraged parents:

> "And this brings me to another area where there is so great a need for that mercy which speaks of forbearance, kindness, clemency, compassion. I speak of the homes of the people."

> "Every child, with few possible exceptions, is the product of a home, be it good, bad, or indifferent. As children grow through the years, their lives, in large measure, become an extension and a reflection of family teaching. If there is harshness, abuse, uncontrolled anger, disloyalty, the fruits will be certain and discernible, and in all likelihood they will be repeated in the generation that follows. If, on the other hand, there is forbearance, forgiveness, respect, consideration, kindness, *mercy, and compassion*, the fruits again will be discernible, and they will be eternally rewarding. They will be positive and sweet and wonderful. *And as mercy*

is given and taught by parents, it will be repeated in the lives and actions of the next generation."

"I speak to fathers and mothers everywhere with a plea to put harshness behind us, to bridle our anger, to lower our voices, and to deal with mercy and love and respect one toward another in our homes." (Blessed are the Merciful, General Conference, April, 1990, Italics added for emphasis)

One last thing I want to say about picking up on the signals of sorrow, regret, and remorse. We have a word or a phrase in our language that is used to express the internal feelings just described; "I'm sorry." It is important to help our children understand the accurate use of this phrase. Its intended meaning is to express the feelings one experiences in relation to the harm or damage their incorrect choices cause. The negative feelings become the catalyst to repair the harm created by the person's wrongful choice. So deep and penetrating should the remorseful feelings be that it would cause someone to seriously consider never repeating the act. The words, "I'm sorry" should be aligned with the decision to never repeat the behavior.

A child who says "I'm sorry," yet continues to repeat the harmful behavior is not using the term accurately. It is in these cases where parents can withhold the blessing of mercy and extend the understanding of justice (Alma 12:34-37).

When a child uses this term incorrectly, it does not mean that they don't feel some sort of regret, embarrassment or shame, but the feeling in some way is not attached to recognizing the feeling of the other person harmed. More likely, the feelings of regret, embarrassment and shame are directed inwardly and thus the child is less likely to change their behavior. In other words, the correlated feelings of the child are more about getting caught and being exposed rather than any real insight or sincerity in how his or her behavior impacted someone else. Being sorry is being sorrowful – but depending on which direction that sorrow is pointed, i.e., toward the feelings of the person harmed or toward one's self, will define whether the phrase is being used accurately. Let us teach our children this important step in the process of repentance.

Principle #10: Kindness – the essential quality that allows our children to tune in when we are teaching them.

I want you to recall why we have been speaking about these principles. We are in the business of developing and training a belief system in our children.

When a parent understands the first three principles spoken of in this chapter, then the focus of their efforts can be properly directed. Paying attention to how we respond to any given situation (i.e. the Primary Issue), understanding that we have no control over our children, and recognizing that we have the power to influence the outcomes we are hoping for in our children, led to the discussion of principles 4-10. Each of these principles is vital in helping things go right. But there is this one principle and attribute, that if developed within us, will more likely allow the reception of the other principles within our children – and that is the principle of kindness.

With specific application, the idea that our children believe that we have enough information to provide direction in their lives (Principle #6), likely would not matter much to them unless they believed we were interested in them. The old saying, "I don't care how much you know until I know how much you care," summarizes this application.

Kindness is a virtue that engenders people toward us. Kindness is an accumulation of several things – not just our benevolent, compassionate care for others. It shows up in our eye contact, our tone of voice, our expressions; our response to difficult situations and our consistent refrain from critical judgment. When our children detect our kindness, there is very little they will keep from us, because we become their safe place of sharing. Jude mentions this in his epistle stating, "And some have compassion, making a difference" (Jude 1:22). Being kind will always make a difference in our relationship with our children, and in turn their developing belief system.

When I became a Venture Scout (that's what 14-15 year old boys were called back then), I recall an experience I had while camping with our new Scout Master. His name was Nelson Lemke. Brother Lemke had recently become reactivated. I knew Brother Lemke personally prior to his coming back – his mother and step-father lived across the street from us. I occasionally would run into him when he would come by. His lifestyle was that of a "hippie;" his clothing, his transportation, and his drug use were all stereotypical of that era and belief system. Upon coming back into the church, Brother Lemke completely changed all of that and his appearance was quite a transformation. What he spoke to us more of was the change he had experienced inside.

When I recall President Ezra Taft Benson's address, "Born of God," I think of Brother Lemke, said President Benson:

> "The Lord works from the inside out. The world works from the outside in. The world would take people out of the slums. Christ takes the slums out of people, and then they take themselves out of the slums. The world would mold men by changing their environment. Christ changes men, who then change their environment. The world would shape human behavior, but Christ can change human nature." (First Presidency Message, Ensign, July 1989)

Being among 14 and 15 year olds, ours was not to consider too heavily about outcomes of our choices and behaviors. Seeing that Brother Lemke was new in the scouting program, I suppose that our scout group was simply involved in the process of breaking him in, not understanding the personal struggle we were creating within him. I don't recall all of the pranks we pulled on him during this campout, but I do recall the one single event that had me stop and think about my personal unkindness and how it impacted Brother Lemke.

The night had been chilly and in the morning we found that the pot of water we left out had some thin pieces of ice floating in it. Brother Lemke had chosen to sleep out under the stars and was still asleep, wrapped in his mummy sleeping bag. The only thing exposed was part of his face. I do not recall who suggested the idea, but certainly I was the one who was holding the pot over Brother Lemke's face beginning to pour the frigid water on him to continue our process of breaking in him. As the water landed on his face, Brother Lemke, without taking any time to undo his sleeping bag, had somehow ensnared me and brought me to the ground. As he held me there, I will never forget the words which came spewing out of his mouth, for these words haunted my very soul, "How come you are making it so hard for me to live the gospel?"

I had never considered the struggle that had developed within Brother Lemke as a result of our behavior collectively, and mine individually. Having already developed a sense of testimony about the importance of the gospel, I found myself stark naked in my conscience that my unkindness had led Brother Lemke to question his association with us; and in extension the church we belonged to. I felt horrible and I knew the intensity of that feeling was being delivered by the Holy Ghost. It was one of those defining moments in which I stopped and considered my ways. I am glad to say that Brother Lemke allowed me to apologize and change the way I had been interacting with him – it allowed our relationship to be strengthened.

In his talk, "The Virtue of Kindness," Elder Joseph B. Wirthlin, of the Quorum of the Twelve Apostles reminded us:

> "Kindness is the essence of a celestial life. Kindness is how a Christlike person treats others. Kindness should permeate all of our words and actions at work, at school, at church, and *especially in our homes."*

> "Kindness is the essence of greatness and the fundamental characteristic of the noblest men and women I have known. Kindness is a passport that opens doors and fashions friends. It softens hearts and molds relationships that can last lifetimes."

> "Kind words not only lift our spirits in the moment they are given, but they can linger with us over the years....."

> "The things you say, the tone of your voice, the anger or calm of your words—*these things are noticed by your children* and by others. They see and learn both the kind and the unkind things we say or do. Nothing

exposes our true selves more than how we treat one another in the home."

"There is no substitute for kindness in the home." (General Conference, April, 2005, Italics added for emphasis)

In maintaining perspective about our roles as parents, it is helpful to remember that our children are on this earth for the very same reason we are. Each comes with their own individual temperaments, strengths, natural gifts and weaknesses, but regardless of their personal make-up, they are still here to develop saving faith in the Lord, Jesus Christ and to work out their salvation in fear and trembling (Philippians 2:12). Our children's willingness to develop such faith and work will largely be influenced by our treatment of them.

One of the greatest ways we can change our attitude to be more kind is to ask ourselves the questions, "How well am I doing in helping my children reach their potential?" and "Do I support them or do I criticize them?" If you are criticizing them you are weakening them and what they believe about themselves. If you are building them up you are strengthening their positive belief system.

As parents, we are not perfect and neither are our children. In every home we will find imperfection. However, the home is where we gather to provide encouragement, support and teach the principles and attributes that will prepare us for our eternal home. Every child will experience a different journey in getting there. Never waste your time in pointing out critically what you find lacking in them. As you build your children you are literally building your eternal family. Our Heavenly Father is kind in His dealings with us. We should be kind to our children. President Gordon B. Hinckley once pointed out:

"Coming closer to home, there is so much of jealousy, pride, arrogance, and carping criticism; fathers who rise in anger over small, inconsequential things and make wives weep and children fear." (The Need for Greater Kindness, General Conference, April, 2005)

President Hinckley then reminded us that "such bitterness and animosity is not part of the gospel of Jesus Christ." After providing an example of kindness exhibited by Joseph Smith, President Hinckley then said, "Brethren, it is this spirit, expressed by the Prophet, which we must cultivate in our lives. We cannot be complacent about it."

In a coming day, each of us will see the effect of the attribute of kindness and the significant difference it will have made in our own eternal relationship of true family. At that time, we will recognize its lasting impact and will measure ourselves against its perfect manifestation.

D&C 133:52 points our minds to this startling moment: "And now the year of my redeemed is come; and *they shall mention the loving kindness of their Lord*, and all that he has bestowed upon them according to his goodness, and according to his *loving kindness*, forever and ever."

May our posterity say to us such kind words; if such shall be the case, then it is safe to say that their personal belief system will be encompassed with truth and strength. Kindness creates confidence in our children and love in our relationships.

Each of the principles mentioned within this chapter engenders the development of healthy principles and attributes in our children. When we are found to be filled with the wisdom and characteristics of these principles, our children have a far greater ability to believe in themselves.

There is tremendous power in correct principles. God, in His great love and wisdom has made available the discovery of correct principles for the purpose of our happiness and in preparation for the next phase of our eternal existence. Principles are natural human laws that mediate our relationships with one another. The family relationships are the most important of all and the principles spoken of in this chapter will get you farther along in developing secure relationships with your children, faster, than any other principles we could discuss, thus increasing your influence with your children more immediately. The reason being is that these principles promote faith in the minds of our children, not fear, doubt and shame. So in review:

1. We can only control ourselves (The Primary Issue)
2. We cannot control our children – doing so builds resentment
3. We have the ability to influence our children and their outcomes – this is where we should be investing our efforts – helping things go right.

Our influence is directly related to our personal values and character:

4. Our keeping of promises to God and our spouse
5. Consistency – especially being consistently honest
6. Our demonstration that we have more knowledge than our children in dealing with relationships and life's challenges
7. Our demonstration that we have the power to provide, protect and lift our children
8. Justice – that we have an idea of what is proper and right, that we act with fairness and are not hypocritical
9. Mercy – that we are longsuffering, patient, and forgiving, thus providing temperance to justice and keeping faith and hope alive in our children's hearts
10. Kindness – the foundational quality that allows our children to tune into us

The Unmaking of America

One way to look at the *power of principles* is to contrast society's that forsake them. While we live in a country that is still considered a place desirous to live, yet we are without doubt witnessing the tipping point of societal decline. In large measure, this decline is a result of rejecting or neglecting true human or moral law. Many of our forefathers recognized that the government they sacrificed to establish would only maintain its powers based upon the virtues and principles of its people. An example of this understanding is found in the following statement by the great revolutionist and patriot Samuel Adams. Five years prior to his death, Mr. Adam's said:

> "A general dissolution of principles and manners will more surely overthrow the liberties of America than the whole force of the common enemy. While the people are virtuous they cannot be subdued; but when once they lose their virtue then will be ready to surrender their liberties to the first external or internal invader." (As quoted in Samuel Adams Heritage Society; http://www.samuel-adams-heritage.com/quotes/morality.html)

I believe that one of the main differences between those that adhere to absolute principles and those that make principles relative is the belief of where principles originate. Those of the absolute camp believe that God is the author and revealer of such truths, while those of the relative camp believe that any law is man-made.

The Book of Mormon is held by Latter Day Saints to be a record of a fallen people and within the recording of that ancient document is provided the reasons why their society failed. Looking to our day (Mormon 8:34-35), the authors of that sacred record wanted us to know what we should be aware of, so as to have a better chance of maintaining our presence upon the land and not become as them. In one of those warnings comes this charge:

> "For behold, at that day shall he [the devil] rage in the hearts of the children of men, and stir them up to anger against that which is *good*."

> "And others will he pacify, and lull them away into carnal security. ..."

> "... wo be unto him that hearkeneth unto the precepts of men, and denieth the power of God. ..." (2 Ne. 28:20–21, 26.)

Principles are *good* as they provide the basis for positive human living. They are also authored by God for the purpose of finding and maintaining happiness. If one dismisses or lacks that understanding then such begin to look to themselves as the source of goodness and security – rejecting any principles that interfere with that objective. Their desire to live without law; has them become a law unto themselves (D&C 88:35; See Also: D&C 1:11, 14-16, 38). Such men and women are found to be active in mocking principles and their drive is to change the laws and turn principles upside down (Isaiah 29:15-16). Of such, Isaiah foretold:

> "Woe unto them that call evil good, and good evil; that put darkness for light, and light for darkness; that put bitter for sweet, and sweet for bitter!" (Isaiah 5:20.)

Members of The Church of Jesus Christ of Latter Day Saints are regularly warned by their leaders to be aware of those that would persuade us to compromise or bend on principle. President Ezra Taft Benson boldly declared to the honest in heart, said he:

> "The Church is founded on eternal truth. We do not compromise principle. We do not surrender our standards regardless of current trends or pressures. Our allegiance to truth as a church is unwavering. Speaking out against immoral or unjust actions has been the burden of prophets and disciples of God from time immemorial. It was for this very reason that many of them were persecuted. Nevertheless, it was their God-given task, as watchmen on the tower, to warn the people." (Ezekiel 3:17-19)

> "We live in an age of appeasement—the sacrificing of principle. Appeasement is not the answer. It is never the right answer." (Watchman, Warn The Wicked, General Conference, April 1973)

There has never been a country like the United States of America. Its greatness is based in the idea that mankind can practice self-control, by adherence to true principles. Katherine Lee Bates, penned such words in America the Beautiful, wrote she:

> "Oh, beautiful for pilgrim feet,
> Whose stern, impassioned stress
> A thoroughfare of freedom beat
> Across the wilderness!
> America! America!
> God mend thine ev'ry flaw,
> **Confirm thy soul in self-control,**
> **Thy liberty in law."**

The freedom to self-govern is an idea that has practically escaped every other nation. Our greatness comes from being free. But that freedom originated, and has been maintained largely due to the trust we as a people have had in God and in the principles which He authored. Our greatness is due to our adherence to these spiritual principles! If we are to remain free, if we are to remain great it will require us to become aware of the powers that have long been at work in destroying these principles. We also must take a self inventory, knowing that revealed principle lays at the foundation of our past achievements, and we ourselves must uphold these basic and fundamental truths if we desire to remain free. Our economy, our communities, and our families are at stake. Economy, community and family are inseparably connected. Each must be in harmony. They become such when we as individuals square our actions with eternal principles or law.

There are men and women, who on a daily basis convene to put into action, the plan to undermine freedom and moral standards. The principles of happiness are time-tested and time-honored. We gain our strength to live happy and free by our adherence to them. There is an ongoing polarity between those that want to pit themselves against principle and those that want to live by principle. Who will win this battle? That is the wrong question. The question is, "Which side will I be found on?" Elder Jeffrey R. Holland provided this insight:

"While we have enemies that desire to overthrow the people that hold to true and correct principles, it is our own consideration and level of devoutness to these principles that will be the greater determining factor upon which our strength is measured." (See: The Cost and Blessing of Discipleship, Elder Jeffrey R. Holland, General Conference, April, 2014)

What might we witness in a society that has lost its moral bearings? What evidence might we point to that supports the idea of societal decline? The following data is vital if we are going to regain our bearings.

One of the startling statistics leading to our difficulties is the decline in traditional family life. In 1950, 78% of the households in America were occupied by married couples. Today the percentage is 48% or less (Married Couples Are No Longer A Majority, Census Finds: Sabrina Tavernise, New York Times, May 26, 2011). The principle of marriage and the rearing of children in an atmosphere of husband and wife cooperation is being ignored and not without some serious implications.

Not too distant past, merely going back to the `1950's, according to a national teacher survey, the problems that teachers were finding most disturbing were:

1. Talking in class
2. Chewing gum
3. Making noise in class
4. Running in the halls
5. Cutting in line
6. Dress code infractions
7. Littering

Today, according to William J. Bennet's book, The Index of Leading Cultural Indicators (1994), suggests that our children are not faring as well:

1. Teen suicide has doubled since 1970
2. Drop-out rate as high as 60% in larger populated areas
3. Sexual activity among 15 year old girls has doubled since 1990
4. 10% of girls from age 15-19 get pregnant every year
5. 60% of all high school seniors say they have drank alcohol
6. 25% of kids do not graduate from high school in America
7. More American youth are convicted of felonies than any other country
8. Every 26 seconds a child runs away from home
9. Every 47 seconds a child is abused or severely neglected
10. Every 56 seconds a child is born to a teenager
11. Every 60 seconds a teen is arrested
12. 3.3 million teens are alcoholics
13. 2.7 million are addicted to drugs
14. Suicide is the third leading cause of death among adolescents.

FACTS WE SHOULD KNOW ABOUT AMERICAN CHILDREN

1 in 2 will live in a single parent family at some point in childhood
1 in 3 is born to unmarried parents
1 in 4 lives with only one parent
1 in 8 is born to a teenage mother
1 in 25 lives with neither parent

Source: *(The State of America's Children, 1998 Yearbook, Children's Defense Fund)*

DIVORCE STATISTICS
Current Family Statistics – 2003

Nearly 7 out of every 10 (68.7%) of children born today will live at some time or another in a single parent home
23.3% living with biological mother (Stepfamily Association)
4.4% living with biological father (Stepfamily Association)
1% Foster Families (U.S. Census Bureau)
3.7% living with non-relatives (U.S. Census Bureau)
6.3% living with grandparents (AARP – U.S. Census Bureau)
30% living in Stepfamilies ** (Stepfamily Association)

(Note: This does not include youth impacted by the death of a loved person such as a sibling or grandparent.)

(** Per the Stepfamily Association, there are no current Census stats available for Stepfamily statistics. However, a survey conducted in 1995 estimated that 30% of all children are living in either a stepfamily or a cohabiting couple).

Children of divorced parents are seven times more likely to suffer from depression in adult life than people of similar age and background whose parents have not divorced. This Israeli study, indicated that the loss of a parent through divorce is more likely to cause depression than loss through death. "The earlier the separation occurred, the more likely it was to have had an influence," researcher Bernard Lerer said.

(Study by Bernard Lerer and Ofer Agid of the Biological Psychiatric Unit at Hadassah Hospital, Jerusalem, as reported in Molecular Psychiatry, 1999)

CUSTODIAL VS. NON-CUSTODIAL STATISTICS
Fathers without visitation or joint custody pay only 44.5% of child support owed, but fathers with visitation pay 79.1% of child support owed.
Fathers with joint custody pay 90.2% of child support owed.
The number of single-parent homes has skyrocketed, displacing many children in this country. Approximately 30% of U.S. families are now being headed by a single parent, and in 80% of those families, the mother is the sole parent. The United States is the world's leader in fatherless families.
Father absence contributes to crime and delinquency. Violent criminals are overwhelmingly males who grew up without fathers.

Source: (U.S. Census Bureau report, "Child Support and Alimony: 1989, released Oct. 11, 1991)

STEP-FAMILY STATISTICS
More than a quarter of today's children will live in a step-family situation. *(Nicholas Zill, Child Trends, Washington, D.C.)*
16% of all families with children at home live in step-families. *(U.S. Census Bureau)*
High divorce and remarriage rates have resulted in about 20% of the children in two-parent households living with one natural parent and one step parent. *(U.S. Census Bureau)*
Slightly more than 40% of all current marriages are second or third marriages. *(U.S. Census Bureau, 1992)*

BEHAVIOR STATISTICS

75% of children/adolescents in chemical dependency hospitals are from single-parent families. *(Center for Disease Control, Atlanta, GA)*

1 out of 5 children have a learning, emotional, or behavioral problem due to the family system changing. *(National Center for Health Statistics)*

More than one half of all youths incarcerated for criminal acts lived in one-parent families when they were children. *(Children's Defense Fund)*

Nine million American children face risk factors that may hinder their ability to become healthy and productive adults. One in seven children deal with at least four of the risk factors, which include growing up in a single-parent household...The survey also indicated that children confronting several risk factors are more likely to experience problems with concentration, communication, and health. *(1999 Kids Count Survey – Annie E. Casey Foundation)*

TEEN PREGNANCY STATISTICS

75% of teenage pregnancies are adolescents from single parent homes *(Children in need: Investment Strategies...Committee for Economic Development)*

Approximately 13% of all babies born in the U.S. are born to adolescent mothers, with one million teens becoming pregnant each year. Explanations for teen pregnancy include the break-up of the American home and parental loss. *(University of Kentucky, Departments of Psychiatry, Ob/Gyn and Psychology)*

THE STATE OF THE FAMILY

"In order to begin to promote marriage, reduce illegitimacy, and encourage families we must curb the trends of *divorce* and fatherlessness. Father absence, a *by product of divorce*, illegitimacy, and the erosion of the traditional family, is responsible for: filling our prisons, causing psychological problems, suicide, psychosis, gang activity, rape, physical and sexual child abuse, violence against women, general violence, alcohol and drug abuse, poverty, lower academic achievement, school drop-outs, relationship instability, gender identity confusion, runaways, homelessness, cigarette smoking, and any number of corrosive social disorders."

Bill Wood
Committee on Ways and Means, Subcommittee on Human Resources

*April 11, 2002*http://waysandmeans.house.gov/legacy/humres/107cong/4-11-02/records/billwood.htm

SUICIDE STATISTICS

Every 78 seconds a teen attempts suicide *(National Center for Health Statistics)*

63% of suicides are individuals from single parent families *(FBI Law Enforcement Bulletin – Investigative Aid)*

"Separation, divorce and unmarried parenthood seemed to be a high risk for children/adolescents in these families for the development of suicidal behavior". *(Atilla Turgay, M.D. American Psychiatric Association's Scientific Meeting, May 1994)*

THE TIPPING POINT

The above cited data would have the honest in heart conclude the correlation between changes in family life and the related, growing dysfunction of society. What allows ongoing, enduring stability in families are the principles that govern healthy relationships.

The only explanation for the startling differences in what used to be expressed concerns and the current concerns is the *lack of principle* in people's lives. Civilizations destroy themselves when they forego principles that mediate human relationships and replace them with self-indulgent behavior disguised in misused phrases of freedom to choose. Neglecting principles creates apathy (Moroni 9:20). Elder Boyd K. Packer prophetically observed:

> "While we pass laws to reduce pollution of the earth, any proposal to protect the moral and spiritual environment is shouted down and marched against as infringing upon liberty, agency, freedom, the right to choose."

> Interesting how one virtue, when given exaggerated or fanatical emphasis, can be used to batter down another, with freedom, a virtue, invoked to protect vice.

> "Those determined to transgress see any regulation of their life-style as interfering with their agency and seek to have their actions condoned by making them legal."

90

"People who are otherwise sensible say, 'I do not intend to indulge, but I vote for freedom of choice for those who do.'" (Our Moral Environment, April Conference, 1992)

The No-Fault divorce laws, which began in California and then swept the nation, are an example of misuse of freedom to choose. Marriage, from a government perspective, is different than marriage from an eternal perspective. But we don't have to wait to die before we recognize the devastation such laws did not foresee.

W. Bradford Wilcox, the director of the National Marriage Project at the University of Virginia and a senior fellow at the Institute for American Values wrote in 2009 an article entitled, "The Evolution of Divorce." I recommend that everyone review his research and then ask themselves whether the principles that establish and maintain marriage are important or not? (http://www.nationalaffairs.com/publications/detail/the-evolution-of-divorce)

As we watch the trends of moral decline in the nations of the earth, I sense that many hardships will continue to be our companion. Those families that will abide the coming storm will be those families that have strengthened themselves by incorporating true principles into their family belief system. Those that can see the stormy clouds out over the horizon are those that already have such principles instilled (Ether 8:22-24). When principles are ignored, governments crumble – leaving behind family governments to fill the void (3 Nephi 7:1-8). Such is the partial fulfillment of the prophecy of Daniel regarding the stone cut out of the mountain without hands that would never be destroyed and fill the whole earth (Daniel 2:34-35,44). That stone is organized in family lines and units, with the king being of the line of David (Ezekiel 37:24-25; Jeremiah 23:5-8; Isaiah 9:6-7). While governments lose their power to sustain themselves, the principled members of the Lord's kingdom will be preserved and protected in direct proportion to the heed they have given to revealed truths and principles.

UNDERMINING OUR INFLUENCE –
THE NO-NO'S OF PARENTING

Since it is in the realm of influence (helping things go right) we will best spend our efforts, it is time to provide you with some tools and strategies that will provide for immediate changes in your home. While we may think that ours is the only home that is struggling with whatever we think we are struggling with, the truth is that every home struggles in similar ways.

Research has shown that some types of parenting interventions are more detrimental than others. The following five parental behaviors have been found to be the most destructive in building and maintaining an influence in our children's lives. These are the No-No's of Parenting:

1) Lying to our children
2) Arguing with our children
3) Criticizing our children
4) Avoiding our children
5) Controlling our children

LYING TO OUR CHILDREN

Obviously, dishonesty at any level will create weakness in the framework of relationships. But I want to speak about a particular type of lying that we do as parents that prevents our children from taking greater responsibility for their own learning and ownership of the outcomes of their own choices.

When the people of King Benjamin gathered for their annual festival, one of the reasons for coming together was to be reminded of and celebrate the kingship of God. In fulfilling this requirement, King Benjamin's address included remarks that highlighted qualities and characteristics of God. As it pertains to our current topic, one of the characteristics highlighted by this beloved leader is God's consistency in doing what He says, taught King Benjamin:

> "And behold, all that he requires of you is to keep his commandments;
> and he has promised you that if ye would keep his commandments ye
> should prosper in the land; and *he never doth vary from that which he
> hath said* ..." (Mosiah 2:22 emphasis added; See Also: D&C 3:1-3)

This principle is the basis upon which our children's adherence turns. When our children learn that "we do not vary from that which we say," children learn to more quickly obey.

One of the complaints I hear often from parents is their disappointment that their children do not do what is expected of them without annoying attempts to dissuade the parent's directive. This could look like delays in responding, pleas to do it at a later time, emotional manipulation, defiance, arguing, or diverting attention away and so forth.

My guess is that parents that experience these annoying attempts have a history of consistent varying from what they say and then end up doing. It is the inconsistency in the parent that produces these repeated strategies, by their children, to avoid taking personal responsibility. The adage, "Say what you mean and mean what you say," can produce more immediate expectations being met and fulfilled, especially if it is framed positively.

If there is anything that is solid about the field of psychology, it is that animals and humans can be conditioned. If you are familiar with operant conditioning, you know that we can associate natural physiological functions, such as salivating with simply ringing a bell, or turning a light on, or even by merely wearing a white lab coat.

When we lie to our children (or vary from what we say), we are conditioning our children to respond in a way that does not have consistent action when we desire it. Think in terms of a slot machine. A person puts in a coin and pulls the handle (or pushes a button) and the machine says "No, not this time." So the person puts another coin in, hoping to get a different answer, but again the answer is "No, not this time." A third attempt is made and with this a few coins are heard to drop. This is observed by the person that "if I keep putting coins in, eventually there is a pay-off." In essence the machine says "No" several times, but then through the relentless effort of the person it says "Yes" once in awhile, or goes against its initial response.

This conditioning is called "Intermittent Conditioning" and it is the most powerful form of conditioning we can use on humans. The idea here is that parenting becomes exponentially easier when our children are conditioned to do what is expected of them the first time we ask them to do something (this is where some of the Love and Logic philosophy integrates). So whether they are coming to us to ask us if they can do something and we respond with a "No" or if we are simply asking them to do something, our answer or our request ought to be coupled with the expectation that we mean what we are saying.

If we begin to act like slot machines, where we may say "No" several times, but then give in when our children insert their metaphorical coins of persistent asking or if we get into the habit of asking our children several times to do something before they respond, then we are conditioning them to delay the response we are looking for. That is our fault, not theirs. This is just another example of how we are developing their belief system. A child that doesn't become aware of the expectation associated with our answer or request believes that all things are negotiable. This is the child that waits until you are raising your voice or threatening them before they begin to get done what you asked them to do the very first time; or the child that doesn't like your answer, "No, not at this time," and continues to insert the coins into your machine until you drop a few coins back – conditioning them to continue to interact in this way with you – aaggh! *The lack of consistency is what creates intermittent conditioning in the child so that he does not take his or her responsibilities seriously.*

Now I am going to share with you what a hundred other parenting books advise – only say things that you are able to follow-through on. This is going to be different for every parent, but what matters is that you don't say something that you are unable or unwilling to do. I can recall when I was six years old and I had accidently kicked a football through our garage window and then lied to my parents about having any knowledge of it. Soon thereafter, my dad told me that he had received information from a neighbor who said that he saw me break the window. Being six and sensing that I was caught, I finally confessed. My dad became enraged and stated loudly, "You are grounded for a year!" I think it lasted a week. But it is statements like these, and usually made in a highly reactive manner, that characterize our inconsistency in what we say.

One time, a child of mine "snuck" playing video games. The manner he employed was filled with calculating and deception (someday he hopes to join the FBI or CIA, so I figure he is just practicing covert operations). When caught, I had a short discussion about the expectations and reasons for the parameters around game playing (actually, I simply asked him to remind me what the family rules were and why they were in place, which he was able to accurately state), and then informed him that he would not be allowed to play for the rest of the year (just a little over two months). Did he bug me about it? Did he try and get that consequence shortened? I suppose he made some attempt (although by his age he already knew that I was consistent in following through with what I say), but I held firm. Come January 1st, everything was back to the normal expectations and he once again took pleasure in playing with the Wii. Sometime in February, it came to my attention that he had "snuck" playing the video games again. I said to him,

> "I enjoy watching to see what may lead to your own learning. One of the reasons, last fall, I chose the two months restriction from game playing was to experiment whether two months was enough to have you take personal responsibility for your impulsiveness and decision making. It appears that time frame was not the right amount of time, and there may be no time that even matters to you, but I am willing to continue to experiment. Since I under-guessed the first time, I am letting you know that you are restricted from video game playing until next year. But come January 1st, all your privileges are restored."

> "By the way," I continued, "I think it is great how far the technology for game playing has come and I certainly enjoy playing them as well.

However, if I discover that you act deceptively in relation to this time of learning, the technology is not as important as my child's ability to demonstrate self-control and balance in his life. I would rather remove the game from the home completely then have to deal with a deteriorating relationship because the game is more important to you than the fundamentals that lead to our having a positive relationship."

"I have no problem with your game playing and I believe that I have been responsible and fair in establishing the guidelines that allow you to use the technology in a healthy way. Whether you decide you want to have the privilege again is up to you. I wonder what you might do?"

Now, words on a page are not adequate in having you understand my non-verbal language when we were having this discussion. Later in this book I am going to talk about non-verbal communication and its importance in delivering the right message. For now, be assured that during this conversation, my son understood my positive feelings for him – he never questioned how I felt about him personally. However in consideration for what I am addressing currently, I did not allow him to play for the rest of the year. I did not vary from what I said. This consistency prevents so many difficulties in parent-child relationships. By the way, his grades improved that year and he gave me no guff about the restriction.

Not all parents are capable of such lengthy restrictions, because they have not learned how to endure their child's disappointments – they can't stand having their child experience almost any amount of pain. That may be partly due to fear that their child will punish them somehow, or from fear of offending their child; or the unhealthy need for the parent to be liked. That is a separate issue from what we are discussing, just simply understand to be able to pick a consequence you are able to follow-through on to eliminate this poor parenting habit is what is important.

Foremost, a parent's responsibility in teaching a child to be honest is for the parent to be and demonstrate honesty at all times. The most common factor I encounter in working with families, whose chief complaint is regarding their child's misbehavior or lack of responsible performance, is the parent's consistent pattern of lying to his or her own child. Almost inevitably, if I point this out to the parent, I receive back an excuse on why the parent lied. Let me provide a case that illustrates this point. Following is an article that I wrote for a website that provides an example of very normal interactions between parents and their children. Because it seems so normal, we may miss or not be able to identify what the problem is in the interaction.

Please note how many times the parents do not follow through or do so inconsistently.

Quit Lying to Your Children
(An Example of How We Lie to our Children)

Some parents confuse the definition of love. Doing everything for our children is not love. Letting our children avoid consequences is not love. Thinking that if we interrupt or save our child suffering from earned consequences will be sufficient in their learning process is not love. Teaching our children to be responsible including being responsible for the management of their own emotions is demonstrating love at a much higher level. What most parents interpret as a demonstration of their love is actually seen as a weak-point by their child that can be exposed and manipulated to their own advantage. Love (as is incorrectly interpreted by so many, well meaning parents) is not enough. A child's esteem is directly related to their belief that they can manage life – but so many of us take away the opportunity for the child to learn the skills of management through the adversity that life naturally provides. When a lesson presents itself, we too frequently disrupt the process.

Jensen is a 13 year old boy. His parents have come to me because of their concern of Jensen's automatic tendency to lie. Jensen's lies are directed, not only to his parent's, but also toward other adults and those in his social group. I asked, "How long have you been lying Jensen?" Jensen replied, "I don't lie!" When I would ask for his parent's to give me an example that would lead to discovering Jensen's lie about lying, Jensen would explain his reasoning for saying or doing something that looked like lying, but in his mind was justifiable and therefore should not be considered as a worthy example of why other's believe he lies [If that just made your head spin, then you are feeling what it is like to be with a liar].

The problem, I discovered in this family, related to the parent's focus of their goal. Inevitably, the goal was on the desired outcome rather than the process. So, if mom or dad want Jensen to pick up his clothes and put them in the dirty laundry hamper, Jensen would continue doing what he wanted to do, with a promise that he would do it later. Sine all the parents wanted was for the clothes to put in the hamper, they allowed Jensen to manipulate them through his lies. Of course, Jensen would manage to forget to do it and mom or dad would end up doing it, with a threat that if they ever did it again that Jensen would receive a consequence. When the next time came up, again the parent's would threaten, but as long as Jensen completed the task, the parent's would not follow through on the consequence. The parents were continually experiencing frustration because they were ignoring the process that kept feeding the problem. Here is an example of that conversation:

> **Mom:** Jensen, are your dirty clothes supposed to be in the bathroom?
> **Jensen:** No.
> **Mom:** Get in there and get those clothes picked up and put in the laundry.
> **Jensen:** O.K. Just let me finish this game.
> **Mom:** Alright, but it better be picked up.
> **Jensen:** Don't worry. I'll get to it right after this game.

Later that evening, after Jensen has already gone to bed, mom discovers the clothes are still on the floor in the bathroom. She picks them up, puts them in the laundry and while going to bed herself, complains to her husband that Jensen forgot to pick up his clothes, as promised. The next day at breakfast:

> **Dad:** Jensen, I understand that you did not pick-up your clothes yesterday even after being told to do so. If you forget to pick up your clothes anymore, then you will lose your video game privileges.
> **Jensen:** O.K. dad. Thanks mom for picking up my clothes.
> **Mom:** You're welcome honey.

Two days later, mom finds dirty clothes that belong to Jensen laying on the floor of his room.

> **Mom:** Jensen, what did your father say about your dirty clothes?
> **Jensen:** I don't know.
> **Mom:** He said that the next time you do not pick up your clothes you will not be able to play video games.
> **Jensen:** Na'ah, he said, "If I leave them in the bathroom."
> **Mom:** That is not what he said!
> **Jensen:** O.K. just let me finish playing this game.
> **Mom:** Do it now or you'll lose your playing time right now.
> **Jensen:** Mom, (a little agitation in his voice) I can't just stop or I'll have to repeat this whole level again. It's taken me a long time to get to this point and I don't want to start all over again. Just let me finish it!
> **Mom:** O.K., but right after that level is done! Wait, can't you just pause it?
> **Jensen:** NO! (This is actually a lie) If I pause it, I will lose whatever I have done on this level.
> **Mom:** O.K. But don't forget this time.

Jensen continues playing and when reaching the end of the level, continues to the next level. Mom questions Jensen about whether he had completed the level and Jensen lies to her and says, "No." Mother tells Jensen to hurry-up. After playing, Jensen heads to his room; looks at his clothes, but rather than bother walking to the laundry room, simply picks the clothes up and stuffs them in his closet. The next day, Jensen has completely forgotten about his clothes. While Jensen is at school, mom finds Jensen's clothes in the closet and out of frustration, picks his clothes up and takes them to the laundry room. Later that day, Jensen goes into his closet to change for Scouts and sees that his clothes are gone. On his way out the door, Jensen, thanks his mother for picking up his clothes and putting them in the laundry.

> **Mom:** Thank you honey, but I was disappointed to find them there in your closet.

Jensen: Oh, I just placed them there because I wanted to get something out of my closet and I simply got distracted. It won't happen again.
Mom: Well, have a good time at Scouts, but next time be more responsible.
Jensen: O.K. mom.

When dad arrives home and asks mom how her day was, she mentions the incident about the clothes. Dad responds with his disappointment, but mom states her opinion that Jensen simply became distracted. Later that evening, after arriving home from Scouts, Jensen asks his dad if he would like to play a video game. Dad responds affirmatively, "But first go take your shower," dad says. Jensen does so and upon exiting the bathroom is seen carrying clothes to the dirty laundry hamper. While dad and Jensen are playing, mom goes into the bathroom and finds Jensen's underwear and socks laying next to the tub.

Mom: Jensen, come and get your dirty clothes out of the bathroom and put them in the dirty clothes hamper.
Jensen: I did mom!
Mom: No, your socks and underwear are still in here.
Jensen: Oh, I'm sorry, I did not see them. I'll get them in a second.
Dad: (sensing mother's frustration) Jensen, didn't I tell you that the next time you forgot your clothes that you would not be able to play video games? You better get in there now and take care of it!

Jensen goes and picks up his remaining clothes and then returns, *resuming play* with dad.

What a nightmare! For thirteen years, Jensen has played his parents in this manner, When pointing out to the parents their inconsistency and idle threats as forms of lying, they simply say, "We know, we know, we should be more consistent, huh? I mean he's a good kid and he does do what we tell him. It's just the lying we can't stand."

It is obvious that these parents are unaware of how they contribute to the problem and until they learn to be consistent in following through on what they say, this frustrating cycle will continue. For thirteen years Jensen has avoided the personal growing responsibility he should have been taking for the management of his own life. He did so because he knew that he could get his parents to continue being responsible for his stuff. One of the outcomes of children that don't learn personal responsibility for the management of their life as a whole is to struggle in transitioning to adulthood.

My oldest boy, when first attending college told us of his roommate that approached him on the first Sunday they were together. This roommate asked my son if he would tie his tie for him. My son asked his roommate who tied his tie for him back home – "My mother," he replied. Though my son was still single he had the wisdom to tell this roommate: "I will tie your tie this one time. If you don't want to learn how to tie your own tie, then I would suggest that you slide the tie just enough to slip it over your head, because I am not going to tie it again for you" – and he didn't. Likely my son's roommate either followed my son's recommendation or found someone else to tie his tie. In time, he would recognize that it is likely easier to learn how to tie one's own tie rather than go through the frustrating experience of finding someone else to do so.

One of our jobs as parents is to prepare our children for the real world. If we don't, it can be a culture shock as they are learning to catch-up on the things they should have learned to master a long time ago. When Jensen reaches adulthood and tells his boss that the report will be done on time, but he believes his boss is like his parents were growing up, he is going to be in for a shock when he sees how his boss is very different than his parents when he doesn't get that report done as promised.

STOP ARGUING WITH YOUR CHILDREN

Prior to my becoming a Marriage and Family Therapist, I owned a construction business that specialized in restoration of different building components. Quite a bit of restoration I performed was for concrete structures. Most of the issues related to these repairs were the effect of rebar becoming corroded and popping the concrete. If you do not know a lot about corrosion, it is an electrolysis reaction in the metal that changes the ionic structure of the rebar. In laymen's terms, some parts of the metal bar would become thinner, while other sections of the same rebar would thicken. The thinning areas would jeopardize the structural integrity of the building, as these were severely weakened areas that could break under the pressure of the weight of the concrete. The thickening areas would push up against the adjacent concrete, causing it to separate from the metal supports and pop at the surface areas. These newly exposed pockets would increase the rate of moisture damage.

Corrosion is like a cancer in buildings and other concrete structures, and the costs for ignoring the signs can become astronomical or even deadly. We hear about bridge and parking structure failures at times in the news. Most of these failures are for the very reason I pointed out.

Corrosion therefore results in weakening relationships of building parts as well as separation of building components that are designed to be in a relationship with one another for the purpose of making the structure strong.

Likewise, contention between us as humans creates the same effect. Arguing, fighting, quarreling and other forms of contention are corrosive. The integrity of our relationships becomes compromised and it goes without saying that our feelings for one another grow apart and our relationships weaken.

Abraham Lincoln once taught:

> "Quarrel not at all. No man resolved to make the most of himself can spare time for personal contention. ..." (Letter to J. M. Cutts, 26 Oct. 1863, in comp. and arr. Ralph B. Winn, New York: New York Philosophical Library, 1959, p. 107.)

Contention is corrosive. It continually weakens our self-concept, our personal sense of power and if continued will result in distancing relationships. The same is true of our children; their personal belief system is negatively impacted when we engage this way. This is one of the contributors to the development of shame, which if reinforced by these chronic negative interactions with one's parents, will have long-term impact on the child's life (well into adulthood). We have very little influence on our children when we engage in arguing as a regular way of interacting with them.

Now that the concept is understood, let's talk about what normal arguing looks like between parents and their children and what to do to stop the corrosive process. When children come to their parents to ask them whether or not they can do something or buy something, parents may respond with the word "No," which immediately leads to the next word or words coming out of the child's mouth – "Why" or "Why not!"

We then gather all of our mental faculties and begin to defend our position, or we simply cut it short by stating, "Because I said so," invoking our parental power. But even being so daring as to push our superior position, yet we are still met with the "whys" and "why not's."

Our children have us so trained that we actually believe we have to explain to them the brilliant reasons for our decision. As we begin to do so, our children begin the process of out-reasoning us (and at times demonstrate greater skill than our own), leading to our bowing to their superior wisdom, or having us erupt in anger as a result of our child's incessant pushing to get what he or she wants.

Now that you are nodding your head and saying, "Yup, yup, that's exactly what it is like," I want you to consider the strategy being so expertly utilized by your child. The reason why your child asks the reason "why" or "why not" isn't because he or she is excited to experience the richness of your wisdom (I mean, really, how many times have you heard a child say – "I never thought of it that way. I can see why you are the parent. You are so wise and I am lucky to have you as my mother"). The reason they use the "W" words is because they do not know what your objections are and until they can hear them then they remain stuck. So they respond, "Why not" and we immediately fall prey to their intention to overcome any objections so they can get what they want.

Before I discuss the strategy that will stop the arguing, I want to say a couple of things that will keep things in perspective. The first is that it is important to teach the "WHY" to your children, because this is what develops moral reasoning due to the law of associative memory. We discussed this principle in the chapter entitled, The Parenting Pyramid, under the heading. "Teaching." So let's say your teenage son asks if he can go over to a young lady's house that he likes; you naturally respond by asking if her parents are home. He tells you that they are not and so you give your answer – "No dear, I don't think it is a good idea." He then immediately goes into the strategy of eliciting your objections with the intention to overcome them. By this time in his life, you should have already been teaching the "why's" of appropriate limits when it comes to spending time with the opposite gender. If you have not, then this scenario obviously opens the door to having that discussion.

However, likely you already have and so you can approach the conversation a couple of ways:

1) "Son, it sounds like you are looking for a reason for my answer. I believe we have spoken about this situation before – can you recall what we discussed?" At that point I just let my child take ownership of recalling the reasons for not being alone with the opposite gender. Now he may say, "I know mom, I get it – there may be a chance to do things we shouldn't be doing at our age. I promise that I will behave – you can trust me." I would then respond, "I'm glad that our previous discussions have allowed you to understand the "why" of this scenario, I also know how hard it is when you like someone that much not to be with them. Since you understand the safe boundaries of boy/girl relationships, do you have any idea of how you can spend time together without crossing those boundaries?" If a parent has taught their child well; and has a secure relationship (we will talk about secure relationships later in the book) with them, the child is more likely at this point to take ownership of his or her choice; and provide safe alternatives. But let's suppose this parent child relationship is not secure and the child does not like the direction his or her parent is trying to steer the conversation (after all, he really wants to be alone with his girlfriend), and persists on changing his parent's mind?

The second response requires you to understand that while your child seems to be intent on getting you to change your mind, in reality, youth do not possess the stamina that comes with maturity. If you will memorize the following two words, *"nevertheless"* and *"regardless,"* I will teach you how to incorporate them in a way that stops the cycle of arguing we have been discussing. The reason this method works is because it follows the rules of an important assertion skill called "Broken Record."

Broken Record is a skill whereby one uses calm repetition (saying what you want over and over again). This skill teaches persistence without you having to rehearse arguments or angry feelings, in order to be "up" dealing with others. This is an example of "Broken Record,"

2) "It sounds like you really want to be with your girlfriend. Those feelings can be very powerful and exciting; *nevertheless*, you are not going over to her house without adults being present."

Your son responds, "Mom, you can trust me. Just this once will you please reconsider?"

"I'm wondering if part of the problem here is that you and she were planning on this and the expectation is now leading to greater disappointment to my answer. I think wanting to be with her is exciting and so I can see my answer is not what you were hoping for, *nevertheless*, you are not going over to her house without adults being present."

Your son comes back with, "I promise to call you every 15 minutes or you can call me whenever you want, that way you know we are not doing anything."

"I believe that you don't have any intention to make a poor choice. Most of us establish a certain point that we won't go beyond, while still allowing some level of sexual excitement. The problem with these limits is that in the heat of the moment, we begin negotiating with ourselves and tell ourselves, 'just a little bit more.' At some point, and we don't know what that point is, we find ourselves in a position we are not prepared for. I hope that my being straight with you allows you to understand that I do understand what you are feeling and wanting. I understand the excitement and the good feelings that come when someone wants to be with us, *nevertheless*, you are not going over to her house without adults being present – I don't think it is wise."

In the example of this second response, we have utilized the word, "*nevertheless*," three times. For most children, their stamina is spent by now. A few (you are probably saying mine) may still have some energy left and continue trying to get us to bend. I will provide you a way to deal with these more willful children, but before I do, I want you to notice what else I am doing in these responses. First of all, I am looking at my child with "smiling eyes," a concept that will be discussed later, but basically sends the message of how much I care for my child. My voice is at a conversational level, it is calm, not defensive or reactive. I have paused from whatever activity I was doing when my child approached me and have given him or her mine undivided attention. Each of these non-verbal communications is being translated faster in my child's brain than any of my verbal communication. Both my non-verbal and verbal communication is congruent and is sending the message that "I care for you immensely."

Typically, when parents are approached by their children that are asking for something that creates concern, our non-verbal language sends a message of uncertainty. If my child senses any level of distress in my non-verbal language, he or she is going to see if they can leverage that distress to their advantage, while ignoring our verbal communications.

The other thing that I am doing in these situations is that I am trying to resonate what my child is feeling or expressing. You will notice how I spoke about my child's wants or feelings associated with his request. So many times our children, in an attempt to manipulate the situation will say, "You don't understand me!" By connecting with their deepest expressions and feelings, our children will recognize that we do understand and that does not become a problematic part of the process.

Now about the willful, persistent child – if after using "*nevertheless*" three or four times does not de-escalate the arguing, I have an honest discussion with my child. It may look something like this:

"Son, is there anything in my behavior or my words that has you believe that I do not understand how important this is to you? I believe the reason you keep on pressing is because you believe that if you keep on asking, I will become frustrated and relent; or perhaps you don't believe that I actually meant what I said. I want you to know that I believe in the principles that have led to my decision. To go against those principles would be going against myself and I will not do that. If on the other hand it is that you do not believe what I said, when I responded with 'No,' then I invite you to ask me again."

At this point your child (son) asks, "May I go over to my girlfriend' s house, even though her parents are not home?"

I smile and respond, "No, I do not think it is wise. Go ahead and ask me again."

Your child replies, "May I go over to my girlfriend's house even though her parents are not home?"

I smile and respond, "No, I do not think it is wise. Would you like to ask me again?

By this point your "willful child" has lost their stamina and will go away: but they will have done so without ill feelings, contention, and argument. Because my verbal and non-verbal communications were respectful, the interaction strengthens the parent-child relationship and the child's self-concept and personal belief are upheld in a positive manner.

As you begin incorporating the word, "*Nevertheless*" on a regular basis, you will recognize that the word is a bit "weird" and it will become very noticeable to your children. Some may get frustrated with the word, for example:

Child: "Mom, may I go to my girlfriend's house?"

Mother: "I can understand the excitement you feel when you get to spend time with her, *nevertheless*, because her parents are not home, I cannot give you permission to do so."

Child (trying to ramp up the contention as manipulation): "I am so sick and tired of that stupid word *"nevertheless!"* That parenting book you bought irritates me! Is that the only word they taught you to use?"

Mother: I can see that the word, *"nevertheless"* is creating some ill feelings, REGARDLESS, you are not going over to your girlfriend's house without her parents being there."

A few paragraphs previously, I stated that I wanted to cover a couple of things to bring understanding to this whole process of avoiding arguments. The first I already mentioned, and that is the importance of teaching the "why." That is an ongoing process and is direct counsel from Heaven (See: Deuteronomy 6:1-9; D&C 68:4; Moses 6:58). The better teachers we are, especially when we teach with the power of the Spirit, the less arguing is going to occur, because of the development of moral reasoning that arises in our children as a result of effective, truthful teaching. They will be less apt to question our reasoning as it will have become their own (More on that concept to come in our chapter on Learning).

The second thing I wanted to mention is the spiritual gift parents have to receive impressions or promptings. All gifts come to us through the Gift of the Holy Ghost. Parents are given the gift of discernment when it comes to their righteous desires for their children. Parents recognize this gift as power to know and understand beyond their own experience. Recognition of this gift is a testimony of divinely coordinated participation in their children's welfare.

Times when this gift is experienced is in times of nurturing or gospel teaching. Discerning a child's need is another time when this gift materializes (Luke 10:42). Our work as parents, being the most important work of righteousness, draws upon Heaven's power and desire.

Parenting is an eternal calling and therefore we are entitled to Heaven's assistance. Never doubt that! We are acting in a sacred partnership to bring about the purposes of the Lord (Moses 1:39; Mosiah 2:17).

One simple story a father told me, illustrates this point. He told me that a young man had come to the house for the purpose of picking up their daughter. This was a first date, and as was the custom of the parents, they invited the young man in to sit and talk for awhile. In the process of conversation, this father received an impression to ask the young man whether or not he had a driver's license and insurance. It turned out that he had neither. They did not go out that evening.

Now there is no way to know whether or not the date would have gone smoothly; without a hitch. Maybe it would have, but the father heeded the impression.

Elder Russell M. Nelson shared this principle and story:

"Children of all ages, learn to listen, and listen to learn from parents... Several years ago, I was invited to give an important lecture at a medical school in New York City. The night before the lecture, Sister Nelson and I were invited to dinner at the home of our host professor. There he proudly introduced us to an honor medical student—his beautiful daughter."

"Some weeks later, that professor telephoned me in an obvious state of grief. I asked, 'What is the matter?'"

"Remember our daughter whom you met at our home?"

"Of course," I replied. "I'll never forget such a stunning young lady."

"Then her father sobbed and said, 'Last night she was killed in an automobile accident!' Trying to gain composure, he continued: 'She asked permission to go to a dance with a certain young man. I didn't have a good feeling about it. I told her so and asked her not to go. She asked, 'Why?' I simply told her that I was uneasy. She had always been an obedient daughter, but she said that if I could not give her a good reason to decline, she wanted to go. And so she did. At the dance, alcoholic beverages were served. Her escort drank a bit—we don't know how much. While returning home, he was driving too fast, missed a turn, and careened through a guardrail into a reservoir below. They were both submerged and taken to their death.'"

"As I shared my feeling of sadness, he concluded: 'My grief is made worse because I had the distinct feeling that trouble lay ahead. Why couldn't I have been more persuasive?'"

"This experience will not have been in vain if others can listen and learn from it. Children, honor your parents, even when they cannot give a satisfactory explanation for their feelings. Please have faith in this scripture, which applies to all age groups: "Hear the instruction of thy father, and forsake not the law of thy mother. (Proverbs 1:8)." (Listen to Learn, General Conference, April 1991)

I teach youth this very important truth:

> "There will be times when your parents may say 'no,' and not have any good reason to do so other than an impression or feeling that comes to them. Your parents are entitled to these special interventions because of their sacred partnership with the Father of your Spirits. It is their duty to take heed to such promptings, because they are accountable to God for the delivery of their special and high calling of being your parent. At these times, will you please acknowledge your approval of this sacred process and be willing to follow their directives without negativity and disappointment. One day you will be entitled to the same gifts and blessings when you become parents yourselves."

The scriptures record a significant warning that came to Joseph, Jesus' earthly father, which led Joseph to leaving his homeland for the purpose of saving Mary and Jesus:

> "Behold, the angel of the Lord appeareth to Joseph in a dream, saying, Arise, and take the young child and his mother, and flee into Egypt, and be thou there until I bring thee word: for Herod will seek the young child to destroy him" (Matthew 2:13).

On a more personal level, I recall when this gift was bestowed upon my own father. The order of my family consisted of four children being born within relatively close time-frames, i.e. 1957, 1959, 1960, and 1961. However, the last two came at greater intervals, 1968 and 1974. The last one was a girl, and her only other sister was the oldest. This meant that at the time of her coming into our family, we already had three teenage boys.

We loved our little sister, but we did not always show such great judgment in how we treated her. If you have ever played water balloon toss, you will recall that the object of the game is to see how far apart you can get tossing the water balloon without it breaking. Our little sister was our water balloon. When she was about three, she would sometimes come out to the driveway where we had an intense basketball game going on. In order to keep her from getting hurt (actually to get her out of the way), we would lift her up to the roofline and tell her to grab the guttering. When her hands were firmly gripped, we would let go and return playing; leaving her hanging there. My mother would become so angry with us, she would pound on the kitchen window yelling and signaling for us to get her down. I can never figure out how that window did not break seeing it took a regular beating.

These are but two examples of many others that led to many scrapes, bumps and bruises on her body. My mother says that during one doctor visit for a normal check-up, the doctor warned her that if he saw any more bruises, he would have to report.

One morning for scripture study, my father substituted reading the scriptures for a dream that he had the night before, followed by a warning. My father indicated to us that the dream he had was different than other dreams. He said this one caused him to abruptly wake up after "its message" wherein sleep fled his body. He said that he pondered what the dream was trying to convey, and after much thought, he believed that the dream was a warning.

Our father told us that we were altogether as a family at an amusement park. He continued:

> "From the parking lot we walked toward the entrance, but in order to get there we had to a cross a bridge that went over a river. He said that two of us were involved in some play with our little sister, which consisted of one of us lifting her over the top rail on the bridge and letting her go, while the other would catch her from the bottom rail. He said that this continued until the one brother missed and my little sister fell into the river below. The brother that missed quickly jumped in with the intent to save her, and my father also jumped to assist with the rescue." Then my father said this. "Your little sister drowned and I was not able to revive her." Then he spoke to us three teen boys and said, "I believe that this dream was a warning and that you boys are to stop being careless with your sister."

He then asked us to consider the message, which we did from that day forward. She is still alive!

If you will teach your children this principle of heavenly inspiration provided parents, it will allow you to handle those special times without the contention that may normally accompany your decision.

These last few paragraphs have been teaching how to avoid arguing when your decision is in opposition to your child's wishes. But I want to make an important observation. I don't want this subject matter to seem like we should say "no" most of the time to our children. We want to say yes to our children much more than we say no. That can be hard for some parents. As we continue to understand human design, family relationships and developing belief systems, we will learn how to handle situations that do not fare so well.

Without going into any depth right now – If our children end up making poor decisions or something goes wrong, when we give them our 'yes's' it becomes a teaching moment. More on that later in the book – I promise.

When we argue with our children, we go against human design, we weaken, or worse, lose our influence with them, and we contribute to creating unhealthy belief systems in our children. The reason for these negative outcomes is in direct proportion to the violation of the principle spoken of by the Savior:

> "For verily, verily I say unto you, he that hath the spirit of contention is not of me, but is of the devil, who is the father of contention, and he stirreth up the hearts of men to contend with anger, one with another."

> "Behold, this is not my doctrine, to stir up the hearts of men with anger, one against another; but this is my doctrine, that such things should be done away." (3 Nephi 11:29-30)

> "The Lord God hath commanded that men...... should not contend one with another." (2 Ne. 26:32.)

Contention, strife and arguing within families is not pleasing to the Lord (Mosiah 4:13-15). The Savior is the Prince of Peace. Many of us hold His priesthood. Such privilege requires us to emulate Him, especially in reference to how we treat our family members.

The purposes of Satan in relation to contention is to "harden the hearts of the people against that which is good and that which is to come" (Helaman 16:22). Not always, but for the most part, show me a child that has hardened their heart against that which is good and who disbelieves the promises contained in the scriptures about that which is to come, and I will show you a parent-child relationship that has been filled with anger, contention and chronic criticism.

The power of divisiveness is such that even the smallest of arguments can create years of regret and severe consequence. Instead, our interactions with our children should lead to our "hearts being knit together in unity and love one towards another" (Mosiah 18:18, 21). Let us shun this spirit of animosity in all of our relationships. If we do so, we will experience greater love for our children (4 Nephi 1:15).

STOP CRITICIZING YOUR CHILDREN

Which is easier for humans to focus on – the negative or the positive? I am sure you got that answer right.

I would like you to do an exercise that may astonish you. I would like you to get a good size plastic bowl. I want the bowl to be light. I then want you to go to the bank and get a hundred dollars in penny roles (that should be 10,000 pennies). As parents, I want one of you to hold the bowl out (your arms or the bowl not resting on anything). The other parent I want you to start dropping pennies in one by one. It does not matter how fast or how slow, but I do not want you to simply open a role and dump it in the bowl. This assignment requires that you drop the pennies one-by-one.

For the parent that is holding the bowl, I want you to convey once every sixty seconds, a number on a scale that represents the difficulty you are having maintaining your strength to uphold this bowl. A Zero is no difficulty at all, while One Hundred is complete collapse.

This experiential activity serves a couple of purposes. First and foremost, single pennies in and of themselves do not weigh much. The beginning of the assignment was likely easy for the bowl holder to maintain his or her position. As time went on, however, the growing number of pennies in the bowl made the ability to maintain position more and more difficult. Second was that as the pennies piled up on themselves, you no longer could see the pennies at the earlier levels, yet you would never mistake the idea that they weren't still there.

So it is with our negative interactions with our children, and especially as it relates to criticism, we lose track of how many times we have dropped metaphorical pennies in our children's bowls, resulting in a growing weight within them, developing a belief system filled with weariness. Let me share with you a story that will help you see what type of criticism I speak of.

Derek is a friend of mine. We used to work together helping young people develop the beliefs, strategies and increasing capacity to overcome addiction. Derek related well with the youth because he too had struggled in his teen and early adult years, so not only could he relate to them, but he was also expert in detecting the attitudes and strategies that kept them stuck.

Derek shared a story several times, which highlights his trappings into addiction. Derek was a pretty good athlete and a phenomenal baseball player. He told us of his dad's presence and support as Derek played and practiced. "He was always there. I can't remember ever a time when he wasn't." So far so good – right?

Derek then tells of this one game, as a means to share what his continual relationship with his father entailed. Derek played third base. Usually, your best players, the ones with the greatest instinct and skill, play in the infield. And so it was with Derek. Anything that came Derek's way was stopped. This particular night he was involved in multiple double plays and he had even fooled a couple of the other team's players, leading to him tagging them out. He had three RBI's this night and scored a couple of times himself. They won the game easily – a terrific night – until his father and Derek walked to the car.

During the game, a batter hit a grounder right toward Derek. Derek stooped, placed his glove low to pick up the ball in order to throw it to first base. Unfortunately, Derek lifted too soon, causing the edge of his glove to slightly come off the ground. The ball hit the edge of Derek's glove instead of the pocket. While it did not get beyond him, it caused Derek to fumble for a moment and when he had gained control, he threw it to first base, but it wasn't in time. Derek was charged with an error.

Derek then qualified this walk to the parking lot with his father by saying this:

> "Now that I am older, I can now see that my father's whole motive and intent was to help me become a better baseball player. My dad played in college and was a pretty good player himself. This was something that we shared together and I know it allowed my dad to feel part of my life."

> "Even though we had a phenomenal game, even though we won handily, and even though I had some pretty good statistics and plays in the game, yet the first words out of my father's mouth were these: 'Son, would you like me to help you understand why you missed that ball?' Why the focus on the one negative part of the game? Why can't he see the positive? These are the thoughts that played over and over in my head as I was growing up with him. No matter what, my father had a way of focusing on the negative. It got to the point that I would dread the walk to the car!"

Derek continued,

> "It appeared to me that I was never good enough, that I could not please my father because of the mistakes I made. There were times where I told myself that I was going to play the perfect game just to see what he would say. Well, I discovered there is no such thing as a perfect game as it appeared that my father would find something 'to help me out with' after the game."

Derek's experience is that of millions of others. Without any intent to harm and only help, parents have this uncanny way of sending the wrong message to their children – "You're not quite good enough."

Elder Jeffrey R. Holland gave this advice:

> "We must be so careful in speaking to a child. What we say or don't say, how we say it and when is so very, very important in shaping a child's view of himself or herself. But it is even more important in shaping that child's faith in us and their faith in God. Be constructive in your comments to a child—always. Never tell them, even in whimsy, that they are fat or dumb or lazy or homely. You would never do that maliciously, but they remember and may struggle for years trying to forget—and to

forgive. And try not to compare your children, even if you think you are skillful at it. You may say most positively that "Susan is pretty and Sandra is bright," but all Susan will remember is that she isn't bright and Sandra that she isn't pretty. Praise each child individually for what that child is, and help him or her escape our culture's obsession with comparing, competing, and never feeling we are "enough." (The Tongue of Angels, General Conference, April 2007)

Words are the tools by which we bring about so many things we are trying to accomplish. Words are powerful, so powerful that they can elicit strong emotional reactions. It is usually in the emotional experience where we interpret our belief system and where behaviors find their strength.

If we are trying to accomplish good in our children, then it is imperative that we send forth words that will result in the good being realized. Either way, our words will return to us void – if our message is more consistently "You're not quite good enough," as our children will struggle with believing in themselves and feeling good about themselves. On the other hand, if we will focus more on their strengths and speak well of them, our children's confidence will wax stronger and stronger.

Criticism in almost any form is typically interpreted as some sort of rejection by us as humans. I don't think that we as parents would intentionally approach our children and say "I REJECT YOU." Unfortunately, our consistent critical remarks are saying exactly that. When that message becomes the child's companion, they begin to battle for a sense of worth and acceptance. If they cannot get that at home they will seek it elsewhere, many times choosing associates who accept them but simultaneously draw them away from the paths of happiness.

The Apostle Paul taught this important principle, "Be not deceived....whatsoever a man soweth, that shall he also reap" (Galatians 6:7). This principle has been titled "The Law of the Harvest" and it serves as an allegorical backdrop in understanding the concept of this section.

The Law of the Harvest ties our interactions with our children and their developing belief system in an unbreakable relationship that will produce a harvest of whatever we spent the most time planting and nurturing. Our family has spent years growing our favorite foods. We are especially glad when our "salsa garden" produces the tomatoes, peppers, onions and cilantro that goes into our homemade salsa. As of yet, and we have been doing this for many years, have we to find a zucchini where we planted a tomato, or parsley where we planted cilantro, and so forth. Our garden harvest reflects our careful choosing of seeds and meticulous attention to fertilizing, watering and weeding.

One of the aspects of bringing in a bountiful harvest is to make sure that we plant intermittently, meaning that we don't plant everything in one day, instead we spread out our planting, as well as our interventions. By doing so, we have a longer season of harvest. So it is with our children. If we only plant one time or water only once, they will not have the wherewithal to become all that they can become. On a regular consistent basis, our interactions should be filled with recognition of all that is good in our children. Our words and non-verbal communication should send forth the needed nurturing, watering, fertilizing and weeding, so that the flow becomes a constant source that they can rely on. If we are not consistent in our garden; when we begin to neglect the vital interactions that provide support for plant growth, we begin to see the ill effects. When we neglect to provide the vital interactions with our children, they likewise wither and struggle to believe in themselves.

As the gardener, you too are learning much about yourself in the process. That is the beautiful relationship between the gardener and his garden. As the gardener learns to be patient, kind and nurturing and attentive, he or she finds confidence that their efforts are bringing about a bountiful harvest. His or her faith in the seeds, water, fertilizer and sunshine, provide the very outcome hoped for.

Faith and confidence likewise increases in us as parents as we learn to be patient, kind, nurturing and attentive to our children's growth and developing belief system.

Foremost, the gardener and happy parent recognize as they focus on their interaction; being intentional with the desired outcome, they too develop as much as their tender young ones. By exercising faith, parents learn the style that brings about the best result, and in turn learn the principles upon which their influence rests (D&C 121:41-42). Wise gardeners and parents testify that by first focusing on their own development, brings about the blessings of their charge.

Active, producing seeds come from framing things positively. Many times as parents we bark orders. "Get the dishes done," "Make your bed," "Fold your laundry," "Quit fighting," etc. Learning how to frame our instructions positively will not only increase cooperation, likewise it will increase our bonds or oneness. Examples may include:

1. Sweetie, let's wash the dishes together so we have enough time to watch a show together. What would you like to watch tonight?
2. After you make your bed, would you like to go over to your friend's house?
3. Thanks so much for helping with the laundry – I like the way you take such good care of your clothes.
4. Hey, it sounds like you two are struggling. If you don't need my help, will you please take it outside until you get it settled? The loud tones hurt my ears.

These approaches are filled with charity, and expectation, without it being demanding. By learning how to frame things positively our outcomes and expectations are more likely to be positive.

Poor harvests come from looking at the negative and harping on it; especially when the harping is filled with criticism. Much of our negative reactions come from our own implicit memories, where our own sense of inferiority or insecurity is being triggered. When things are not going the way we want them, or we feel like we are not a very good parent, it is easy to look outside of ourselves for the reasons of our stress. Yet, we alone are responsible for our thoughts and actions. And that inner emotion, such as anger, embarrassment or insecurity is the product of our own thought processes and not caused by our children's actions. By understanding this, it becomes easier to stay positive because it puts the control within you.

President Spencer W. Kimball reminded the saints of this truth when he said:

> "I remind you ... that regardless of your present age, you are building your life; ... it can be full of joy and happiness, or it can be full of misery. It all depends upon you and your attitudes, for your altitude, or the height you climb, is dependent upon your attitude or your response to situations" (in Conference Report, Oct. 1974, 112–13; or Ensign, Nov. 1974, 80).

Finally, let me turn to a couple of scriptures which counsel us regarding the things that come from our mouth. The first comes from the writings of the Apostle Paul:

> "Let no corrupt communication proceed out of your mouth, but that which is good to the use of edifying, that it may minister grace unto the hearers." (Ephesians 4:29)

And then the Apostle James:

> "For in many things we offend all. *If any man offend not in word, the same is a perfect man* and able also to bridle the whole body."

> "Behold, we put bits in the horses' mouths, that they may obey us; and we turn about their whole body."

> "Behold also the ships, which though they be so great, and are driven of fierce winds, yet are they turned about with a very small helm, whithersoever the governor listeth."

> "Even so the tongue is a little member, and boasteth great things. Behold, how great a matter a little fire kindleth!" (James 3:2-5)

In this last verse, it is apparent that James is aware of the contention and destruction our words can create in another. How many times does a parent have to speak condescendingly, negatively, blamingly and critically before their child feels the heat of anger that comes from being rejected.

James then points out the great hypocrisy that so many of us fall prey to. With the words that fall from our tongue:

> "Therewith bless we God, even the Father; and therewith curse we men, which are made after the similitude of God."

> "Out of the same mouth proceedeth blessing and cursing. My brethren, these things ought not so to be."

> "Doth a fountain send forth at the same place sweet water and bitter?" (James 3:9-11)

How can we kneel in the morning and praise Father in Heaven with our words of gratitude, patiently bearing all that He sees fit to have us experience and then through the course of the day curse His creation? Every child, every parent, every person is His creation. For those that find high regard for any artist and then detest the works of the artist is seen to be foolish. Thereby James concludes:

> "This wisdom descendeth not from above, but is earthly, sensual, devilish."

> "For where envying and strife is, there is confusion and every evil work."

> "But the wisdom that is from above is first pure, then peaceable, gentle, easy to be entreated, full of mercy and good fruits, without partiality, and *without hypocrisy*"

> "And the fruit of righteousness is sown in peace of them that make peace." (James 3:15-18)

May we as parents make peace with our children, may our motives be pure, may our approach be gentle, may our children feel mercy because of our kind, uplifting words and may we bring in the harvest of good things because we have sown good things. For those that will learn to refrain from criticism will find themselves as a fountain that sends forth sweet water.

STOP AVOIDING OUR CHILDREN

There were a bunch of old ads run by the church with the byline of, "Family, It's About Time." If there is any single factor that sends the message that our children matter and that we are interested in knowing them, it is the time we make for them. Acceptance; feeling like we are included is an important component of healthy belief systems.

When I was in my youth, there was a song titled, "Cats in the Cradle" by Harry Chapin. This song told a story about a father who never made time for his child – while the child kept promising to be just like his dad when he himself grew up. As the father retires, he finds himself with more time and desires to connect with his son. But his son is now in the middle of his own career, raising his own family and does not have time for his father. It was a powerful message, mostly because it touched the experience of so many.

One of the great universal regrets of those parting mortality is the wish that they had spent more time with the one's they loved. Life has a distinct way of pulling on us, especially when it comes to the need to provide. Unfortunately, most of us don't experience the discernment of what matters most in life until we are about to go out of it.

If we that still have much time could take counsel from those whose time is nearly spent, we would do well in creating greater balance that affords the making of memories, the moments of being present when our children need a listening ear, and developing those bonds that have eternal significance.

I once knew a young man of 16 who just shut down. He did not care about anything. At night, when he would wake up due to the need to go use the restroom, he didn't even care and would wet the bed. Darren was born of a relationship between an American military officer and an English woman, while the father was stationed over seas. After discovering her pregnancy, these two wed, believing that it was important for the child they had produced. However, the marriage did not make it very long and upon return to the United States, this father brought with him his son. Within four months of their return, the father married again and then left his son with his new bride, while he worked and lived abroad.

In time, Darren began taking his anger out on his step-mother. Frequent calls were made between the parents, but very little interaction by the father with either one. The phone calls were mostly to discuss Darren's growing anger, depression, defiance, and self-harm. At age 15, Darren's father placed Darren in a residential center, telling his son that as soon as he could get control of his behavior, he would have him return home.

When it came time for family therapy, two appointments were scheduled, one with his step-mother and the other with his father. A good percentage of the time when his father was called, his dad did not answer and weeks would go by before contact was successful.

115

I am sure as you read this account, you are experiencing some emotion, and likely you have connected Darren's struggles with the lack of interest his father displays. Let me share with you some of the personal beliefs that Darren developed, beliefs which were uncovered during the process of therapy:

1. I was a mistake
2. I am not worth knowing
3. I am unimportant
4. No one would even miss me if I ended my life
5. I am less than any other human

Is it easy to see how his behavior is connected with his personal belief system? Is it likewise easy to see how parents contribute to a child's developing belief system? After Darren had been institutionalized for a year and a half he began to decline even more. Rage became his companion and it was obvious that the course of intervention was adding to the detrimental effects of his life. When I consulted with his case manager (the state he was from was paying for his care), and provided the broader picture, Darren was brought back home and his father was made to become accountable to family court. The source of Darren's problems was not Darren's doings; they were his dad's. The failure to show interest in his child collapsed any sense of worth or importance in Darren.

Again, this is a big story and likely none of you are this extreme in avoiding your children. However, to some degree or another, when we fail to connect on a regular and healthy basis, our children will have similar ways of looking at themselves. Their sense of self is largely dependent upon the way they perceive our view of them.

Now, spending time with our children does not require heroic, time consuming efforts. Being able to connect on a regular basis can be very simple. Our intentional choice to connect with our children daily is what matters. As a child walks by and we reach out to bring them into our arms; or seeking out our children when we get home from work and showing interest in their day or what they may be doing currently; inviting them to come and help with dinner and talking about whatever they want to talk about; plopping down and playing video games or watching the show they are viewing; or simply looking in their eyes and expressing your joy for their being a part of your life, each of these small gestures will have your children experience the feeling of being wanted, of being included, and of their importance to someone else.

If every once in awhile we go the extra mile and demonstrate our heightened fondness for them by taking the time to be just with them, this too solidifies their belief that they matter and are thought of. Taking our child on a business trip, or sending them on a scavenger hunt where they find tickets to an event they have been telling you about, showing up at school at lunch time and taking them out to eat, helping them practice a sport; or going sight-seeing with them are examples of individual expressions of their importance to you.

The larger perspective here is the idea that families are designed to be eternal – that our associations will have no end. Preparing for that reality does not begin after we die, that preparation begins today. How awful it would be to find ourselves at the end of our lives strangers to one another. Everything we are doing with our families in mortality is an investment of our eternal possibilities.

Of course it would look and feel silly if we are trying to take time to be with one another without also talking to one another. Talking, listening, encouraging and learning together are the very reasons we are spending time with each other. These devices strengthen our relationships, wherein the desire to spend eternity with one another grows. I want to be with people who want me to be with them – that makes perfect sense. I want to be with people who I know and trust and love – that is what develops from our behaviors and communications with one another.

The great human need is to be understood, to be included and to feel that one matters. Time, and especially time where children can feel that they have connected emotionally with us, that their thoughts and feelings are acceptable to us, and they perceive their importance to us – will all lead to our growing influence in their lives.

STOP CONTROLLING YOUR CHILDREN

I have pondered from time-to-time about the connection between a desire to control and the feeling of rage when unable to. This is a daily occurrence in the human experience; just a few minutes in front of the news will remind us of this condition. Every evening, during any newscast, we have examples of tragedies that are traced back to the emotion of anger.

We hear of parents, or of boyfriends or girlfriends that lose control when they feel helpless in controlling the crying of a young child. Gang related activity is on the rise, which is fueled by anger due to missing fathers or violent upbringings. Jealousy, a form of unbridled anger, is the cause for many murders or cases of missing persons. Of course we hear of wars and rumors of wars, all encased in attitudes of anger and control.

In each of the cases mentioned, it is easy to detect how someone rapidly escalates negative thoughts when they believed they had no control and the ensuing feeling of anger.

For those that set their hearts upon wickedness, Nephi tells us that they will experience rage and anger against that which is good and those that embody it (2 Nephi 28:20). Is it because they want their existence and their manner of living not to be judged as wrong or unacceptable and by extension them being viewed as wrong or unacceptable? Such perception is the real cause of their anger. Yielding to the influence of Satan by surrendering our self-control is the thought process that leads to angry feelings. Those undesired feelings are designed to point us back to the path of happiness, instead so many continue to step on the thorns found off of the path, experiencing the intensifying pain, and then look back at those still on the path, who are beckoning to them to return, and blaming them for the thorns now embedded in their feet.

The dramatic stage of pre-existent war appears to be connected to the rejection of control over other's, and their God-given right to agency, expression of will, and choice of paths one desires to pursue. Satan's expert combining of fear reducing philosophy and the desire for each of us to be like our Heavenly Parent's prepared the stage that ultimately led to a battle where one third of the hosts of heaven lost the very thing the rest of us so valiantly fought to preserve. As soon as someone buys into such enticing promises, their capacity to choose takes an immediate hit. Likewise, those that call good evil and evil good (Isaiah 5:20), diminish their strength to avoid being controlled. Of this latter group, John Wooden addressed with this insightful saying, "Discipline yourself and others won't need to" (What I've Learned, Esquire Magazine, February 2000). The world is filled with people who, rather than focusing on self-discipline, instead are waging war against the principles that, if adopted and obeyed, will lead to greater happiness and freedom. It sounds like a continuation of the same war!

Knowing the connection with agency and emotional experience, especially understanding the anger that results when feeling compelled to do something, we are in a better position to evaluate our interactions with our children. Are we continuing the pre-existent war in our own homes? Are we cutting-off our children's agency with the argument that we know what is best for them and justifying our control as a means to an end? Do we feel so deprived of any sense of importance that we substitute our calling as a parent as a means to satisfy that which is missing? Are we in the habit of "making" our children appear a certain way so that others will not evaluate us as failures as parents? Character always is more concerning than our reputation. All such motivation is housed in fear, not faith. Such parenting will directly interfere in the progress of what our children are designed to become and will severely impact their understanding of celestial living. Faith, not force is the best means in having our children develop a healthy sense of agency:

Celestial living requires that each of us is able to stand independent because of our development of understanding of principles that mediate happiness. As a parent, I am heavily involved in teaching correct principles and allowing my children to experience the outcomes associated with their interaction with those principles, whether their interaction goes against or stands in alliance with revealed truth. My role is not to become the enforcer. My role is to help observe for my children what they may not fully observe for themselves as they experience the outcomes of their choices. Through consistent, kind observing, I act as a guide so that my children develop greater capacity to mature and be trusted with greater latitude as they become better observers of the connection between abiding by principles and the happiness derived from doing so.

George Farling put it simply when he stated, "Choice is an element of human dignity. Without the power of choice, a man is a lot less than a man. Without the exercise of choice a man never discovers what he can be or what he can do. Choice is the key to the future." (George E. Farling, "Youth Can't, But Must," Weslyan Methodist)

As you recall, in the pre-mortal realm, one of the consequences attached to those who advocated for controlling others and stripping them of their agency was to be "thrust down" becoming subject to the Devil's authority (Isaiah 14:12-14; Abraham 3:28;D&C 76:25-27, Moses 4:1,3-4). Ironically, their opposition to the true principle of agency was enabled by the power of their own choice (D&C 29:36-37). Among other things, the pre-mortal conflict stemmed from a rejection of eternal law, namely that of agency. Agency is a vital element in proving that we want Eternal Life. Agency is the gift and power that enables making the record perfectly clear (Exodus 32:33; Revelation 3:5; 20:12; D&C 128:6-7; Alma 5:58; and D&C 88:2). So critical is this principle that we should be very cautious in our interactions with others. Those that did not keep their first estate, in part due to their rejection of this eternal principle, had serious penalties attached to their rebellion. We too should be wary in tampering with someone else's agency as the same issues and the same salvation is at stake here in our second estate (Abraham 3:26).

When we practice compulsion upon others in any degree of unrighteousness, Heaven's aid and power are withdrawn (D&C 121:37); this includes interaction with our children. Likewise, we can expect some negative outcomes in our relationship with our children. These negative outcomes are natural consequences to the breaking of divine law, as well as human design. In an article that appeared in the June issue of the Ensign back in 1986, the author highlighted some of the natural consequences we could expect:

> "For one thing, we may succeed in making our child obey us at that moment, but if he does not understand the reason for his behavior he will not appreciate its importance. And since he has felt a threat instead of love, sooner or later he will rebel against what he perceives as tyranny. The decisions he makes thereafter will be based on an emotional rejection of authority rather than a rational acceptance of righteous values and principles."

> "Another reason parents should avoid exercising unrighteous dominion is that their children will see them as unreasonable. One of the main causes of interpersonal conflict is poor communication, and communication between children and parents is limited—if not

completely blocked—when parents refuse to listen to and reason with their children."

Faithful parenting does not go unnoticed by the world. Many have wondered why the Latter Day Saints, in general, produce children of confidence and character. Elder Boyd K. Packer relates an experience with a high ranking general:

> "I have a message for parents about the education of your children. Several weeks ago I had in my office a four-star general and his wife; they were very impressive people. They admire the Church because of the conduct of our youth. The general's wife mentioned her children, of whom she is justly proud. But she expressed a deep concern. 'Tell me,' she said, 'how you are able to control your youth and build such character as we have seen in your young men?'"

> "I was interested in her use of the word 'control'. The answer, I told them, centered in the doctrines of the gospel. They were interested; so I spoke briefly of the doctrine of agency. I said we develop control by teaching freedom. Perhaps at first they thought we start at the wrong end of the subject. A four-star general is nothing if not a disciplinarian. But when one understands the gospel, it becomes very clear that the best control is self-control."

> "It may seem unusual at first to foster self-control by centering on freedom of choice, but it is a very sound doctrinal approach." (Agency and Control, General Conference, April, 1983)

The promise of this approach to teaching is the constant divine help that supports our efforts (D&C 88:78). Again, we are not parenting alone – we are acting in concert with God and He is sending forth the understanding that accompanies obedience to his ways. We must have faith in this process.

One of the ways to foster the outcomes of good choices is to provide good choices. So many times we couch our choices in "choose the right or get into trouble for choosing the wrong." To a child, this reasoning is not the most inspiring method of discovery and commitment. One of the ways we can promote good choices is to leverage our children's desires with an expectation. For example, our child may come to us and ask, "May I go over to my friend's house for the afternoon?" Our reply can promote immediate compliance, "Sure honey, AS SOON AS you get the dishwasher emptied." Many parents would be tempted to say, "No you can't because you did not get the dishwasher emptied when I told you to do so earlier." This phrase, AS SOON AS, should become part of every parent's arsenal. It is amazing to see the energy level toward duty when affixed with desired choice. Most importantly, the approach empowers our children to do what we want them to do without threat of consequence.

Later, as we discuss child development and learning, we will revisit issues of control and how these approaches to parenting bump against human design and develop unhealthy belief systems. For now, let me just state clearly that the message that children get about themselves, when not permitted to practice their agency is that their ability to problem solve is inadequate, that their thoughts and feelings are unimportant and inconsistent with reality, and that their acceptance is conditioned upon doing things their parent's way. None of these beliefs will act in the child's behalf to develop the confidence and capacity to choose well. Instead, our children will experience underlying anger by not having a sense of control of their own lives.

FUNCTIONAL VS. DYSFUNCTIONAL

Healthy families have the capacity to organize and reorganize as they grow and change. Children are supported and nurtured. Above all, children get the message that, despite mistakes and inappropriate behavior, they are worthwhile human beings who deserve love – and they are indeed loved. (Dr. James Jones, Ph.D.)

It is often heard said, "I came from a dysfunctional home." Some people use the phrase jokingly to make an awkward moment seem more accepting. Others may use it to explain why they have become who they are. Whatever the reason, it is important to know that some families do function better than other families, yet all families have struggles.

This chapter is going to look at what functional families do well and how, when faced with struggles, are they able to find the resources to move beyond the difficulty presenting itself.

It is best to start with a working definition of functional and dysfunctional so as to begin assessing our own families approach to issues and struggles, which inevitably arise in every home.

Definition of:

Functional – recognize there is a problem and gather resources to overcome or improve the situation;
Dysfunctional – recognize there is a problem and ignore it, hoping that it will resolve itself.

The following ideas were inspired by James McArthur, PhD., the Director of Counseling at BYU. I would recommend that you review his article, (Ensign, February 2009) that perhaps you might gain more insight to this topic.

What is it about Dysfunctional Families that keep them from developing the resources that would allow them to live more harmoniously and more effectively? It has been my experience that such families are led by individuals that lack either understanding or faith or both. That lack of understanding can come from their own childhood experiences, which interfere with their ability to parent in a better way. Many times it is the doubt expressed that things can't really change – after all, someone might conclude, "I've been living this way for years. I really doubt that I can change these attitudes and habits."

In many cases, but not always, parents of Dysfunctional Families have had poor examples themselves. They are merely continuing the same parenting approach that was modeled for them and they are likely to have left over struggles of their own as a result.

Regardless, in the Day of Restoration (Psalm 14; Isaiah 35; Acts 3:19); the Dispensation of the Fullness of Times (Ephesians 1:10), there is no excuse or reason to maintain such unhealthy systems. The knowledge of the purpose of family has been restored back to the earth along with all of the principles that allow us to strengthen our homes, preparing us for the promises of eternal life, whereby we may be exalted to live forever in our family units. Therefore the beginning of required change is to believe in the revelations concerning the purpose of families; restored in these latter days and then begin to act in harmony with the principles associated with family life. The ancient counselor put it simply:

> "A wise man will hear, and will increase learning; and a man of understanding shall attain unto wise counsels."

> "The fear of the Lord is the beginning of knowledge: but fools despise wisdom and instruction." (Proverbs 1:5,7)

Following then are some of the basic truths that have been restored concerning Functional Families. Both scripture and research methods support these outlined characteristics and if you desire to have a more effective family then this is a good place to begin your learning. As you work to implement these characteristics into your own home, your understanding will increase.

2) In the functional family, parents focus their energy on teaching their children correct principles and allowing them to exercise their agency.

This concept has already been covered in the Chapter: The Power of Principles. More will be discussed when we cover Child Development and Learning. However let me just use this moment to remind you of the two following truths.

Principles are discoverable. Our opportunity as parents is to find those moments when children experience the effects of correct principles. As we do this consistently, our children will learn the benefit of obedience to these natural human laws and in so doing adopt them as a valuable resource in guiding their choices. This is called moral reasoning. This whole process is inherent because of the Light of Christ, which is present in every individual (Moroni 7:16, 18; John 1:4, 9). Conscience or moral reasoning is a manifestation of the Light of Christ.

Usually when someone experiences a consequence when interacting with principles there is a feeling associated with that consequence. Like a script, when we recognize these feelings, it is our cue to assist our child in associating their emotional experience with the keeping or breaking of human law (principle). As we observe our children's outcomes based upon their experience, including their emotional outcome, we assist our children in observing themselves, what works and what doesn't. Here are a couple of examples:

3) Suzy has come home from school on Monday and is obviously upset about something that happened that day –

Parent: Honey, it looks like something did not go well today?

Suzy: I can't believe how shallow my friends are.

Parent: Help me understand.

Suzy: Remember last Saturday when I had plans to go see Wicked with Sarah and Layne?

Parent: Yes

Suzy: Well, when Bobby Patterson called me on Friday to go on a date with him Saturday night, I of course wanted to go with Bobby more. I have had a crush on him forever and I couldn't believe he even knew I existed. So I texted Sarah and Layne to let them know I couldn't make it because of my date with Bobby. I guess I should have known then something wasn't right.

Parent: What do you mean?

Suzy: Well Layne simply texted back, "Have Fun," and when I texted her back to give me a call, she responded by saying that she was working until late. I never heard more from her. And Sarah did not respond immediately. It was on Saturday that she texted me and wished me "Good Luck."

Parent: Was this unusual of Sarah and Layne?

Suzy: No, recently there have been other times I have had to back out on plans because something else came up. But this was Bobby Patterson. I was hoping they could be excited for me and understanding.

Parent: Is that what led to today?

Suzy: Yeah, when I saw them at school they both acted cool towards me. I mean, they weren't really unfriendly; they just weren't their same selves. When I asked them about the play they said they really enjoyed it, but then did not elaborate much. They didn't even ask me about my date with Bobby.

Parent: Well, it looks like you didn't enjoy how they treated you.

Suzy: No, I didn't. I have had different thoughts about how I should respond or feel. Some of that has been, well if they can't be happy for me, maybe I should consider different friends. Another response I had was that I should take a look at myself and how I choose to be a friend to them.

Parent: I noticed you said there have been other times that you had to back out on plans. I'm wondering if it isn't just Bobby Patterson, but a collective experience of being backed out on that has made them feel less important?

Suzy: Do you think?

Parent: Suzy, one of the principles related to friendship is that of loyalty and commitment. It is important that when we make a commitment to someone that we do all in our power to fulfill that commitment. When we begin developing a reputation of saying one thing but doing another, people can become wary of us. I think any friend can understand backing out of a commitment once in awhile, but if it becomes more consistent than not, then likely we are going to experience a negative consequence in how others feel about us – resulting in some of the feelings you are currently experiencing.

Suzy: Perhaps I have not been so considerate lately and have placed my wants ahead of theirs.

Parent: Suzy, I know you better than any of your friends. I think you are a good friend to others and I know how much you like your friendships. I think this is why you are having such a negative emotion. Have you been able to identify the feeling you are having?

Suzy: Some of it is shame for not being more sensitive to what I was doing, but the other is fear that I will lose Sarah and Layne as friends. I love them.

Parent: Do you like feeling fear and shame?

Suzy: No! They are awful feelings.

Parent: If you could choose to replace those feelings with something else, what would you choose?

Suzy: A clear conscience and assurance that Sarah and Layne want me to be their friend.

Parent: Do you have any idea on how to get those feelings?

Suzy: I guess I should go to them and tell them that I recognize that my recent choices have caused strain on our friendships and take accountability. I then need to demonstrate consistency in what it means to be loyal and the importance of commitments.

Parent: Well, it sounds like you have some insight on how to turn your negative experience into something more desired.

2) Johnny comes to the dinner table and before sitting down, gives his sister a squeeze, his younger brother a quick messing of the hair and to the baby a big kiss on her cheeks. Dad notices this positive interaction and wonders what has led to these good feelings –

Parent: Is it me or are you in a really good mood?

Johnny: No dad, you have noticed correctly.

Parent: Want to share? Did a pretty girl give you a kiss?

Johnny: Well that would have been the icing on the cake, but no, it had nothing to do with a girl.

Parent: I'm listening and very interested.

Johnny: Well, I have been struggling over a decision that is pressing itself on me. Should I go to college right after high school or prepare to go on a mission? It makes it harder when I have so many friends that have decided to go on a mission coming out of high school.

Parent: Well, what did you decide?

Johnny: Before I tell you that, I want to share what happened to me while I was making the decision, because that is why I feel so good.

Parent: Would you like to share with us now?

Johnny: Sure, but let's bless the food first. (After prayer is said)

Johnny: I know that God cares for me personally. I have had too many experiences to doubt that truth. But did He care enough about this personal decision to provide me any insight? I went to Him in prayer and told him that I wanted to do what He wanted, but also wanted to know, which decision would be better for me? I don't know my future like He does and so I wanted some help. Well yesterday my school counselor called me in and invited me into her office. Waiting for me on the phone was the Dean of Engineering and Technology at Harvard University. Apparently my school counselor contacted him to let him know of my dilemma. He told me that whatever I decide, Harvard wanted me to come there – that he believed that I would really be an asset. He said that he has had several experiences with Mormon young adults after having returned from their mission call and that he likes what he sees. I thanked him for his time. The impression I got while walking home from school was that Heavenly Father wanted me to be calm in my decision – that I had no need to fear.

Parent: It sounds like you have learned about the principle of prayer and continue to have faith in it. I also recognize the positive feelings that have resulted from your faith in that principle. Do you recognize that your feelings are connected with prayer?

Johnny: Yes, and as I said before – this is not the first time.

The way Father in Heaven has designed our existence and environment is in a manner where our obedience or disobedience to law will bring with it consequences, positive or negative. These consequences are to be relied on and perhaps provide the best form of learning, next to study and faith (D&C 88:118; 109:7, 14). At the conclusion of this book we will discuss quite a bit about consequences – here we are simply introducing the idea that learning through the presence of consequences is what leads to understanding. Shielding our children from the effects of consequences will stunt their learning. Not paying attention to our children's emotions and helping observe for them what they are experiencing are missed opportunities to help our children begin to value principles. Principles, when internalized, provide for a moral compass. It is imperative that we allow consequences to teach the truth about principles.

When we help observe for our children, we increase their understanding. This is an important aspect of developing wisdom. As the wise counselor suggested, "With all thy getting get understanding." (Prov. 4:7) - Understanding of what? An understanding of who we are and the purpose of our being here experiencing mortality. Within the mortal experience are opportunities for our understanding to increase and become solidified. As we learn and apply the principles which govern happiness, we come to know of the truth of our divine potential. This understanding is enhanced when someone is able to experience the outcomes associated with correct principles. Parents become the key in helping their children make these associations.

2. In the functional family, parents intentionally strengthen their families.

As every parent knows, each child has there own temperament, personality, strengths and limitations. One may excel in academics, while another becomes frustrated with the amount of time it takes to learn things. One may do well socially, while another prefers one or two friends, or even isolation. One child may have had several spiritual experiences, while another seems so bored at church. One may like competitive sports and another likes animal husbandry. Regardless, every child has needs (this fits within the framework of human design). To some it may be more time with a particular parent, to another to diversify the day's activities instead of spending so many hours playing video games, or perhaps one needs to begin developing better spiritual habits. This is part of the assignment given to parents – to attune to each child's experience and thoughtfully plan how to strengthen one's children.

Another intentional way parents strengthen their families is by "planning time together." Some wise parents have adopted what is affectionately known as the – 7-7-7 Rule – Every 7 days, the parents go on a date, every 7 weeks they (the parents) go away for a weekend, and every 7 months they gather their children up and go on a small trip. Each of these is intended on developing good memories that in turn keep the family desirous to be with each other.

The most profound way to strengthen family relationships is to become highly aware of the non-verbal cues and the words that are being sent to one another. These non-verbal and verbal cues include our time, the tone in our voice, and the positive messages we send. These are the food of healthy attachment that build trust and love with each other. In the chapter that discusses Attachment, each of these will be gone over in more detail.

It is simply important to know that our children develop a sense of "I" or "Identity" based upon our interactions with them. Being short-tempered, impatient, unavailable and consistently disappointed will send one message. Being attuned, available, interested and a good listener will send an important message about their value and purpose.

Most importantly, your children need to know that you think of them often and that those thoughts are positive and accepting. Whether it is through notes, a text, or by your voice – please regularly tell your children that you think of them and that you are glad to be their parent. This strengthens them!

3. In the functional family, relationships are of supreme importance.

One of the greatest questions we can ask our children from time-to-time is this, "Hey, I wanted to check-in with you. How are you and I doing? It is important to me that our relationship is on a good path. Is there anything I can be doing better or is there something you would like to discuss with me?"

This intervention sends the message that our relationship with our children is of a very high priority. Obviously spending time with our children, surprising them with taking a day off to be just with them, maybe sending flowers to your girls, tickling them, doing a project with them, and so on, likewise send the message of the relationship being valuable to you.

4) In the functional family, parents are active teachers.

In developing a healthy belief system in our children necessitates our teaching them the truth about who they are and why they are here on earth. They need to understand about their eternal existence, including the doctrine of the pre-existence, the reason for mortality and the potential for celestial glory in the next life. They need to be taught concerning their spiritual heritage (Hebrews 12:9), about Jesus Christ and the Atonement, and every other true doctrine and principle that promotes a positive, truthful image. It is from these eternal concepts that faith develops in the mind of our children and empowers them to act in a way that invites the Holy Ghost into their lives. When our children have come to understand the way in which the Holy Ghost manifests His influence, then we have parented well and our children understand their nature, their relationship with God, and the desire to walk the path of happiness is strengthened.

Other things we should be teaching our children are to live peacefully with their family, peers and in their community. Teaching them how to look beyond themselves and get out once and a while and serve others. Teaching them appropriate boundaries so that others do not intrude on their feelings, thoughts, and rights; helping them develop good social skills so that they will be liked by others and invited to be part of the group; teaching them how to become good learners, teaching them about how to care for themselves; and teaching them how to be assertive. All of these things good parents do intentionally and throughout the course of their child's upbringing.

In all of these things, remember, our children are practicing and need our kind feedback. If they decide to make choices that are contrary to what we are teaching, or resist certain things we are attempting them to do, we should be longsuffering, not short and agitated. They will more likely continue trying to learn when we demonstrate unconditional love in the process.

5) In the functional family, parents lead by example.

Do I want my child to learn patience? – Then we as parents need to demonstrate patience. Snapping at our children, having tones of disinterest and impatience, or cutting off our children's communications, simply train our children to do the same.

Do I want my child to learn balance? – Then we as parents need to demonstrate balance in our own lives. Are we too spiritual all the time, are we unable to lighten up, are we working way too much, do we spend more time sitting down 'vegging out' than we do getting up and being active, do our hobbies appear to be more important than anything else we do? There are many parts to being human and it is important that we teach children how to nourish all of the parts, not just one or two.

What do our shelves look like? What do our children have first hand access to? Do they have a library card, or membership with Kindle or one of the reader's programs? Are our homes filled with uplifting magazines that relate stories of human experiences filled with hope and spiritual learning?

Pride and Prejudice should be in every home's library, as well as The Swiss Family Robinson, To Kill A Mockingbird, Animal Farm, Where The Red Fern Grows and the like. One of my favorite stories is Charles Dickens', A Christmas Carol. I have read Harry Potter, and Hunger Games alike, and as interesting as these collections are, I don't believe they compare to classics such as A Christmas Carol. While many modern children's literature are filled with intrigue, and sometimes moral leanings, yet they are usually coupled with many other ideas and plots that do not leave someone feeling uplifted.

Scrooge is a miserable, negative thinking; I can't stand being around you kind of character. Sound like any of your children? He walks through life in isolation and experiences some sort of importance by being able to control others through money. He is so self-absorbed with his own pain from unresolved issues that he can't see or even begin to understand the needs of those around him, including family members.

Then comes this scene that just captures our attention when Scrooge arrives at his home Christmas Eve. Everything is dark and you can sense Scrooge's anxiety. He doesn't really like this part of his day and it is in this moment when his old partner, Jacob Marley, begins to make contact with him. Scrooge is an expert at denying reality and it takes several attempts before Jacob won't have anymore of it. Jacob is on a mission and it appears that his motive is love.

When my mother was passing she made this comment to me, she said, "Larry, I can't do much to help my family while in this old, worn out body. I will be able to do much more from the other side of the veil." I believe that is true and it is kind of fun to link that concept with this part of the story.

129

So through the multi-locked and bolted door comes Scrooge's old partner. Those locks and bolts tell us a lot about Scrooge's insecurities, about the way he has lived his life, afraid of life. When Scrooge gazes on Jacob Marley, he is intrigued by the chains that bind him down. "What are these chains," Scrooge inquires. "These are the chains that I forged in life, link-by-link, they represent the manner in which I treated mankind." Scrooge replies that Jacob was a good businessman, upon, which Jacob laments, "Humankind was my business," an acknowledgment that he always understood that he had neglected that which was of most importance in life.

Scrooge asks what the nature of the visit is and Jacob says that he is interested in Scrooge's welfare, telling Ebenezer that his chains were as long as the ones observed seven years ago. Ebenezer is no position to properly evaluate his current condition, nor the necessary intervention that might lead to fulfilling Jacob Marley's mission.

Can you see the application in those children that struggle similarly? The ones that are filled with insecurity that would rather be alone than experience the stress of fitting in. Children today also go to dark places, for example their rooms, never being with anyone and living a life of illusion through their video games or television. As we begin to worry about their manner of functioning we seek out help, but then experience a lot of resistance. The child has no ability to evaluate what is best for him or her; they simply don't want things to change due to the heightened stress that comes with having to face their issues.

I'm sure that parents wished they had what Jacob Marley was about to use as an intervention – the ghosts that are going to go through a cognitive/post-traumatic therapy session with Old Scrooge. How nice that would be for us to leave our children in their bedroom one night and let the ghosts take care of everything!

Now, I doubt Dickens was a psychotherapist, but he certainly had an intuitive mind when it came to the development of his story line. How ingenious it was for the first ghost to demand of Scrooge to visit his past. Does Scrooge want to? No, he is insisting that he doesn't want to be reminded of the pain of not being wanted as a child. There is something in the nature of Ebenezer and his father's relationship that had Ebenezer not think well of himself. It grows apparent that his primary relationship with his father sets in motion a general guard against all relationships.

But what does Scrooge discover? He discovers that a relationship with money is rewarding and does not require risk. It enables him to be in control of relationships. I see that all the time with individuals that have suffered significant abuse, their relief does not come in the form of another relationship but in the satisfaction of things. As long as I have enough money, I can continue to buy my happiness – who needs the risk of being let down in a relationship.

One of the things Scrooge realizes about his past is that he had experiences and relationships that sent another message than the one received by his father. Good Ol' Fezziwig made him smile and not be so serious and stiff all of the time. His beautiful fiancé delighted his heart, until he returned to his automatic thoughts of relationships being hurtful. Scrooge placed his heart on money, lost balance and perspective and failed to estimate that not all relationships were going to be like his and his dad's relationship, in spite of the exceptions. Scrooge began to live his life in fear, not faith. For years he placed his trust into one thing – a thing that could not look into his eye lovingly, a thing that could not speak sweetly of things that were admired in him, a thing that could not wrap its arms around Ebenezer, providing the touch that all humans crave. Ebenezer rejected the meaning of all of the other good relationships he experienced and in its stead placed the message he received from his father as his core belief.

Though no real lesson came of this first experience with the Ghost of Christmas Past, yet for the first time in many years, Scrooge has his awareness raised of the unresolved pain, the unresolved trauma that has kept him stuck emotionally. What the experience did provide was the perfect preparation of the next Counselor, the Ghost of Christmas Present.

Still being the crotchety person he is, and throwing some attitude at his new visitor, the Ghost of Christmas Present shows Scrooge that his moody manipulations had no power over his presence, nor would it prevent what Ebenezer was going to have to see. The self-absorbed, low self-esteem miser was going to finally be forced to see what Jacob Marley was trying to help him understand – that humankind should be everyone's business. Scrooge is faced with seeing the hardships his controlling, stingy ways has on a loyal employee, to the extent that a child will die because the family cannot afford the proper medical care. He sees that the joy he believes that is produced by vast amounts of wealth is nothing in comparison to the joy his nephew experiences because of his happy home. He also recognizes what others really feel about him as he acts in his insecure, domineering fashion. Indeed, Scrooge begins to see the connection between his earliest primary relationship and the belief system that developed therefrom with his current relationships with everyone. Scrooge's heart begins to feel, his mind begins to ponder, and suddenly Ebenezer is faced with reality instead of the illusion he has created by his negative, doubting thoughts.

Unlike the experience with the first visitor, Ebenezer is not begging to return to his room because he is overwhelmed with the new perspective shed. His sudden return is a surprise. For a moment he is left to ponder his growing enlightenment, when suddenly a ghost, much unlike the one's previously beheld, appears but does little to communicate with Scrooge. Scrooge is left to himself to come to himself (Luke 15:17), and as he does so he begins to question whether he had sinned against humanity too much to turn things around. This becomes the gnawing of his soul. He experiences excruciating pain of both mind and body, when suddenly he remembers the message of

131

his late partner, Jacob Marley. This is a chance to change, to live in faith, not fear. He begins to question the present spirit and asks, "Are these shadows of things as they are to be or are they shadows of what may be?" At this moment, Scrooge enters into a covenant with the Ghost of Christmas Future wherein he promises to change and engage mankind in a manner that lifts and eases burdens. At the moment of giving his word, Scrooge is transported back to his bedroom.

In that moment, Scrooge recognizes that the visions have carried him through the night. As he opens his window, likely for the first time in years, we are introduced to a scene that causes us to feel the joy of the renewed countenance. Who doesn't love this endearing moment when Scrooge, dancing and leaping and feeling giddy, looks down on the street below and asks a boy there, "What day is it?" The boy's reply, "Why it's Christmas Day!" Ebenezer is so tickled that he exclaims, "I have not missed it!" and then proceeds to do what comes from healthy self-esteem, he attunes himself to the needs, wants and feelings of others, Because of his own renewed being, he no longer lives in fear, but in faith. Because of the good that Ebenezer begins to perform, it was recognized that he had kept his word and thus changed what may have been into the blessing of families and generations to come.

In my opinion, there has never been a better story of human redemption penned by mortal man. The only other story of redemption that is greater is the one that is recorded in the scriptures. The story is uplifting and realistic to human experience. It is a classic that helps us teach vital life lessons. Between Hunger Games and this classic story, it is A Christmas Carol that I would rather have in my child's mind as a resource.

One last way we set an example for our children is in the way we treat our spouse. This relationship demonstrates and sets the tone for how we want our children to experience their relationships. In the Chapter, Parenting Pyramid, we discussed some realities of the husband/wife relationship and its example and impact on all family relationships. It is impossible to fool our children – they intuitively sense happiness or tension in the primary relationship of the home.

President John Taylor emphasized this point when he said,

> "Husbands, do you love your wives and treat them right, or do you think that you yourselves are some great moguls who have a right to crowd upon them? ... You ought to treat them with all kindness, with mercy and long suffering, and not be harsh and bitter, or in any way desirous to display your authority. Then, you wives, treat your husband's right, and try to make them happy and comfortable. Endeavor to make your homes a little heaven, and try to cherish the good Spirit of God. Then let us as parents train up our children in the fear of God and teach them the laws of life. If you do, we will have peace in our bosoms, peace in our families, and peace in our surroundings."

"Do away with unkind or harsh words, and do not allow hard feelings to exist in your hearts, or find place in your habitations. Love one another, and by each trying to enhance the welfare of the other, that element will characterize the family circle, and your children will partake of the same feeling, and they in turn will imitate your good example, and perpetuate the things they learn at home." (As quoted in Teachings of the Prophets, John Taylor, Chapter 21, Pg. 191-199)

I think the horse is dead and I am sorry for beating it, but it is important to realize that your relationship with your spouse and children are what sets in place their belief about themselves and whether they can exercise faith in their relationships. Our example is supreme!

6) In the functional family, parents teach their children faith.

In the book, Lectures on Faith, prepared by the early leaders of the church we find the following question and answer:

Question: What does it mean to work by faith?

"We answer—we understand that when a man works by faith he works by mental exertion instead of physical force. It is by words (thoughts), instead of exerting his physical powers, with which every being works when he works by faith." (Lectures on Faith, Salt Lake City: Deseret Book Co., 1985, p. 72.)

There is much good that comes from mental exertion. The ability to picture what one wants to become and then organize and plan how to bring that picture into fruition is the basis of our thoughts. Our thoughts are powerful tools by which we engage faith.

Faith comes by hearing truth and believing in it – without having to have a perfect knowledge of things (Alma 32:21). In developing faith in Christ, one must first hear of Him; His plan of happiness through legally authorized administrators (Romans 10:14-17) and then must exert (thoughts) words in the form of prayer, asking for spiritual confirmation (James 1:5; Moroni 10:4). However, in order for the petition to be recognized as truly faithful an individual must ask with a sincere heart, with real intent, believing in Christ, or as James puts it:

"But let him ask in faith, nothing wavering. For he that wavereth is like a wave of the sea driven with the wind and tossed."

"For let not that man think that he shall receive any thing of the Lord." (James 1:6-7)

Real intent means you really intend on doing something with the information, it is not for intellectual enhancement alone. Sincerity recognizes the changes one will have to make in his or her life, when spiritual confirmation comes. When someone has prepared themselves such, then the promise is true:

> "... he will manifest the truth of it unto you by the power of the Holy Ghost. And by the power of the Holy Ghost ye may know the truth of all things." (Moroni 10:4-5; See Also: John 14:26; 15:26)

Faith that leads to salvation must be centered in Christ. But faith in other truths is likewise vital if we are going to lead a life of fulfillment, hope, and purpose. The exercise of faith in things "hoped for, but not seen" unlocks the power of faith. As you act upon your belief, you do so in recognition of your dependence upon God; that he is the faithful steward of your faith. He is waiting to stretch you beyond any conceived ability. It will require repeated practice to walk to the edge of your understanding, knowing that your journey is prompted by the smallest of impressions and whisperings from the Comforter. In time, you will clearly discern what is and is not His promptings, because through effort and exercise it becomes evident.

As your faith increases, so does your character and your power. Character and power are inseparably connected. When one learns of truth and true principles, he or she is obligated in the exercise of faith to have complete integrity to that truth. To do otherwise is to create doubt and fear. Going against truth will always lead to decreasing faith, and thereby decreasing personal power. To lack integrity is to hold to opposing ideas and thoughts, of what has been revealed. You cannot exercise faith in falsehoods!

Faith requires many correct decisions. We call this obedience. Consistent obedience forges a character resistant to the eroding influences of worldly appetites, pleasure and sin. It provides an inner strength that has been developed by countless good decisions. Character is not developed in a moment of great challenge. It is in the great challenge where character is manifest. Character is a measurement of your faith.

Character is evidence of the process of tapping into the power of Heaven and God's grace. He is able to improve us; make our weak things become strong, and form us into His complete likeness, not because we willed it, but because of His Divine help – unlocked in the exercise of faith. All those that have walked the path of humility, seeking to submit their will to the Father's have understood this sacred process. It is something difficult to explain to someone that has never experienced it. But all are invited to do so (Matthew 11:28-30).

Pure faith manifests itself with complete power. Scripture informs us of this ultimate power:

".... There is nothing that the Lord thy God shall take in his heart to do but what he will do it." (Abraham 3:17)

As God thinks and speaks, so shall it be accomplished, because of the attribute of faith that dwells in Him independently. He has shared with us this truth and has told us upon which principles faith is established and harnessed.

With faith, we can purpose things in our heart, and then exercise the right thoughts (words) and mental exertion to do them. Remember, faith is not simply positive thinking. Faith taps into real Divine sources, which are always true and correct. Also remember, there is no faith in falsehoods. Faith is an alignment with God's will. It is our coming into unity and partnership with His desire and purpose for us. As we do so, His promises and blessings become operative and we experience His strength through us.

> Remember that without faith you can do nothing; therefore ask in faith. Trifle not with these things; do not ask for that which you ought not. (D&C 8:10)

For those that seem to struggle obtaining this type of faith, there may be obstacles that are preventing its development. Evaluate your children to see if any of the following may be stumbling blocks:

1. Has he or she has not developed the spiritual habits that allow them to exercise faith
2. Unworthiness – has not repented
3. Pride and arrogance
4. The illusion of self-sufficiency (i.e., financial success, academic achievement, fame and/or popularity)
5. Religious fanaticism – measuring righteousness by appearance and comparing self to others, being judgmental (Alma 31;16-17; Matthew 6:5)
6. Addictive behavior, including drugs, alcohol, prescription medications, tobacco, shopping, stealing, gambling, masturbation, pornography, hoarding, etc.
7. Entertaining immoral thoughts through written material or media
8. Mental health struggles – anxiety, depression, mood dysregulation, fear, doubt, guilt, bitterness, resentment, low self-concept

Again, faith is a real power, and parents that teach their children to have faith in the Lord, Jesus Christ and all other true principles, will have their children believing in themselves, in their potential and in their ability to bless and lift others.

There is nothing we do without first believing that there is some desired outcome that will be fulfilled or benefit gained. The mere reading of this book is initiated by some

135

level of faith that you will gain something from its contents; otherwise you would not be so engaged.

This concept is critical for our children to understand. I have met way too many young people who are devoid of understanding faith and its power to generate activity that leads to desired outcomes. One way I help parents teach their children this concept of action connected with belief is through a parable I call:

The Parable of the Fast Food Restaurant

How many of you have ever eaten at a fast food restaurant? Do you recall where you were when you made the decision to go there?

Most likely, the decision to move toward the fast food restaurant was made in a location, where the fast food restaurant was unseen – like maybe you were at school or at a gym playing ball. The point is, the restaurant was not visible to your eyes, therefore you were exercising faith, which is to "believe in something that is true, even though we cannot see it" (Hebrews 11:1; Alma 32:21).

Let me ask you a question. What is the reason you go to a fast food restaurant anyway? The answers are usually as follows:

1. I like the way the food tastes
2. It is convenient
3. It doesn't cost much
4. I don't have to do much clean-up afterwards
5. It is quick

However, none of these answers is the real reason why someone decides to go to the fast food restaurant. These are simply ancillary to the real reason why anyone would begin moving toward the fast food restaurant.

The real reason why someone would act and move toward the eating establishment is because they actually believe that when they arrive, there would be food to eat. Without this central belief, none of the other reasons would even matter.

But how did you know that the fast food restaurant would be there when you arrived or that there would be food available? Well, there would have to have been enough evidence to suggest to your mind that it would be there. So let's review the evidence.

Have you ever been to that fast food restaurant before? How many times? You see, the more times you went the stronger the evidence.

Have you ever driven by the restaurant and noticed others there eating. How many times have you driven by and saw people eating? You see the more times you had that experience, it would strengthen the evidence.

Have you ever heard any advertisements on the radio or television stating that if you come they will have food for you? How many commercials have you heard?

What about that sign in front of the establishment that says "Over 99 Billion Served?" That is a lot of people that have always found food when they went there.

Has there been even one time when you went when they did not have food?

As you can see, your going to a fast food restaurant is an act of faith; all generated from a belief, based upon experience that both the establishment is in its same location and when you arrive, there is food there. Without that faith, there would be no cause of action.

Faith is the foundation for all action. When this principle is understood, it removes the obstacles preventing effort. The, "It's too hard," "I can't understand what the teacher is trying to teach," "I can't, I don't know how," "They'll just laugh at me," etc. When someone believes that with personal effort and support that they can accomplish anything they purpose in their heart to do, they then can get busy (action) to have their faith become realized.

7. In the functional family, parents teach accountability (Actions) – Accountability does not take into consideration one's motive or intent. Accountability focuses on behavior. When someone says, "I didn't mean it" or "It was an accident" it is irrelevant.

Everyone one of us will hurt or damage another person or thing. Accountability is about repairing the damage or hurt. Accountability is about standing up and saying 'I did something wrong and I want to make it right. I want to restore that which was lost due to my actions.'

A child that is filled with shame may want to avoid taking accountability, because he or she perceives the process as reinforcement of being a bad person. Such children are tired of feeling bad about feeling bad and therefore avoid ownership. What they do not understand is that the self-learning and feelings associated with personal accountability counters the deep shame they are experiencing. This is one of the reasons why wise parents teach this principle to their children. Its effects are far more reaching than a few words from parents encouraging it. This is one of those principles where knowledge comes after doing it (John 7:17).

My family had gone to Cambria for a week to spend time at a beach house. Unfortunately, I had to work and so I was assigned the "feed the pets" duty. The first morning I went into Micah's room to feed the fish. The aquarium sat on his dresser adjacent to the window. After feeding the fish, I decided to open the blinds to allow natural light to fill the room. Upon opening the blind, I noticed a bb size hole in the window.

When my family returned from the trip, I gathered my boys together and simply asked, "Does anyone know anything about the bb size hole in Micah's window?" I knew that non-verbal language would indict the guilty one and sure enough Carey squirmed a bit. I said, "Carey, it appears from your body movement that you might know something about this." Carey confirmed that it was he that had unloaded the little ball while in the backyard goofing off. I could tell by the look on his face that he was worried. I said, "Carey, your heart must have sunk when you realized what had happened. I imagine that there was some concern on whether you were in trouble or not. Carey, you're not in trouble and I never became angry." I continued, "I know you well enough that I concluded it was likely an accident. I don't believe you intended on breaking the window." I hugged him and looked at him with "smiling eyes" so that he was assured of my admiration for him.

"Carey," I said, "this has now become a teaching moment and I would like you to learn the lesson and principle of accountability. Accountability is when we take ownership of any harm or damage we may have caused due to our actions. It is important that we recognize when we have done something harmful, and more importantly that we care how it may have affected others. Based upon that care we demonstrate our sincerity by doing all in our power to restore or repair the damage caused. Accountability has nothing to do with our motives or intentions. Accidents and mistakes are not reasons to avoid being accountable."

I then encouraged Carey to measure the window and call at least three glass repair businesses to obtain pricing. I then told him that he was free to choose whatever bid he would like. I then said, "After you have selected the estimate, you will need to go and earn the money to pay the contractor."

Carey was faithful in this discharge and Carey earned the money for the repair. I asked Carey how he felt about what he had accomplished. Carey indicated that it felt good to have taken the responsibility to be accountable for his actions. Carey learned something about himself that day as well as an important lesson in life. There is nothing in my words that could have matched the feeling he had for following through on this project. He learned the value of money. He learned that mistakes happen, but it is not the end of the world, nor do they define him. He learned that positive feelings arise and confidence increases when we take care to repair our mistakes. He learned how to take an active role in problem solving and decision making. This one single event allowed my son to evaluate himself realistically and conclude that he was a positive, capable, and responsible individual. When someone feels those highly-reinforcing positive emotions, self-esteem is intact and healthy.

I told this story in one of my parenting workshops and then later received the following email from a couple that had attended:

"My husband and I attended your recent parenting workshop, "The Art of Effective Parenting." We wanted to let you know how your concepts helped us with a recent event."

"I have been puzzled about our boy's bathroom. Lately it has smelled like urine. And yet when I inspect it, I can't seem to locate its source. I go into the cupboard and pull out the Clorox wipes, wipe everything down, and yet the odor continues to linger. I began wondering if this is just how boy's bathrooms smell."

"Well, you know how the Clorox wipes containers are. Sometimes the tab does not grab hold of the next sheet and so you have to push your fingers down inside to grab the wipes and lift the next one up. The wipes were almost gone and so in order to get my fingers on the wipes, I turned the container upside down while I pushed my fingers past the tab. In doing so, yellow liquid began to pour out onto my hand and onto the floor. I had located the source!"

"I told my husband about what I had discovered and asked him what he thought we should do. He replied, 'If it works for a bb hole in the window, it should work for a container of wipes.' The light went on and we both knew this was going to be one of those teaching moments you emphasized in your workshop."

"Like you, we lined up our three young boys and asked, "Does anyone know anything about the pee-pee in the Clorox wipes container?" We simply watched the reaction of the three boys and easily concluded that Nathan knew something about it. With some gentle prompting, Nathan, our four year old, confessed that he used the container instead of the toilet one time. We told him that we were not upset, but then explained that he would have to take accountability for damaging wipes that did not belong to him. The price tag was still on the container and so we told Nathan that he would have to go and earn $2.57 so that he could replace what he had damaged. My husband suggested that he could go around the neighborhood and ask if anyone had any work that he could do to earn some money."

"It was agreed that he would be out the next morning trying to find work. That evening I got on Facebook and let my friends know what had happened and told them to expect a cute, blond-haired four year old looking for work."

"Nathan was at it by mid-morning and was finding success in getting work to earn money. Now four-year olds don't really understand money. All Nathan knew was that his pocket was beginning to fill up. One door Nathan knocked on was that of our friend Steve. Nathan told him what he was doing and asked Steve if he had any work for him. Steve asked Nathan, "Do you think you could empty 29 bottles of water and then use the hose to refill each one?" Nathan shook his head affirmatively and Steve showed Nathan where the bottles were stored. Nathan took each gallon container out to Steve's back patio, emptied each one and then refilled every one. Afterwards, Steve showed Nathan how to use a medicine dropper to put a couple of drops of bleach in each bottle. Steve said that Nathan had really gotten into his work as was evidenced by his wet clothes. Afterwards, Steve pulled out 29 pennies and paid Nathan one penny for each bottle. As Nathan's hands began to have difficulty holding that many coins, Nathan exclaimed, 'Thank you, this is the most money I have made all day!'"

"Well, Nathan earned all of the money, but rather than just pay me, Nathan insisted that I drive him to Walmart because he wanted to buy the new wipes himself. I grabbed a shopping cart on our arrival, because I was going to pick-up a few things. When we got the cleaning aisle, Nathan took a Clorox container from the shelf, but rather than put it in the cart, he held onto it. When we got to the check-out stand, Nathan put the container on the conveyor belt. He told the checker about what he had done and then he reached into his pocket and pulled out all of this change he had earned earlier in the day and handed it to the lady."

"I could sense that my son was feeling something positive in this moment. After he paid for the Clorox wipes, he gave them to me and said he was sorry and that he wouldn't ever do that again. I grabbed him and hugged him and we had, what you call, 'a tender moment.'"

"One of many similar comments I received back on Facebook was, 'Where did you learn how to do this – this is incredible!'"

"Thank you Larry for helping us learn how to shape a positive belief system in our children."

What a powerful teaching moment for a four-year-old. This early in life his parents are providing lessons that will shape his truthful sense of self, and teach him about the feelings of others. I believe most parents would have simply become angry and punished their child. Which approach do you think will have the greatest impact on developing a positive personal belief system?

7) **In the functional family, parents teach responsibility and life skills** – For chores, clothing, emotions, socialization, organization – so they can take care of themselves when they leave home.

My mom was a wise old bird. She saw to it, by the time we were 18 that we knew how to do all things, both inside and outside of the house in order to take care of ourselves. Their was no discrimination, boys and girls alike learned how to take care of the yard and learned how to keep the inside of the house tip-top.

She started involving us in these responsibilities from when we were young. She did not make the mistake of waiting until we were teens to begin the process. I believe that is an important factor, as little children don't really discern that what is being asked of them is work – for a younger child it is simply being with mommy or daddy and a means to please them. Young children love to do things that make their parents happy and sit-up and take notice. In the process, there is no question of chores being optional, it is simply what we do. However, if we wait until children are older to begin doling out domestic assignments, they will resist because it is change.

Now my mom did this in a way that reminds me of Mr. Miyagi's approach to teaching Daniel-son karate. If you recall the movie, "The Karate Kid," Mr. Miyagi has Daniel-son come to his place and wax old cars, sand wood decks and paint fences. However, Mr. Miyagi had Daniel-son do these chores in a very specific way. It wasn't until weeks of doing these difficult tasks for Mr. Miyagi that Daniel-son questions Mr. Miyagi's intent.

Mr. Miyagi then engages Daniel-son in a fight, where Mr. Miyagi begins to punch or kick at Daniel-son. As he is doing so, Mr. Miyagi barks out signals that tell Daniel-son to mimic the same moves he had learned while doing all of the work for Mr. Miyagi. Daniel-son comes to the realization that the work was simply training him in the moves of karate. Likewise my mom's method had us realize, after we hit adulthood, how prepared we were for life.

When it was time for dinner, my mom would call for each of us to come to the kitchen to help. We learned how to chop and slice, brown meat, cook bacon, make a salad, cook pasta, make garlic bread and all of the techniques utilized in the preparation of food. Day after day, week after week, month after month, and year after year, we spent time in the kitchen helping prepare the food. By the time we were 18, we had no difficulty in planning, shopping for and making meals. I and some of my siblings were thankful we knew how to cook, because it seemed that we married spouses that were not so good at it.

141

Each of us learned how to do laundry, sorting, soaking, treating stains, when to use bleach, how to fold our clothes, ironing and so forth. While I was not taught how to sew, per se, I was taught how to hem pants, sew on buttons, and make small repairs with a needle and thread. I was taught how to care for my clothes so that they would last. I knew how to shine my shoes as well.

I learned that there are things that we do at regular intervals to maintain good health, like washing bedding, dusting, vacuuming, sweeping and mopping floors. I learned how to clean windows and clean out roof gutters.

I learned about the importance of personal hygiene, and was surprised by some girls I kissed that did not. Nothing worse than to kiss someone with bad breath due to poor oral health. My hair was not greasy, and while I had some acne, I was faithful in washing my face to help remove excess oil. My nails were trimmed, my hair combed (actually styled – it was the 80's) and deodorant, always deodorant!

There was nothing I couldn't do in the yard. I knew how to edge and mow, rake and sweep. Weeding, fertilizing, trimming, aerating and watering were all skills I learned.

Then there was that special week every year – Spring Cleaning! Everything was pulled out of cupboards and drawers so that they could be wiped out. New drawer linings were installed, the exterior of the house was washed, curtains and pillows were laundered, walls were wiped down, the silver polished, screens scrubbed clean, floors stripped of wax and then sealed again, items that were still in good condition but no longer useful were gathered and donated.

We had a garden and learned how to keep it pest free and weed free. We learned how to can, dehydrate and freeze to add to our food storage.

We learned how to take care of cars, by washing, waxing and vacuuming, changing fluids on a regular basis and tuning them up.

We learned how to keep things tidy and organized. Our beds were made, our closets kept neat. We were taught to not bring out every toy we had at the same time. When finished with some toys, we had to clean them up and put them back before we were permitted to bring out new toys. Clothes thrown all over the floor, towels not replaced neatly, wash rags not wrung out is not something one would not find in our home, at least not for days on end.

The consistent pattern shown to us by our parents prepared us for the real world. There was not one single activity of domestic work that was overwhelming. Each of these activities in and of themselves was small and not much to be made of – even though we would complain from time-to-time. Yet, the doing of the small things over and over again brought to pass a very big thing (Alma 37:6), the skill sets to be more self-sufficient; the confidence to meet the real world when it came time to be on our own, and the pride that comes from accomplishment.

I have passed this legacy on to my own children and they too experience the confidence that comes from hard work. While in college, my oldest son used his skills to prepare meals in the basement of his dormitory, which resulted in many young ladies coming and partaking of the feast – it demonstrated that he would be a good catch, and it allowed my son to meet many young women – not a bad result from such a small thing such as cooking.

Likewise, it is important that parents teach their children manners and appropriate social customs. If parents will spend time looking in their children's eyes while growing up, children will learn how to do the same. How many youth have I counseled that struggle with issues of fitting in, ADHD, academic functioning, and feeling better about themselves that also struggle with eye contact – ALL OF THEM! Eye contact or the lack thereof is significant in the development of personal belief systems. Eye contact, allows for unconscious assessment of how others view us. That is part of our human design and our society is going to pay the penalty for encouraging poor eye contact and less social interaction through modern technology. The increasing number of mass killings and plots to hurt, maim and kill will continue to rise because of our turning our backs on what is important in developing healthy self-esteem and empathy for others.

According to neurobiologist, Dr. Allan N. Schore, the non-verbal communication of "mutual gaze" is essential to the proper development of the infant and child brain. Dr. Schore states:

> "In later years this connection remains crucial to the development of minds, hearts and spirits of our growing children. Making eye contact is not giving a casual, distracted glance. It is the act of attending to another with the heart and mind. It is giving the kind of focused attention that says, 'I see you. You are important to me.'" (Relational Trauma and the Developing Right Brain, The Neurobiology of Broken Attachment Bonds, Relational Trauma in Infancy, 2010, 19-47).

By striving to more fully and intentionally look in our children's eyes, in the manner described above, will nourish our children's sense of worth and deepen our feelings with one another.

Teaching our children how to greet others, how to start a conversation, how to be sensitive to other's social mores', how to be kind and cooperative are things that parents are responsible for so their children will experience social acceptance. Parents should teach their children about cultures, political view points, and other social issues so that their children become interesting and are able to express opinions and be informed. In this process, parents should also be teaching their children respect for all

143

people and develop a spirit of inclusiveness – not judging others as inferior just because their beliefs and customs seem foreign (1 Samuel 16:7).

We have become an instant gratification, pill-popping, throw-away society. In the midst of it all, our emotional regulation systems have been trained to disengage, thereby increasing the number of people that suffer from mood swings and instability, anger, anxiety, depression, and shame. The day of blaming all of these issues on genetics is over. Every respectable researcher, therapist, medically trained personnel and prophet know that children's brains learn to regulate from the environment they are raised in. If I have a parent that experiences anxiety, their children's brain will synchronize to that anxiety. One of the greatest and most important achievements of human development is that of emotional regulation.

Human design is such that in the mind-body connect, the mind is supposed to be the master of the body. When a person struggles with emotional regulation, it is because their mind trained their body to become the master over the mind. I have already touched on this in the Chapter: Setting the Stage, but more details will be discussed in learning and development. But for the person that struggles with emotional regulation, it is because the person believes what their negative emotion is telling them.

8) In the functional family, parents teach communication – openness, assertiveness, active listening, positive feedback; not stuffing feelings

In any relationship that is found wanting, we can be assured that communication is likewise found wanting; especially impacted are those relationships that matter the most. If there be hardships and negative feelings between spouses or parents and children, then we will see a history of repeated failed emotional communication in the wake of such relationships.

Children learn how to communicate from their parents. Communication is a skill. If a parent has not acquired the skill themselves, they will find it difficult to teach their children. Likewise, without the ability to communicate well, the parent-child relationship will suffer. Of all the communication styles, assertiveness is the highest form used by mankind.

Assertiveness means that we have an opinion, we care for ourselves, we want to stand up and be counted and we want others to know what we are experiencing. To assert one's self means that I have respect, not just for myself, but also for the person or people I am communicating with. At no time do I take a superior, aggressive or victim position. The message I send is that I am just as interested to hear what others are experiencing and when my time comes, to share what I am aware of inside my own experience.

Awareness includes six areas, 1) What I observe or notice, 2) What I think, 3), What I feel, 4) What I need, 5) What I want for myself, what I want for the other person I am speaking with and others that may be impacted, and 6) What my behaviors are, including what I used to do, what I am willing to do now, and what I am going to do in the future.

Active listening is likewise a skill that is part of the communication process. Active listeners are able to forego their own experience momentarily so that he or she may attune themselves fully to the other person and the experience being shared. The active listener is confident that by becoming an effective listener, he or she earns the right to be heard, when that time comes. In the meantime the active listener is trying to "go deep" into the experience of the other person, looking for underlying needs or emotions being expressed. At no time does the active listener block communication by 1) Interrupting or cutting-off the other's communication, 2) Being distracted, 3) Being impatient, 4) Giving answers to quickly, 5) Assuming that one understands what the other person is saying, 6) Tuning out something that one disagrees with, 7) Forming a rebuttal in one's head while the speaker is talking, 8) Wanting to change or fix the other's person's perception, and/or 9) Completing other people's sentences.

Life has the uncanny ability to keep us busy and distracted. However, if we learn that our parental guidance is of supreme importance then we will learn to listen when our children desire to be heard.

Our children desire to share their stories, their thoughts and feelings when they observe that we care and want to hear them. Sometimes they will tell us things that we may not want to hear, but are we sending the message that we are ashamed of them when such courage is being displayed? Our character really matters in such moments. Our ability to attune to and understand their feelings, their decision making process, their moment of weakness in terms of Heavenly Father's plan (Moses 6:55) can provide the very loving reassurance they seek in their unhappy experience.

Active listeners are able to help direct better conversations because of their awareness of the six areas we as humans communicate. While listening to a person share their experience, they may recognize that the person left out voiced wants or feelings. By simply asking, "How do you feel about what you just shared," or "Help me understand what you want" are great conversation builders and are introduced simply because active listeners are likewise skilled in communicating the six areas of awareness.

Families that do well have an understanding that lines of communication are open and welcome. When individuals in families stuff their awareness and experience, it is because communication has been hurtful and judgmental, or the person wanting to share does not experience being understood, or what they are sharing is perceived to be unimportant to another person. When someone experiences repeated let-downs in their sharing, it is natural that such an individual will begin to suppress their inner experience. Healthy family communications will send the message of personal importance – thus developing positive belief systems.

Conversations that are full of criticism, contempt, defensiveness and stonewalling (i.e., withdrawal of sharing thoughts and feelings) will create fragile relationships. Instead, we should always look for the good and the positive in each situation and with each person we are communicating with.

We are of the same species as God. Inherent in each of us is the capacity to become like Him and master the mannerisms of His perfection. In Isaiah 55, we are introduced to one of the things in which He does very well:

> "For my thoughts are not your thoughts, neither are your ways my ways, saith the Lord."

> "For as the heavens are higher than the earth, so are my ways higher than your ways, and my thoughts than your thoughts."

> "For as the rain cometh down, and the snow from heaven, and returneth not thither, but watereth the earth, and maketh it bring forth and bud, that it may give seed to the sower, and bread to the eater:"

> "*So shall my word be that goeth forth out of my mouth: it shall not return unto me void, but it shall accomplish that which I please, and it shall prosper in the thing whereto I sent it.*" (Isaiah 55:8-11; Italics added for emphasis)

The gift of communication is priceless. Our Father in Heaven uses his words in such a way that bring about His righteous purposes. His communications with us are at the core of our relationship with Him. He has told us repeatedly of His great love for us. He is found constantly encouraging us. He has always spoken the truth; and His pleasant voice is that of perfect mildness (Helaman 5:30).

His countenance shines with glory and radiates perfect love. Because we are made in His image, we have the capacity to communicate as He does, both verbally and non-verbally. Our children will be strengthened in their life course by what and how we communicate with them.

His pattern of prayer helps us understand that listening to our children and accepting them for who they are, and what they are experiencing, is what allows them to learn wisdom from us. When we go to Heavenly Father in prayer, it is because of our soul's sincere desire to be understood and our willingness to listen to His Spirit's promptings to become better at understanding His desires for us. You will notice that in prayer, He does not dominate the conversation, nor does He spend much energy in telling us what we have done wrong. Instead, His focus is on our feeling His love. When we feel His love, we desire to change – not just because it is the right thing, but because we desire to show our love for Him (1 John 4:19). If for a moment we do detect some chastisement, remember, such moments are a demonstration of His love not rejection (Hebrews 12:5-6).

Elder L. Lionel Kendrick summed up this message of Godlike communication when he taught:

> "Heavenly Father has given us a priceless gift in our capacity to communicate with each other. Our communications are at the core of our relationships with others. If we are to return home safely to Heavenly Father, we must develop righteous relationships with His children here in mortality."

> "Our communications reflect in our countenance. Therefore, we must be careful not only what we communicate, but also how we do so. Souls can be strengthened or shattered by the message and the manner in which we communicate."

> "Christlike communications are expressed in tones of love rather than loudness. They are intended to be helpful rather than hurtful. They tend to bind us together rather than to drive us apart. They tend to build rather than to belittle."

> "Christlike communications are expressions of affection and not anger, truth and not fabrication, compassion and not contention, respect and not ridicule, counsel and not criticism, correction and not condemnation. They are spoken with clarity and not with confusion. They may be tender or they may be tough, but they must always be tempered."

> "The real challenge that we face in our communications with [our children] is to condition our hearts to have Christlike feelings for [them]."

> "When we develop this concern for the condition of [our children], we then will communicate with them as the Savior would. We will then warm the hearts of those who may be suffering in silence. As [our children present with] special needs along life's way, we can then make their journey brighter by the things that we say."

> "Christlike communications will help us to develop righteous relationships and ultimately to return to our heavenly home safely. May we treasure the divine gift of communication, and may we use it wisely to build and to assist [our children] on this marvelous journey through

mortality..." (Christlike Communications, General Conference, October, 1988; thoughts in parenthesis intended to direct the information directly to our children)

9) In the functional family, parents are empathetic to feelings – feelings are not "Its" they are "Me's." When we minimize our children's feelings we are minimizing them.

Some are better at feelings than others. Some can become very uncomfortable when it comes to dealing with feelings. However, feelings are part of human design and are the means by which important information is communicated and understood; especially spiritual communication and understanding (Luke 24:32).

As our children experience life, they will experience highs and lows, positives and negatives, triumphs and defeats. Regardless of the internal feeling, our ability to attune to and feel as they feel allows us to connect to one another.

In the Garden of Gethsemane, Christ's compassion for each of us was perfected. It was there that he felt of all of our infirmities, our doubts, our weaknesses, our dislikes, our so easily besetting sins, our fears, our pain and sorrows. In this incomprehensible moment and later on the cross, Christ experienced it all! Because of the Great Atoning Sacrifice, He now knows how to succor us perfectly because He identifies with us perfectly (Alma 7:12).

Such spiritual insight strengthens us when we wait on the Lord's promised relief, because we know, He knows, from His personal experience how to help and heal us. His choosing to succor us from his own learning allows for mutual identification.

In essence, none of our children will have different feelings than our own. There is a finite experience of emotion and therefore it allows us to identify with others. Regardless of their expressed or unexpressed emotion, our ability to demonstrate empathy for these emotions frees our children of isolating experiences. By recognizing and sharing in their emotions provides the ability to have close relationships. It also provides the ability for children to regulate better, knowing that their experience is not an exception. Such personal, parental succoring will teach our children greater control of their inner experiences.

10)   In the functional family, parents are supportive of kid's interests – strengthening children's self-concepts through supporting development.

Parents recognize individual strengths and talents within their children. Many times, such personal gifts provide direction and purpose in life. Likewise, Heavenly Father uses such strengths and gifts to bring about His purposes (1 Samuel 16:11-12).

When developing a sense of self, children begin to recognize some of these same talents and interests and by increasing their development find inner strength and confidence in their quest to master their physical environment.

At other times, children will try things that may not seem so natural with varying results. At times such trying will lead to further development and growth, while other times it will result in a "I went and saw, but do not like what I see" experience.

Some parents believe that by putting their children in so many things will have them become more liked, or more acceptable to the world. Playing sports all year round, specialized coaching, weightlifting and conditioning, mastering several musical instruments, taking voice and dance lessons, getting their children a tutor so they can excel academically, beauty pageants, science fairs, traveling the world, attending self-improvement conferences, and so on and so forth, ad nauseum.

Usually such monumental efforts send the wrong message. It usually sends the message that if I am not on the top, then I am on the bottom; so such children struggle with the weight of perfectionism. It also takes away from healthy balance. Children need lots of free time to be with friends, to be lazy, to read; to explore, to serve and the like. The pressure of always performing will wear children out and likely cause a rift in the parent-child relationship.

When there is more than one child in the home, and the philosophy is to have all of our children excel in so many things, the nature of parenting turns from being present to being a chauffeur, a personal assistant, a manager and an agent. It creates too much stress on the entire family structure.

Here is my advice, allow your children to have a voice in their development. Let them know that doing nothing most of the time is out of the question. Heavenly Father did not want us to come here to bury our talents (Matthew 25:29-30). He wants us to show an increase in that which He has blessed us with. Help your children identify strengths and gifts they already manifest, but also ask them what kind of things they think they might be interested in trying.

Also, help them understand that as anyone pursues interests, at times those interests may turn out to not be as interesting as originally thought. Here it is important to instill an understanding of commitment and follow through. Let's say your son decides he would like to try tackle football. As he gets into the first weeks of conditioning, he may have never considered the will power it takes to go and exhaust himself everyday. He may not like it and shortly thereafter comes to you and says, "I don't think I like football after all," hoping that you will give him permission to 'quit.'

This is an important learning moment, because we do not want to teach our children that when something gets tough, or if there is something we don't like that we should

149

just quit. That is not a habit you want your children to get in. I have told my children that when they decide to do something they have to stay committed long enough to either fulfill an obligation or to go the distance to ensure that their experience is enough to make the appropriate decision. In the example just cited, I would have my son understand that if during the season, any part of the season, if he decides football is not for him that he will remain a part of the team because of the commitment he made to his coach and teammates and in so doing still give his very best effort. If he cannot make this commitment then I don't support the activity.

The principle of commitment is part of real life experience. It teaches someone how to go the distance and helps a person learn that they have internal resources to manage hard or difficult circumstances. Most people discover that commitment allows for greater perspective and a belief that one can find good and strength in almost any situation. It develops confidence and reveals an important truth, that belief coupled with effort provides the pathway for desired outcomes. This truth is usually the difference between success and failure and acts as the leveling agent between potential and outcome.

What my children do without being nagged, nudged or induced are the things that I find easy to support. When it came to musical practice, for example, I had one son that would only practice when asked, another that started with great enthusiasm and then lost momentum and a third son that we had to ask to stop practicing after a couple of hours of playing practically everyday.

Provide limits on how many activities a child can participate in at any given time frame. Tell them that you will support one or two activities beyond some of the regular things they do, like scouting, young men and young women. Maybe a job and athletics or dance lessons and guitar lessons, but to do scouts, have a job, be in a play, participate in hip-hop classes, meet weekly with the ward organist to learn how to play the organ, have daily basketball practice and babysit on the weekend is way too much, especially if all six children are doing the same thing.

Elder Neal A. Maxwell put it this way with regard to over-parenting:

> "There are wise limits in daily life. For instance, how many of the various "lessons" for their children can young parents sustain, financially as well as transportationally? How much such "good" can their children actually stand? We sometimes do so much for our children that we can do nothing with them."

Coping with an ever growing burden of schedules and accomplishment can upset the balance and harmony we seek. In the midst of either doing or being all for everyone else can lead to becoming overwhelmed and eventually being defeated. Common to human experience are keeping up with the demands of relationship, employment, individual

150

refreshment, family and church responsibilities. One way to keep things in perspective and perhaps priority is to understand the message of the oxygen mask deployed on airplanes when the cabin pressure is disrupted. We must first put on our own mask so that we can help others. If we are passed out, we are no good to others needing our assistance. The gospel helps in this process as it defines those things that need our greatest attention. Our happy relationships with our family members goes farther in keeping us refreshed than it is for our children to live a perfect life.

Of all of the talents our children should learn to develop is the talent of spirituality. If they are of the House of Israel, it is because their pre-existent course signified the development of this talent. Mortality is but a continuation of eternal life, and the blessings of the Covenant were assured because of this pre-earthly progress to believe. Our responsibility as parents is to reinforce this attribute throughout their stay with us so that their talent to believe and obey will assure them of greater blessings in the next stage of progression.

So within all of the scheduling, teach your children to schedule time to build upon their pre-existent talent of spirituality, the ability to believe and obey. Such will add to their own understanding of personal worth, value and purpose. Failure to transmit testimony will in one short generation impact generations to come.

11) **In the functional family, parents are gentle, not harsh** – not provoking anger in our children.

Of all things that lead to growing resentment and anger in our children, is primarily harshness in our interactions with them. Harsh tones, harsh judgments and evaluations, and harsh labels.

The ancient counselor taught, "A soft answer turneth away wrath: but grievous words stir up anger" (Proverbs 15:1). Likewise, when we act in ways that send such profound disapproval of the child's existence, we also "provoke them to anger"

From anger comes discouragement (Colossians 3:21), an internal struggle steeped in doubt about one's acceptability and capability. How many times do our imperfect children set off in us our own imperfections? If we are to refrain from harshness in dealing with our children's misgivings, what do we do in these decisive moments?

A son once said to his father, "I don't feel like I am ever good enough. I never hear what you like about me," to which the father replied, "I would gladly tell you when you are doing well, if you would ever do anything that deserves such attention." The emotional reaction was clear – this young man became discouraged and then angry! One can discern immediately the difference between splinters and planks in this example (Matthew 7:3-5).

151

Louis C. Shimon penned these words:

> "Wouldn't this old world be better
> If the folks we meet would say:
> 'I know something good about you,'
> And then treat us that way?"

Consistent harsh dealings with our children sap them of vitality to believe in themselves and to act in the true nature of their Divine heritage. Harshness sends the message of continual disappointment and failing. As parents, we have the responsibility to dispel such poor tactics. Every word and every act influences the thinking and attitude of our children. It is in the family that our children learn the primary dealings of sociality. If we can temper our disappointments when our children perform less than what we expect, looking first at our own imperfections, recognizing that all fall short, and then in gentleness demonstrate their worthiness and acceptability, we will witness them rise to be a blessing to their own family (your grandchildren) and to society at large.

It appears that the Savior may have had this concept in mind when he so boldly declared:

> "And whosoever shall offend one of these little ones that believe in me, it
> is better for him that a millstone were hanged about his neck, and he
> were cast into the sea." (Matthew 18:6)

Children thrive upon the happy and accepting countenances of their parents. Smiles bring closeness. Frowns bring uncertainty. Generous praise lifts hearts. Contemptuous judgments deflate souls. Kind tones are sweet melodies to the ears and heart. Harsh tones reverberate darkness to the mind.

We can discipline, but when coupled with severity, correction is not usually the outcome, but resentment. It is self defeating and aggravates the problem. Be gentle, not harsh and you will find that your children will respond to your approving nature.

12)   In the functional family, parents teach mutual respect – Receiving respect is an innate desire of every person.

"Don't you ever talk to me like that! I don't deserve to be treated that way – I am your mother!" Sound familiar? Typically, demanding respect will get us continued disrespect – it displays failings in our relationships. When a parent finds themselves in a position demanding respect then something has gone wrong.

Nurturing respect comes from the idea that every person deserves to be treated decently simply because of their inherent worth and our association with one another

152

as part of God's family. Without this understanding, it would be difficult to find the motivation to cultivate respectful interactions.

Yet, even without knowledge of the family relationship of every being, many have stumbled upon universal truths that speak to the importance of developing respect for others. Some have termed this universal truth as Karma, while others have simply described it in terms of "What goes around comes around." Whatever the reasoning to develop consideration for others; those that understand and live by this concept seem to do better relationally.

I have counseled with many parents who were beside themselves because one or more of their teenagers were becoming more and more disrespectful with them as the parent. Sadly, but not without understanding, the majority of such cases was simply a manifestation of long-term parenting that was absent of respect for their children.

My roots come from the South. I was raised with southernly manners. When it came time to get up from the dinner table, I was expected to ask, "May I please be excused from the table?" Or if any adult called to me, I would respond, "Yes Sir" or "Yes Ma'am" before engaging in any conversation with them. Of course other words I learned were "please," "thank you," and "may I." Each of these social skills and manners favored me among my peers and adults. I recognized that others showed me a greater level of respect, because I demonstrated the same towards them.

There is a plaque that hangs on a wall in our home that says, "Raise your children so that others will like them." This serves as a regular reminder to teach and monitor our children's interactions with others, as well as our parental interactions with them.

One type of respect is the kind that we give to others when we act with politeness, civility, and with good manners. These can be people put in authority over us, or even strangers that we are meeting for the first time.

The other type of respect is the one we feel toward someone because of the way they conduct their life and the way they interact with others. We recognize that they are a person of honor, a person that lives high standards and so we naturally produce feelings of respect for them.

There is a hope in each of us as parents that our children will show respect toward us because of the mere fact that we are human, but more so because they admire us because of our character and the way we interact with them and others. Children are always watching!

Many errors we fall into for not giving respect are merely rationalizations of poor behavior we find ourselves engaged in. One of these errors is to look at the behavior of another person, concluding that they deserved the disrespect we showed them.

Another error is when we come across a person that makes us feel uncomfortable due to their being different, this can be people that are slower, have disorders that create uneasy interactions, or some sort of physical characteristic that is pronounced. In other words, if others would not behave badly or appear or act differently then I would not behave badly. This way of thinking obviously is trying to shift responsibility for our behavior to someone else. It makes us think that we are not responsible for our poor behavior or justifies our disrespect.

Other forms of disrespect are displayed in prejudice, gossip, ridicule, bullying, and resentment. Most of these are learned in the home, while some develop due to peer interaction. To counter the source and display of such forms of disrespect we must set the proper example ourselves. We must also teach correct principles and provide stories and examples that invite our children to want to live in a manner of respect. Having your children place themselves in another's position and asking how they might feel if they were shown the same disrespect can assist in having your child see the importance of this concept.

The reality is that your children see disrespect displayed in greater amounts in today's world. The world is filled with contention, hatred, war, fraud, corruption, misuse of authority, murders, envying, strife, pride and other forms of disrespect. Each of the negative feelings we experience due to these realities is the Light of Christ encouraging us to seek peace. Why? Because we are literally the children of God (Matthew 5:9). Our divine heritage includes having dwelt with God, our Heavenly Father and His Beloved Son, The Prince of Peace. That time spent with them allowed our true selves to recognize that living peacefully was better than living with discord. Teaching and learning respect for one's self and for others is the pathway that leads to ultimate peace. Where God and Christ dwell, there is no discord, but oneness. Our ability to live peacefully requires our becoming peacemakers.

A parent that yells to demand respect is a parent that has failed to become a peacemaker. He or she will need to change their own interaction, their own behaviors that will warrant honor and respect from their children. There is no other way. It will require parents to check themselves with regard to their tones, their facial expressions, their selected words when engaging with their children.

13) **In the functional family, parents follow through on consequences** – allowing children to learn from their own experience (Moses 6:55-56; Abraham 3:24-26)

Mortality is meant to be a school. Learning from the lessons of life provides wisdom, knowledge and experience that assist us in repeating thoughts and behaviors that bring positive results and likewise, avoiding those that bring disappointment, heartache, and sorrow. The learning we do as a result of our mortal schooling will ultimately prepare us for our growing responsibility beyond this life. The more we acquire here, whether that be knowledge, character development (i.e., meekness and humility), saving faith, and strong relationships, the better prepared we will be in our transition (D&C 130:18-19; Matthew 6:20, D&C 130:2).

Every conference and from scriptural accounts, we are reminded that we are temporary traveler's here in mortality and that our talents, gifts and blessings are not designed for mortal experience and accomplishment only. We are reminded that our real purpose reaches far beyond the mortal experience and that our energies are to be enlisted in developing our eternal capacity.

Effective parents teach the connection between choice and consequence, which acts symmetrically in developing faith within our children. When our children come to understand that there are predictable outcomes associated with their choice, it provides them with a sense of control and the ability to act in faith.

In one of the later chapters we are going to speak specifically about consequences; however, our purpose here in this brief section is to highlight how our children's experiences, when handled well by us, their parents, develops the capacity to shape attitudes and skills that lead to resiliency in our children.

Our children are going to have both positive and negative consequences as they go through the school of life. Life has a way of teaching our children cause and effect, *if* we allow consequences to teach. The parent that does not allow their child to experience the outcome of their choices is cutting off the development of resiliency that is linked to the belief that one is capable, even after getting knocked down.

In following chapters, you will learn how to handle well the setbacks and triumphs experienced by your children. Your purposeful interaction will help develop this resiliency, which is vital in meeting life's challenges. Those that have acquired this ability recognize that challenges will present themselves, but more importantly, they believe they can cope with whatever comes their way.

Other confidence building attributes related to resiliency are not having negative experiences or personal limitations define us. Instead, the child that has developed the skills and attitudes of resiliency makes a conscious effort to improve and overcome weaknesses and past defeats. Resilient children believe that they can influence different outcomes, or use their creative mind to plan and strategize on having better outcomes. They do not become stuck like so many children that spend their energy in blaming others or making excuses for their failures. Resilient children focus on what is in their control. Lastly, children that develop resiliency also believe that life has purpose and meaning. They wake up everyday and organize their thoughts and behaviors to align with that purpose. They also adopt principles associated with that healthy belief system.

All of these benefits from simply developing a belief that one can bounce back and succeed where once failure was experienced! What parent would not want their child to develop such a positive trait? And yet, over and over again, parents interrupt this process by not allowing their children to experience the consequences from their choices. Functional parent's follow-through on the consequences associated with their child's choice, so that their children may gain and grow stronger in the midst of life's experiences. When consequences are allowed to be experienced, children naturally learn accountability and responsibility for their lives.

14) **In the functional family, parents have family councils – everyone is invited to contribute. Children are asked to be the experts of their relationships. (What do they see works well, what solutions would they offer)**

There was a Council in Heaven and we were all invited to participate in that family council (Abraham 3:21-28; Moses 4:1-4). That pre-earth council acts as a spiritual pattern for our earthly homes.

Family councils are not established so that father and mother can dictate their agenda. It is instead a place of learning, a place of shared ideas, and a time when the family government is operating toward shared purpose, interest, and outcome.

In every family, issues arise. The family council is a time where invested members assist with meeting those issues in a way that maintains unity in the family system. When we ask our children to provide input in whatever issue is being discussed it sets within them an idea that they have part ownership of the good outcomes sought for. It also sends a message that their thoughts and opinions matter.

As parents, we spend a lot of time, mainly due to our greater experience, in solving relational issues between siblings. Family councils are a good place to have children become experts of their relationships, by providing their own plan to improve relationships.

Family councils are also a place to recognize efforts and accomplishments in our children's lives. It is a time where we can plan, synchronize calendars, demonstrate respect and love, and interact in a way that invites the Spirit to be present.

Following is a story that highlights an effective family council:

> "Our family had a large irrigated farm, in combination with a dry farm and a dairy farm, in Lewiston, Utah. Throughout my childhood, our family prospered and enjoyed many of the good things life has to offer. But when I was in my early years of high school, we had some financial problems. We suffered a year of severe drought followed by two or three more dry years. Our crops were a total failure. At this same time, many

of our crops were infested with new insects. All the farms in the area were affected, and many other farmers were having difficulties. Mortgage payments that had not been met the previous years mounted and some farmers lost their homes."

"At this time my oldest brother, Eldred, was serving as a missionary in Germany and had to have a specified amount of money sent to him each month. As children we knew that we were experiencing financial problems, but we did not realize the extent or the seriousness of them."

"One evening in the spring, my father and mother called the family together for a family council. We sensed the seriousness of it immediately. We gathered in our front room, and Father took charge. Calling the family to attention, he said that we were meeting about a very serious matter and asked Mother to open with prayer. He then told us of our financial difficulties. It is the only time that I remember hearing a full disclosure of our financial standing. He listed our assets, our liabilities, our expected income for the year, and our essential minimal family needs, and he showed us that our income could not possibly meet our requirements. Prior to the meeting he and mother had met with the banker who held the mortgage on the home and had worked out a plan whereby the home could be saved from foreclosure. We would have to pay the interest payment each month until fall and then make a larger payment with our cash crop in November. The monthly milk check had to cover these interest payments as well as provide the money to be sent to our missionary."

"Mother and Father presented two options to us as a family. First, we could let the bank take over our home, find some place to live, and continue to run the farm. Second, we could meet these monthly interest obligations with nothing left over for other family expenses. Through the summer we could not buy clothing, we could spend no money on recreation and almost nothing on gas for the car; in fact, it would be difficult to get food staples needed to supplement our garden produce. Since the payment in the fall would leave us again with no extra money, we would have to continue this tight economy for at least a year, maybe more."

"After presenting our problem, Father asked each of us to express our thoughts. He wanted us to be part of the decision making. Each of us in our turn answered that we would like to save our home, and we all pledged ourselves to sacrifice our wants; even the smallest children said they would not ask for anything that was not absolutely necessary. Mother and Father said that they wanted the same thing that we wanted, and with tears in their eyes thanked us for being such good, cooperative children, and also thanked us for the hard work that we had done on the farm."

"After the decision was made, we all knelt together and Father said a prayer. He thanked the Lord for our many blessings and asked his help in carrying out the plans we had made that evening. We felt that the Lord would indeed help us if we would do our part. That night our love for each other was surpassed only by our love for our Heavenly Father. I had a lump in my throat that would not go away as I prayed fervently for help in carrying out my part in the plans that we had set."

"In the following years and through the Great Depression, as we struggled to get an education, to serve our church, to maintain our ideals and our standard of living, I had many occasions to reflect upon that family council and the tremendous impact for good that it had upon me. I accepted the difficult times with the assurance that our entire family was working together toward a common goal—and we were succeeding." (The Meeting That Saved Our Home, Thora B. Watson, Ensign, February, 1985)

In families that hold councils, children of these homes come to believe that there are resources and support for meeting the demands of life's challenges. They learn that unity is better than dissension, and that they have the personal means to contribute valued information and expertise. Such inclusiveness strengthens bonds, increases respect, and produces critical thinking. A child who experiences this on a regular basis comes to develop a perspective that all things are possible to them that believe (Mark 9:23).

THE FAMILY GOVERNMENT

"All great change in America begins at the dinner table." (Ronald Reagan)

Government is necessary in the lives of men, as it ideally provides for protection from harm, establishes rules that support positive social interaction, and if established on correct principles, promotes individual achievement and happiness.

In our school systems we are required to study different types of government and the impact such governments have on the world, both foreign and domestic. When we are employed, we operate under the company's government to ensure that our quest for economic prosperity is maintained. When we attend our spiritual centers, we recognize that there are hierarchy's and established rules for moral conduct. In short, we understand the importance of government in many aspects of our lives. Proper government provides the foundation for mutual cooperation in accomplishing the desired outcome of the entity.

Unfortunately, most families spend little effort in teaching about and reinforcing the importance of their *family government* and the associated benefits of good government in the home. Most families simply assume that parents rule and kids drool. After all, there is usually quite a discrepancy between adults and children in relation to knowledge, strength, capability and resources.

This book is not designed to dictate what the best family government is, with the hopes that every family will adopt the same structure. What this book will do is reference some interesting research that will guide the reader into looking introspectively in order to determine whether their style of governing is influencing the family to have the best outcomes. Because every family is structured around the personalities that are present in their home, the different human characteristics do involve themselves in the outcomes hoped for; a little more on that in a moment.

First of all, we have already established that the most important subset in a family is that of the husband and wife. The better this subset is; the better it functions, the greater positive impact it has on the family as a whole. So, let's first look at what research has indicated in relation to parenting styles in determining effect on children outcomes. After looking at the research, we will then present the idea on how to teach about your family government so that things are clearly understood by everyone in the home.

Diana Baumrind, a researcher and psychologist, specializing in child development, looked at different parenting styles and originally came up with three classifications.

They are as follows:

1) Authoritarian (Too Hard)
2) Permissive (Too Soft)
3) Authoritative (Just Right)

Without going into too much detail, the **Authoritarian style** has as its characteristics parents that are controlling, demanding, unwilling to listen, and rigid in their beliefs and manners. Some of the way these parents interact is with harshness, sometimes abusive, becoming personal in their attacks. In other words, when disciplining their child their voice is typically raised and their focus is less on the child's behavior, and instead more focused on the child's character.

The **Permissive style** typically lacks real structure and the parent's demands on their children are low. This parenting style tries to lessen any confrontation, allowing children to believe that they are on equal ground with their parents (friends). Children of this parenting system can easily learn how to manipulate their parent's emotions in order to obtain what they want. Without any real rules or structure, these children tend to funneling their self-interests through their parent's cooperation (spoiled).

The **Authoritative style** presents itself with confident parents that recognize their role as more than someone who sets rules; they recognize that they are in the business of developing a belief system. This parent avoids control and does not react to their child's expression of self-will as a personal attack against them or the system. This parent is clear in the rules and expectations of the home and of their child's behavior, but remains kind, while still being firm.

This parent recognizes that their children are *practicing* and testing how to live life in a positive manner and therefore uses the child's experiences (both positive and negative) to guide their child in deciding what attitudes, beliefs and behaviors get them the best result, believing that the child can and will make the correct choices based upon those experiences. This process requires attentive parents that can *observe* for the child, what the child is experiencing based upon their *practicing*. We'll talk more about this *observing* later.

Dr. Baumrind did finally develop a fourth classification of parenting styles and called it **Uninvolved parenting style** (Just Wrong). Uninvolved parenting *may* take care of a child's basic temporal needs, but fails to take interest in the child's other areas of development. In a sense, these parents are detached from their children's lives intellectually and emotionally. The extreme of Uninvolved parenting is severe neglect or rejection.

Probably as you could guess, the Authoritative style (Just Right) tended to have children that were happier, more capable and successful. The Authoritarian style (Too

Hard) led to children that were more obedient and proficient, but ranked lower in happiness, social competence and self-esteem. The Permissive style (Too Soft) had children that ranked low in happiness and self-regulation. These had difficulty with authority and doing well academically. Finally, the Uninvolved style (Just Wrong) ranked the lowest across all domains. Issues related to low self-esteem, self-control and competency all had higher correlation rates associated with this style of parenting.

Earlier we discussed the *human principle of influence* (helping things go right). All of Dr. Baumrind's results are couched in terms of correlation studies. It is the correlation of parenting styles that manifest the truth of the principle of influence. The reason why there is not enough supportive research to make cause and effect determinations is because one always has to take into account the complexity of human personality, brain development, significant events in a person's experience, etc. It would be too difficult to try and control for this human diversity. Therefore, understand that while you can learn the most effective parenting style and be consistent in that style, there may be variables that lead to your child struggling anyway. But the point is simply this; there are high correlation studies that emphasize the importance of the Authoritative style in having the outcomes we are hoping for in our children.

There are so many areas of study in the field of psychology, but the one that is making drastic headway in helping us understand the power of influence is that of the Attachment Field. How we connect to our children appears to be critical in our influence as parents and likely plays a significant role when understanding the different parenting styles. Dan Siegel, M.D, and Mary Hartzell, M.Ed. wrote an excellent book that addresses attachment and our ability to understand ourselves so that we can connect in a healthy way with our children. I highly recommend it to parents. It is called "Parenting from the Inside Out."

So that you can get a taste of the impact of these different parenting styles, let me ask you some questions, and by your honest responses you will probably discern why certain parenting styles provide for better outcomes compared to others.

CLUSTER 1

Do you enjoy someone controlling you? Do you enjoy being cut-off when you are trying to explain things? Do you like it when someone tells you over and over again what a failure you are, or how stupid you are? Do you enjoy harsh punishments, restrictions, and things being taken away constantly? Do you enjoy being yelled at or belittled? Do you enjoy being labeled? Do you enjoy feeling like you are never good enough or are the cause for so much unhappiness in the lives of your family?

The above questions are related to the *Authoritarian style* of parenting. It is very difficult to connect with a parent that influences you to believe that you are the bane of their existence. Feelings of deep hurt and anger would likely lead to a child *avoiding* their parent.

CLUSTER 2

Would you enjoy not having enough information to know how to handle life in a positive manner? Would you experience confidence in your life if no one helped you understand the importance of limits? Would you be annoyed if your parents were regularly seeking approval from you regarding your relationship with them? Would your self-esteem struggle if you came to believe that your worth was attached to and measured by what you have rather than who you are? Would you develop uncertainty and perhaps fear about how to manage life when you have to help your parent – parent?

The above questions are related to the *Permissive style* of parenting. You would likely be filled with mixed emotions about your parents, at times being confused; at times having good interactions, while other times feeling empty and without direction. Uncertainty in relationships would create *ambivalence* in the parent-child relationship.

CLUSTER 3

Would you like to feel unimportant? Would you like to feel incapable? Would you enjoy wondering how or if you fit in? Would you like your life if you did not know when you were going to eat again? If needing help with homework and your parents weren't willing to help you learn, would that create good feelings inside? Being left to fend for yourself and likely take care of your siblings, would that bring joy during your childhood? Would you like to consistently fear your parents?

The above questions are related to the *Uninvolved parenting style*. Your ability to trust authority figures would be severely disrupted and your limitations in knowing how to take care of yourself developmentally and emotionally would likely lead to *disorganized* attaching patterns.

CLUSTER 4

Finally, how would you enjoy knowing that your parents take a deep interest in you? How would you enjoy being listened to and understood? Do you enjoy the security that comes from parents that demonstrate good judgment and teach you in a way that invites your willingness to experiment with different ways of doing things? What would it be like to know that your parents trust your ability to learn from your own experiences? Would you like having parents that teach the "why" of how they formed their rules and expectations? Would you enjoy having parents that have a sense of being fair and reasonable? Would you appreciate the help in learning how to fit in and how to develop a good work ethic?

The above questions are all related to the *Authoritative style* of parenting. This type of parenting is most likely to assist in forming very **secure** attachments.

Hopefully by answering the questions and reflecting on how you would feel based upon the impact of the various styles, you will see the wisdom of and have a desire to begin to adopt the *Authoritative parenting style*.

From these different parenting styles would emerge different types of family government; some that exhibited tyrannical characteristics, others that allowed its members to become indulgent, some that would be filled with chaos, and those that would provide and teach correct principles and allow its members to govern themselves based upon their own experience.

Dr. James Jones, a psychologist that specialized in family relationships looked at the Authoritative style of parenting and developed a family government based upon the characteristics present in that style. He called it "The Loving Trust Model." In describing this style of government, Dr. Jones stated that this is the structure that makes sense. The formulation of the government is built and maintained on the following truths:

> "Parents rightly maintain position of authority in the home due to their more extensive capacity to provide, and their wisdom obtained through extensive experience. Children sustain them in this role by consent because of these attributes. Parents regard their children as a sacred treasure and place their roles as teachers, nurturers, etc. as one of their highest priorities. Parents allow their children to gain experience through trying and encourage growth through these experiences."

Now that we have looked at parenting styles and their impact on the development of the government of the family, let's look at how to teach the members of the family about our family government.

ESTABLISHING CORRECT STRUCTURE – ROLES AND RESPONSIBILITIES:

Begin with convening a family council and explain that you are going to discuss the family government. Invite your children to discuss what they think your roles as dad and mom are individually, as well as the roles you play as parents.

You may begin by simply asking, "What do you see dad do a lot of that helps the family?" As the children identify the things that you do you can assist them by affirming their perception that these are your roles and responsibilities.

After these are clearly established, ask the following question, "How do dad's roles and responsibilities help others in the family?" You might ask them, "What if dad did not fulfill these roles and responsibilities – what would your lives be like? How would you be affected?

After the children recognize the importance of dad's roles and responsibilities, you might ask, "How is dad doing in fulfilling his roles and responsibilities? If you could give me a grade A through F, how would you grade me?

Allow the children to provide a grade, and then have dad take accountability for those areas that may have been identified in need of improvement. This model's for the children how good governments operate – by returning and reporting – and then offering solutions to improve.

Once dad's roles and responsibilities in the family government are established, then move to mom and go through the same process. After mom is finished, it is now important that the children have a correct understanding of your *role as parents,* being a shared responsibility and though your responsibilities and roles may differ somewhat, they work collectively for the whole and are complimentary in nature (See: Moses 5:1-2; D&C 25:5-9).

To do this, repeat the same process above, drawing out those characteristics, attributes and duties that compliment each other to create a whole. This process helps your children recognize that you are both on the same page and support each other in the roles and responsibilities you each assume.

Now comes the greatest part of the discussion, the part where the children get to clearly state what roles and responsibilities they play and hold in this family government. Ask your children if they believe they play an important role in the family government. If they hem and haw a bit, ask what they spend most of their time doing. Most children recognize that the majority of their time is spent in learning, whether that is academics, athletics, music or dance, etc. They also likely have regular chores that assist the family.

Once they begin to define their roles and responsibilities, now ask them to give themselves a grade on how they think they are doing with contributing to the family government. It is important that mom and dad also provide a grade for each child. When all is said and done, it may look something like this:

Example:
Dad – Inherently the provider and protector (A-)
Mom – Inherently the nurturer, environment setter (A+)
Parents – Equal partners, presides in the home, teachers and
        modelers (B+)
Children – Responsible toward helping and learning (B)

164

THIS OPERATES IN BOTH DIRECTIONS

These concepts (roles and responsibilities) have to be taught and consistently reinforced. Children need to understand that what they do *matters as much* to the parents as what the parents do for them. By teaching this truth, children gain a greater sense of being needed and do better in fulfilling their roles and responsibilities, especially if we praise them in doing so. Kids love to be noticed for doing right things. Many problems can be easily remedied by returning to the proper structure. So again – cliff notes on this process:

- Start by having a family council and *Lay It Out*
- Have children repeat back what they understand the structure to be
- Ask the children if they think you as parents have fulfilled your roles as spelled out and take accountability for your own shortcomings
- Have children clearly state what their own roles and responsibilities are
- State how those will impact you as the parents
- Ask the children if there is anything they need from you to assist them in fulfilling their responsibilities and roles.

In the coming years and months there will be ample opportunity to return to the fundamentals of the family government both formally and informally. We as humans learn by repetition and as the children grow, revisiting this discussion formally will assist in retention as well as making adaptations based upon family circumstances. More importantly will be the *informal references* to this concept, which will instill in real-time applications the importance of everyone fulfilling their responsibilities to the best of their abilities, so that the entire family entity can achieve its stated purpose.

After teaching this concept to his family, a father helped one of his sons recognize the importance of keeping up with his studies rather than waiting until the end of the quarter to get his work in. The father reminded his son that during the family council (previously held) that his son had clearly stated that he (meaning the son) never had to worry about having food, clothes or shelter and had given his dad an 'A' for his effort. The father told his son that having no anxiety throughout the day was a benefit his child enjoyed because of dad's efforts. The father then said to his son,

> "Son, let me remind you of the importance of each family member's efforts in doing their very best. When you delay your assignments you create some stress on your parents, the stress directly related to the frenzy created at the end of the quarter as you are trying to figure out how to get it all done, as well as the stress on your parent's concerns of whether you are developing the habits you will need in order to do well in life. Sometimes it is difficult for your dad to focus on things at work when he knows his son is struggling and is behind in his responsibilities. Let me remind you, what you do with your responsibilities has as much impact

165

on your parents as what we do has on you. Son, I would like you to take your role in the family importantly and help your mother and father by being responsible for organizing yourself better. Just as you enjoy being stress free about our obligations, we deserve to be stress free about yours. Now, how can I help you become better organized?"

The great blessings that attend our children's minds in establishing clear roles and responsibilities in the family government is that a child experiences the feeling of being needed; that their contributions to the family are important and recognized as valuable. It provides them with a sense of empowerment and control and of course the desire to create respectful relationships. Such children are naturally more cooperative and responsible. Each of these traits and internal experiences shape positive belief systems.

In today's society this is especially important because many times children do not connect their efforts in family responsibility or academic achievement as having any real impact on how the family functions.

Just a couple of generations back, children did not struggle with making the connection on how their responsibilities affected the family. Most of America was still living on small farms or ranches. More Americans were growing their own food and raising livestock as a means to support the needs of their family. Therefore, there was a more direct and noticeable difference if children did not do their chores. If Mary did not get the cow milked, there was no cream to make butter. If Johnny did not harvest the wheat, then there was no flour to make bread and so on.

There was no mistaking that their individual efforts were meaningful to the family. Those conditions allowed children in the family to recognize that their roles and responsibilities were greatly needed and that their efforts had significant meaning within the family system. More importantly is the fact that many times children had to combine their efforts and work together to get the outcome they needed. That too is a family responsibility, to learn how to create a spirit of cooperation and respect between family members. Again easier when living the way they did a couple of generations back as compared to today's generation.

Today's generation can get lost in that understanding because of the great ease it is to get the necessities of life. The "need" is not as distinctly discerned by children today, for example, how does making a bed or wiping a mirror, or taking the dog for a walk translate in the child's mind as being significantly impactful? How does getting an A on a test, compared to a D really affect the family's ability to do better?

Now the human condition has not changed, in that, when any of us are experiencing a need, we seem to put in the mental and physical work it takes to meet that need. Establishing a clear family government as described provides some impetus in creating that need.

CHILD DEVELOPMENT AND CHARACTER BUILDING

I have stated at least a couple of times that this book is going to teach about human design. Our growing understanding of this design provides the insight we need as parents to influence the outcomes we hope for. To understand *why we do what we do* in relation to our children is far more valuable than simply memorizing a few parenting interventions that may lead to a desired behavior change in our kids. When we can get to the real source of behavior change then we don't need to memorize parenting tricks – the real source of all behavior is *what one believes about themselves*.

Personal belief is an ongoing process and function of childhood. There is a reason why we have our children for 18 years. Being able to decipher and decode human development is a skill every parent ought to acquire. Having this information drives the *"why we do what we do"* at any given moment of their development, thus developing the belief systems that will produce happy, healthy and functional individuals.

Eric Erickson, an American Developmental Psychologist, discovered that there are tasks, which include skills, beliefs and attitudes that each of us must master if we are going to create the aptitude to live our lives well. If we fail to master these tasks then we will become stymied and until such mastery occurs, these unresolved tasks will continue to negatively impact our lives. They do so in the realm of self-esteem or self-concept.

As parents, it is helpful to understand these developmental tasks, when they begin to occur and how we can influence our children in mastering the tasks needed to deal with the world in a positive manner. Please recall that brain development is an ongoing process so that we can be sensitive to our child's limitations during this process. At the end of each section, I will include a brief synopsis of the child's brain based upon the ages being discussed. This information is very helpful for parents in understanding how to better interact with their children. A child's developing brain is exactly that – developing. It is far different from the adult brain. How it perceives, how it processes; its limitations provides insight to parent's repeated frustration of why the child does not see things the same way the parents do. Following are Eric Erickson's stages of development. We are only going to focus on the stages from birth through adolescence.

TRUST vs. MISTRUST – Infant – (In-utero to the 1st year or so of life)

A child begins to create a sense of self and his or her environment even while in-utero. The rapidly dividing process and differentiation of cellular activity of the forming baby is driven by both genetic encoding and environmental signals. Both parent's DNA are providing information to their newly forming child. Much of that information is the passing on of the parent's own learning, experience and belief, (i.e., the parent's implicit memory). In addition, cellular and genetic development is constantly receiving information from the environment creating cellular communication and changes in genetic expressions during the child's development. Environmental signaling continues to act as *genetic engineering* in the developing process.

Babies are amazingly receptive to this process of signaling. Their brain development provides the basis for acquiring information, but in large measure is a canvas that is waiting to be designed upon. Our interactions as parents is what begins and has the largest influence on what that picture ends up looking like. In-utero, the baby's developing sensory system is picking up on the mother's emotions, her voice, her heart rhythm, her relationships with others, her laziness or industriousness, her positive or negative thoughts and the corresponding levels of stress or calmness she is experiencing. Each of these factors is shaping the child's sense of "I" as well as a sense of control over the environment. If mother's basic experience is filled with high levels of stress, then insecurity and uncertainty becomes the child's perception of the environment. As mother's stress rises, so does the baby's. If mother struggles with depression or anxiety, these also send signals to the baby's cells and they (meaning the cells) begin to communicate with each other in correspondence with the anxiety or depression.

Any of these negative signals are going to be interpreted as "I'm not sure I can trust." "I can't seem to get control of these negative feelings, these higher levels of stress – the world does not seem like a safe and loving place to be". Because the infant is powerless to change these experiences, they begin to not trust themselves. Likewise they begin to fill with doubt in relation to mother's ability to take care of his or her needs.

After the baby is born, the environmental influences increase in how the baby will respond to the ability to trust. Again, newborns are highly sensitive to their environment. In order then to assist our newborns in mastering trust requires an environment of maximum comfort with minimum inconsistency. We must attune to the child's needs and meet them consistently. If their diaper is messy, we must change it relatively quickly, if they are hungry, we must stop our other activities and feed them, if they are tired we must hold and rock them, having them fall asleep within the security of our touch, when our child becomes frightened we are able to quickly make our presence known and provide the comfort he or she seeks. Our interaction stimulates the neurobiological framework that provides the *belief* that the child can trust itself, its environment and his or her caretakers. We cannot spoil an infant, in fact, we are literally preparing them for the next phase of task mastery, which requires their ability to trust the environment enough to begin to explore greater separation from his or her parents.

One insight I might offer here is to understand that the parent's experience of trust with one another is present in these ongoing signals we are sending our children. Whether we are aware of it or not, the parent's association with each other establishes the depth of developing intimacy in all of the family relationships. The greater the intimacy experienced between the parents the greater the trust that can be experienced by all family members. Lawful associations allow for greater intimacy, while unlawful associations introduce mistrust, insecurity and doubt within the family system.

Brain Development: A child is born with 100 billion neural connections. These are waiting for stimulation from the environment so that more connections that will enhance the child's development will occur. For pathways not receiving stimulation, the brain has a way of deleting or pruning these off. We should be aware of this part of human design so that our intentional interaction is providing sufficient stimulation.

During this first phase, it is believed by most researchers that the child does not see itself as separate from his or her caregivers. Some of that introspection comes from the fact that the hippocampus has not matured enough to create mental models of autobiographical information. The child likely perceives the big people in his or her life as an extension of self. Therefore, the responsive or non-responsive actions produced by the child's distress (i.e., hunger, tired, messy diaper, etc.) are interpreted as the child's ability or inability to have some control in their environment. The greater consistency and comfort builds trust in the child's perceived environmental control.

AUTONOMY vs. SHAME & DOUBT – Toddler (18 mo. – 3 years)

There is a term in the field of psychology called "Individuation." Individuation is considered a high level of functioning where a person is able to balance between being on their own and the ability to reconnect with relationships without experiencing high levels of stress either way. Object Relations Theory has us understand a little bit of what is going on in this process and provides a basis for the next developmental skill that needs to be mastered.

Around the age of two, the hippocampus develops enough to begin the process of storing memories as a *connected* story or narrative. In this storing of information, the child begins to be more highly attuned to the idea that if mommy or daddy leave the room that in time they will return. Making this *connection* of leaving and returning begins to provide the narrative that the young child is still safe in these brief separations. The child begins to perceive that out of sight does not mean out of mind. If mommy or daddy has left the room and the child begins to feel insecure, the child signals the distress and mommy and daddy quickly emerge. This repeated experience strengthens the child's concept that he or she is being thought of and cared for even if not in the direct presence of the parents. This begins to provide the structure or scaffolding of separateness from parents.

There can be extremes in feelings being experienced by the young child during this stage of development. Because the child begins to see him or herself as separate from

169

their parents, a conflicted internal experience of wanting to develop a higher order of autonomy verses remaining close begins to emerge. As parents act in a supportive manner when this distress occurs, provides greater belief in the child that he or she is going to be alright with longer periods of separation.

If a parent is not supportive and comforting during these internal struggles, the child begins to experience fear of separation and may become more clingy and dependent.

In essence, the internal working mental model that allows a child to progress to more independence is the idea in the child's mind that though physically absent, the child knows that their parents are aware of them and continue to act consistently toward the child's needs. By knowing this, the child is able to explore more, is able to practice doing more on their own, while maintaining the ability to choose closeness at any time by moving toward their parent. This moving toward and away from one's parent, in a kind of dance, sets the process of individuation in motion. This process fully matures in young adulthood if the child has successfully mastered the other higher order tasks. In another chapter, I more fully detail what autonomy looks like as the child grows older.

We must provide the environment that allows the child to practice autonomy. Sometimes parents, because of the two years just spent in being highly nurturing, fear somewhat for the child's expressed desire for greater separation. Parent's fears of their child getting hurt can creep in and compel the parent to be very cautious – too cautious. The parent will interfere with the child's attempts at autonomy by continuously interrupting many of his or her activities.

"I am what I can do" is the motto for this stage. If I am not allowed to do anything then I begin to believe that I'm not capable. I will begin to doubt my judgment and my abilities because I never develop enough experience to have me believe otherwise. An example of this may show up in the child's increasing ability to climb. A 2-3 year old may spot some homemade cookies on the counter. The child begins to focus on how to get to them and understands that climbing may produce the outcome they are hoping for. As they begin to climb, the parent cuts-off the attempt by physically interfering with the child's climbing by grabbing him and placing him back on the ground. Usually this is followed with a "no-no, we don't climb on the counters." If this continues as a regular pattern, meaning the child's attempts to master their physical environment are interrupted and made to seem bad, the child begins to doubt their decision making ability. Being too overprotective or being harshly criticized for mistakes or accidents will produce shame and doubt as a core belief in the child. The child needs to develop a sense of control and mastery of the physical environment by their physical explorations and manipulations.

A few reading this book, after completing the last paragraph are wondering if I am saying we should allow our children to climb counters to get cookies. What I am saying is that if the majority of our toddler's attempts to master the physical environment are interrupted and are made to seem like the child is in trouble or has done something wrong, will impact how the child perceives his or her efforts. In the case of the cookie, it may be wise for the parent to teach the young toddler to ask for the cookie. After all, this is a form of how we master our environment.

Another way we as parents' cut-off the development of autonomy in our children is through how we interact with our child's thoughts, feelings and motivation. If we keep cutting these off (i.e., thoughts, feelings and motivation), the child will experience doubt and shame in his or her abilities.

How does someone gain confidence in them self if they are constantly questioning their thinking skills or are not sure their feelings are appropriate expressions based upon the circumstances? And yet many parents interact with their children in a way that causes that confusion. For example, a child's perception is different from an adult's – that has a lot to do with the child's brain being underdeveloped as well as the difference in life experience. A child will share his or her experience and then a parent will quickly chime in – "That's not the way it happened." Or a child will have gone through a process of critical thinking to find a solution to a problem, only to be met with – "Why are you doing it that way?" followed by – "You should do it this way." Likewise, a young child may fall down and scrape their knee and begin to cry because of the experience – when suddenly they hear a parent say – "Oh stop your crying. It doesn't hurt. It's just a little scrape."

These continuous responses begin to develop doubt in the child's mind as to their thoughts and feelings being able to be trusted. It creates the child to say, "Well, I can't break away from my parents because obviously my thoughts and feelings are inadequate to meet life's challenges." If this is the pattern of conversation between a parent and young child, the child will not seek growing autonomy, and will experience personal shame and doubt because of being inadequate. Their motivation has been smashed.

So you may be asking, "Well, I want my child to see things in a way that will help them do better – what do you suggest?" You will notice in the above examples that the parent is simply cutting off the child's thoughts and feelings, declaring them to be inaccurate. One way we help our children develop better ways of looking at things is to share our "stories" with them. I might say, "Oh, I am so glad to hear what you thought of that crash we saw today. There are some things I must have missed. I was focusing on how everyone was alright, because they were wearing their seat belts." In this way, our better power of perception can assist the child in shaping that experience, where now he or she has become greater aware of what happened, without being criticized in what he or she may have missed. Same thing with the emotion associated with the scraped knee – "Oh that looks like it hurt sweetie. Let's take a look. Oh it doesn't look bad at all. That's the kind of scrape that stops hurting real fast. Have you noticed how the pain has gone down?"

171

These shared "stories or narratives" assist our children in developing better assessments of their situation without creating doubt about how they have perceived things.

Now, one more bit of information that should make you smile – the favorite word used at this age is "No!" This is the child's declaration that he or she does have their own will. When we hear this word it should send signals of joy to us as parents, because the child is putting into action the idea that one day they will leave our home as they recognize their growing autonomy.

Brain Development: Maturing hippocampal function – Creates the ability for the child to recognize their interactions as more sequential because experiences are beginning to be stored as retrievable information. This provides the ability for the child to see themselves as separate from others.

INITIATIVE vs. GUILT – Preschool (3-6 years old)
Up until this point of development, a large measure of our children's activities has been centered in mimicking adult behavior. Practicing by observing is a way that little people learn about themselves, their connections with others and the development of creating their own ideas. And that is what the next stage is all about, is beginning to create things of our own making and not simply mimicking behavior. Becoming creative is the definition of 'Initiative.'

"I am what I can imagine" is the motto for this stage. The favorite word is "Why." With increasing cognitive abilities, greater ability to create begins to form. The child has a greater sense of agency and has an opportunity to learn through our responses to their questions – if we listen and take the time to answer it encourages greater decision making ability (thus developing the child's capacity to become more creative and independent). If we treat the questions as if they are annoying, likely a child will continue to feel dependent upon the adult. If we end up saving the child they will turn it into guilt later. This can simply be a parent taking what the child has produced and making corrections to it (i.e., the parent does most of the work on a project due at school, because the parent wants his or her child to feel good by having others compliment the project).

By either consistent fixing of their creativity or if we don't show support for their creativity, they too will likely experience guilt or feeling bad as a mainstay to their self-esteem. So let me be clear about how guilt is being defined by Dr. Erickson – what he is saying is that the child begins to feel bad about them self, in relation to the negative feedback they receive through their efforts to create. This bad feeling isn't so much about having done something wrong that needs to be corrected, it is about not being good enough to have others take notice and provide positive feedback.

To help parents understand what it looks like to be positive about our child's creations, I share this story about my daughter Lauren when she was about four years old:

> One late afternoon after coming home from college, I came into the house, and after turning the corner I noticed that there was a good size mural on the wall, drawn in crayons. Now, we had just finished painting the house inside and out (fortunately I had used a semi-gloss on this one wall).
>
> As I took a closer look at what had been drawn, I began to recognize something sweet and special about this drawing. I got down on my knees and called Lauren over. When she arrived, I put my arm around her and pulling her in tight asked, "Lauren, were you thinking about your dad today?" She replied, "Uh-huh." I said, "I thought maybe you had." I continued, "I noticed that you have drawn a picture of a man with brown hair, a mustache and blue eyes (that was me) as well as a little girl with brown curly hair and big brown eyes (that was her). I also noticed that the man and little girl are holding hands and both are smiling" (in fact everything in the picture was smiling – the bird flying upside down, the sun, the cloud, the trees, etc.).
>
> I questioned further, "Is that a picture of me and you?" Lauren, staying very close, smiled and said "Yes." I then asked Lauren, "Lauren, do you know that dad thinks about you during the day as well?" She replied, "You do?" I said, "Yes, and whenever I do I feel exactly the same way you drew me – happy!" Lauren and I hugged (this is one of those tender moments that I refer to often in my teaching).
>
> Take a moment and try and experience this from Lauren's perspective. Do you see how I am receiving her creativity? Do you think there is anything in that interaction that would have made her feel bad about what she had created? I think you get what I am saying.
>
> Now, of course I didn't want her to be drawing on the walls and so I asked her, "Lauren, do you like drawing pictures for dad? "She responded, "Uh-huh." I said, "Did you know that at the store are these really big pads of paper that you can draw lots and lots of pictures? Her eyes lit up a bit. I said, "If you keep drawing on the walls, then you are going to run out of room, but we can just keep buying as much paper as we need – would you like to do that? Lauren responded affirmatively. I then asked, "Would you like to go to the store tonight to get that paper and maybe some more color pencils and crayons?" She became very

excited. "Well before we go, will you help daddy clean this wall? As soon as we are done we'll leave."

Lauren and I began cleaning the wall. It wasn't long before I looked over and saw this skinny little, four year old arm looking kind of tired. I said, "Honey, your arm looks like it is getting tired." Lauren replied immediately and emotionally, "I'll never draw on a wall again!"

With a big smile on my face, I thought to myself, it couldn't have worked out better. After the wall was clean, I kept my word and we went to the store to buy the supplies. I have wondered, when I reflect on this tender memory, what it is Lauren believed about herself because of that encounter. I think it is safe to say that she believed she was acceptable. Every interaction we have with our children sends them a message about their personal belief system.

Brain Development: This stage of development is the beginning of what is termed as 'magical thinking.' Young children do not possess the discernment at this age of what is real or fantasy. That is why it is very important to monitor what children read, watch and listen to. If we fill their magical thinking with shows of violence they will act out violence. In addition, Delta and Theta Waves are the prominent wave length during these years. What this means in laymen's terms is that you can practically download into the child's brain whatever it is you would like them to believe. There is really no interference in doing so. This is why a fat man in a red suit can get into a sleigh pulled by eight tiny reindeer that fly and in one night visit every child's house and out of one single bag have all the toys necessary and whether there is a chimney or not, this jolly old elf can slip in and out of the children's houses.

This is also why we admire a child's ability to believe. This is child-like faith.

INDUSTRY vs. INFERIORITY – (School Age 6-12 years)

Learning to earn, learning to be responsible; learning skills that build confidence is the focus of these next few years. Up until the beginning of school, most of a child's increasing confidence in being able to manage their environment has come through play. Their continued mastering of the environment now begins through their ability to learn and to develop higher skill sets (including social). It is through the child's sustained effort where a sense of personal capability is developed. Personal capability is the opposite of feeling and believing that one is inferior.

The idea that a child is now going to be contending in a classroom with other children in relation to acquiring knowledge, putting a portion of it into long-term memory, and then being able to retrieve that information at time of assessment (testing); and then having to be accountable for those outcomes, among peers, teachers and parents, is quite a shift in responsibility.

It is important for parents to understand that the current education system is established in such a way where only a certain percentage would test well. Part of the reason for this is due to a child's personal neural wiring, which manifests in a learning style, but also because current classroom models do not create the ideal setting for learning.

To give you an idea of what I am talking about, let us look at animals that are kept in a zoo as compared to those that roam free. In many comparative studies, it is found that those animals that roam free have larger brains (i.e., more neural connections) than those of caged animals. It isn't too far reaching to suggest that free roaming animals experience more and therefore would produce many more neural connections than their counterpart. More neural connections translate into more resources being available to assess and solve. A lot of these differences being contrasted are associated with greater experience, *but also greater input from all of the animal's sensory systems.*

In today's classroom setting, optimal sensory input is ignored. The more we can engage all of the senses in learning, the greater capacity to store information in a highly retrievable manner (free roaming animals). The more neural connections we are making, the greater the learning that is occurring. The research is pretty clear on this and that is why you find some children having a difficult time – to sit, listen, listen, listen and actually recall enough information to perform well on a test. Many children learn better through "doing" or even through "physical breaks," (i.e., exercise, play and such) or "naps," (remember kindergarten?) and otherwise. Very few classrooms accommodate the various ways that children learn.

Well what if your child is one of those that learn better through complete sensory input, like kinesthetically? Will they do as well in the traditional classroom setting? Of course not! It does not mean that they aren't bright enough, but it doesn't matter, because they must perform based upon the shoebox mentality. As they continue to get grades that are less than their peers – more likely than not the child will begin to believe that he or she is inferior, especially when beginning to receive so much negative attention because of their struggles to perform better (i.e., counselor intervention, teacher reports, parents nagging their child, etc.). Jane Elliot's Brown Eyed/Blue Eyed Experiment in 1970 demonstrated very well how children are susceptible to immediate doubt about worth and feelings of inferiority when they don't believe that they are as good as other peers.

There are other likely contributors to a child's inability to do well in a classroom setting. Without a doubt, we are living in a time when we are seeing soaring rates of inattentiveness, hyper-arousal, poor social functioning, greater rates of anxiety and depression, all of which leads a child to struggling with issues related to a low self-concept. These conditions do not exist in a vacuum, issues related to environmental toxins, soaring rates of psycho-medications, T.V, programming (i.e., meaning how story lines are focused on for a few seconds and then the scene jumps to another story line for just a few seconds, and so on and so on). This type of programming teaches brains how *not* to focus for long on any one thing. In addition, astronomical rates of children no longer living with both parents; and technology that addicts the child's brain and then isolates him or her, preventing the child from practicing normal social interactions, which pro-social interactions are what give us the good feedback we are all needing, and because it is happening less and less, children today are experiencing much more emotional instability than at any time in the past!

Of all of this that I am speaking of, the research indicates that the number one indicator for academic success is the emotional stability of the home. Many families no longer understand what it means to be a family – and the children become the biggest losers.

Regardless, this is the developmental task for approximately six years, to learn how to put forth organizational skills, social skills, learning skills and testing skills in an environment where children are pitted against other children in recognition that one's industry does produce the outcome sufficient where the child believes that he or she is capable.

Since parents play the most significant role in influencing the mastery of each task, a couple of parenting mistakes that contribute to a child feeling inferior are:

1) Providing everything for the child; and
2) Using things in substitution for your time with them.

By using things instead of time – what does a child learn about him or herself?

We are all highly programmed to be in relationships and yet many families don't plan time together and many homes now have both parents working just to make ends meet. Such conditions can create a sense of concern about how one fits in. Some parents, in order to make up for this lack of time, will substitute things for their time.

When this comes to be a significant pattern, in subtle ways, the child begins to measure his or value based upon getting things. Instead of developing a meaningful relationship with a person, they sense their value in the possessions they acquire. One of the big problems that arise is that the child may not develop much respect for the parent relationship, but rather insists that the parent keep buying things. The disrespect, (i.e., not doing chores, dropping grades, being sassy, making poor decisions, running with the wrong crowd, etc.) has the parent begin to take things away. The implicit memory tells the child that the parent does not value the child as a result, because up to this point the child is measuring parental acceptance through stuff.

In essence the child has learned to rely on objects (rather than the parental relationship) to measure self-value. The insistence to keep things flowing is the goal of the child. If I am not getting more, what does that say about my worth? Entitlement is the attitude we begin detecting, but underneath it all is unhealthy esteem and a feeling of being inferior.

A funny, but poignant scene that exaggerates this point is an opening scene in one of the Harry Potter movies, where Harry's cousin is having a birthday and he demands to know how many presents his parents bought him. The parents begin to feel uncomfortable, because every year they have purchased at least one more present than the year before. When the character discovers that there is one less present than the year before he becomes highly agitated and disrespectful toward his parents. His parents insisting that the value of this year's gifts exceed last year, produces no calming influence. The child insists on quantity – not too of an unrealistic outcome!

By providing everything for the child – what does the child come to believe about him or herself?

In large measure, children become entitled and the child begins to feel incapable. If the child cannot master becoming more responsible for its outcomes it will believe that he or she is inferior. If the parents are solving, doing, giving everything, and saving as regular interactions with the child, the child does not learn how to become more responsible for his or her outcomes and instead creates a dependence on the parents.

Bishop H. David Burton commented about this very topic when he said:

> "Parents who have been successful in acquiring more often have a difficult time saying no to the demands of overindulged children. Their children run the risk of not learning important values like hard work, delayed gratification, honesty, and compassion. Affluent parents can and do raise well-adjusted, loving, and value-centered children, but the struggle to set limits, make do with less, and avoid the pitfalls of "more, more, more" has never been more difficult. It is hard to say no to more when you can afford to say yes."

> "Parents are rightfully anxious about the future. It is difficult to say no to more sports equipment, electronics, lessons, clothes, team participation, et cetera, when parents believe more will help children thrive in an increasingly competitive world. Young people seem to want more, partly because there is infinitely more to catch their eye....."

> "Fewer and fewer parents ask their children to do chores around the house because they think they are already overwhelmed by social and academic pressures. But children devoid of responsibilities risk never learning that every individual can be of service and that life has meaning

beyond their own happiness." (More Holiness Give Me, General Conference, October 2004)

With such interference in developing the belief that one can eventually break away from one's parent, the child enters adolescence uncertain about his or her capacity, acceptance, and confidence, especially in comparison to his or her peers. Youth that struggle with self-confidence easily recognize their peers that do not, and in doing so simply reinforces their negative view of self. On the other hand, if a child is able to further master his or her physical environment through industry, then the task of forming a realistic identity in adolescence is more likely.

Brain Development: Near the end of this stage, children begin to think more logically, calculate and question. This is why a fat man in a red suit *cannot* get into a sleigh pulled by eight tiny reindeer that fly and in one night visit every child's house and out of one single bag have all the toys necessary and whether there is a chimney or not, this jolly old elf *cannot* slip in and out of the children's houses.

IDENTITY vs. ROLE CONFUSION – Adolescent (12-18 years)

This stage of development finds the child trying to integrate many roles (child, sibling, student, athlete, worker, member of the church etc.) into a self-image under role model and peer pressure.

If the child's environment has been emotionally disruptive or the environment has not allowed him or her to master the previous tasks, this can become a scary time. "I am what I am based upon what I believe about myself, what I have experienced, etc." Much of that belief is based in the tasks associated with child development. If the tasks have been sufficiently mastered along the way, then the child believes well of him or herself. On the other hand, if the child has become stymied in mastering these tasks, the child believes that he or she has little value. This latter group is just simply looking for acceptance, (i.e., how do I fit in?) no matter who is giving it.

On every school campus is that one group who will accept anybody. This is the group that formed due to a shared characteristic of stunted emotional development. Most in this group have experienced the same feelings of not being good enough, not being smart enough; not being acceptable enough. One of the hallmarks of this group is to teach how substances can free one self of uncomfortable feelings. A child that has not mastered the earlier developmental tasks is going to find such a group inviting, because, 1) some one is willing to pay attention to them, without judgment or criticism, and, 2) they come to realize the power behind substance (self-medication) use, freeing them of the stress associated with unhealthy esteem. It is in adolescence that we may first begin to notice exactly how a child does feel about him or herself by his or her associations.

Now, that is not to say that those that have done well in mastering the earlier developmental tasks won't have struggles – many do. Children that have a good sense of confidence and self-worth may still experiment. Remember, they are just practicing. What looks like rebellion, is more likely experimentation of identity formation. In our fear and concern, we may interact in a way that creates tension in the parent child relationship. If we continue to handle the *practicing* (i.e., rebellion) incorrectly, it can end up having the child make the final decision of a role that will cause a lot of pain and anguish. The key is to rely on the child's internal moorings and notice the positive, rather than become critical of choices that seem to betray a good upbringing.

Brain Development: The adolescent brain begins to develop the ability to use abstract thinking. This is one feature that separates adults from children in their perception of the environment. Remember, however, that this is just the beginning of this ability. Strengthening abstract thinking comes from our teaching of principles using everyday experience. This is what the Master did when he taught in parables. Likening one thing to something else, in order to firmly plant principles in our children's minds has its greatest potential during this phase of child development.

THE IMPACT OF BECOMING STYMIED

You may be asking, "How crucial is it for children to master these tasks?" or "Is this part of human design really that vital or critical?"

Barry is a 50 year old client. Barry's father was a military officer and rarely spent any time home because of the demands of his assignments. Barry's mother unfortunately died, when Barry was just 3. Barry's father remarried not too long thereafter because he wasn't willing to alter his military career path in order to take care of his children.

Barry's new step-mother beat Barry from 3 years old until he was 11 years old. While Barry likely developed a level of trust (Embryonic development – 18 months), and to a degree autonomy (18 months – 3 years), when with his real mother, Barry's new experiences (i.e., mother dying and step-mother's abuse), likely impacted both of those tasks. At a time he should be developing initiative (3 years – 6 years) and industry (6 years – 12 years), instead Barry experienced rejection of anything he had to offer and because of the trauma he was experiencing on a regular basis created a neural system that was on high alert. Such conditions would have never developed the confidence and calmness in order for Barry to well in school – and he did not.

When Barry was 11 years old, his father came home one night and at the dinner table, Barry's father noticed some bruising and cuts on Barry. Barry's father commented, "Barry, you need to be more careful, you really hurt yourself." Barry's brother piped in with great intensity, "You don't get it dad, your wife has been beating Barry since he was 3!"

Dad missed all of this because of his great absence, but he did not miss the idea that he didn't want his children to be abused physically. Barry's dad divorced the horrid woman, only to marry again in two months to another woman that had different, but just as disturbing problems, which further impacted Barry's ability to master any of these tasks.

Barry himself went on to have multiple marriages and other significant relationship issues. Today, Barry is a server in a restaurant and is struggling with addiction.

When I began to explain these developmental tasks, I wrote them on a board so that Barry could visualize what we were discussing. With regard to identifying the task to be mastered vs. what would fill in if a child became stymied, I had the following:

Task Mastery		Task Stymied
1. Trust	vs.	Mistrust
2. Autonomy	vs.	Shame and Doubt
3. Initiative	vs.	Guilt
4. Industry	vs.	Inferiority
5. Identity	vs.	Role Confusion

Barry said, "You can just erase everything on the left. Everything on the right is a perfect description of what I have experienced my entire life." What personal belief system did Barry have, what was his core template concerning himself based upon the interference with human design and purpose? More importantly, as the reader, are you detecting the connection with Barry's continued disruptions in relationships and career because of his belief system?

If you are reading this book it is because you either have children or intend on having them and want to become a better parent or be prepared when you do. If you ignore any aspect of human design you will not get the outcomes you are hoping for. This chapter explained a part of our human design – it is real and it matters. Some of you are now going over in your head about what your child needs to strengthen based upon this information, or are recognizing the effects of these things in your own life.
The good news is that we have the capacity to go back and master those tasks that are underdeveloped or lacking – it is never too late. Doing so leads to healthy belief systems, because each task is based in true human law and potential.

HEALTHY OR SECURE ATTACHMENT
(The basis of emotional stability in children and adults)

One of the primary areas that we as parents hone in on in determining how well our children are doing is in the area of academics. It would be reasonable to conclude that a child's success in the classroom is mostly dependent upon IQ or good genes, or developing the skills to organize, plan, focus and prepare. However the research indicates otherwise. In his book, Brain Rules, John Medina, summarizes the research with this one statement:

> "The emotional stability of the home is the single greatest predictor of academic success. If you want your kid to get into Harvard, go home and love your spouse." (Brain Rules, Pear Press, 2008)

What creates emotional stability?

In a revelation given to some of the early leaders of the Restored Church, the Lord provided the following counsel:

> "Wherefore, be not weary in well-doing, for ye are laying the foundation of a great work. And *out of small things* proceedeth that which is great." (D&C 64:33)

Secure attachments provide the foundation for the great work that we do in our families and like the scripture indicates about anything momentous, secure attachments don't just happen; there are repeated, consistent, *small things* we do that end up producing a great relationship.

Humans have the highest capacity to form connections with one another, which if accomplished, provides for all of the important social needs that lead to healthy and positive belief systems. It is within our relationships that we sense our importance; our value and meaning in this mortal experience we are having. It is in our relationships that we learn so many skills which lead to feelings of capability. It is in our relationships where we experience a continual flow of necessary intellectual and emotional support that lifts our spirits and has us experience the noblest and deepest sense of joy (2 Nephi 2:25). Whether in mortality or in the eternities, a *fullness of joy* will only be experienced within the context of relationships (Psalm 35:9; 2 Nephi 5:27; Mosiah 2:41; 3 Nephi 17:18-20; 4 Nephi 1:15-16).

I think that some of the greatest insight that has come out of John Gottman's studies and the continuing development of the attachment field that follows John Bowlby's work is a clear understanding that healthy connection happens at the emotional level.

Dan Siegel points out that:

> "As parents we want to have loving, and meaningful relationships with our children. Understanding the role that emotions play in how we connect to each other can help us do just that. It is through the sharing of emotion that we build connections with others. Communication that involves an awareness of our own emotions, an ability to respectfully share our emotions, and an empathic understanding of our children's emotions lays a foundation that supports the building of lifelong relationships with our children."

> "Emotions shape both our internal and our interpersonal experiences and they fill our minds with a sense of what has meaning. When we are aware of our emotions and are able to share them with others, our daily lives are enriched because it is through the sharing of emotions that we deepen our connections with others." (Parenting from the Inside Out, Pg 53)

When I see relationships that are struggling, and of course here we are speaking of the parent-child relationship, then I know that the relationship has failed to produce sufficient, successful emotional communication.

All insecure attachments arise from repeated experiences of *failed emotional communications*. Therefore, secure attachments arise from repeated experiences of successful *emotional* communications. Collectively, successful emotional communications are what allow us to attune to one another and feel connected.

Successful emotional communication begins by understanding how both verbal and non-verbal communication influences human experience. Studies indicate that 93% of our communication occurs at a non-verbal level, and yet most of us never pay much attention to what our non-verbal communication looks like and the messages that we are sending on a continuous regular basis.

For example, at times I work with clients that struggle with social confidence. Such individuals contribute to their own problems by their repeated non-verbal message of "I don't want to be known." These people hang out in corners, in back rows, in dark movie houses, and in their homes. Their whole body tenses when approached or engaged. Their smile is uncomfortable and awkward and eye-contact is flitting and fleeting. Many times their voice sounds weak, or they may laugh nervously. They usually have not developed the resources to have engaging conversation, leaving the other person to produce the energy to create any resemblance of an interaction. These people wait for others to initiate contact and can become easily offended if someone doesn't maintain their original interest in the relationship or they may come to overwhelm the friendship because they have been starving for human connection for a long time. The collective message of all of their non-verbal cueing is "I am insecure" which has others deliberately assess whether they want to develop a relationship with someone that puts forth little energy in sustaining a meaningful bond.

If we are going to increase confidence in our relationship with our children, we must learn how to align our internal state with theirs. In his research on emotional communication between parents and infants, Dr. Ed Tronick developed a study called the *Still Face Experiment* (You Tube, type in: "Still Face Experiment," if you would like to see the interaction of the mother and her infant). In this study, a mother and her infant are seen engaging in a normal dance of eye contact, sounds, interested tones, very expressive facial gestures and mother following her child's forms of social cueing (affective behavior, i.e., pointing, reaching out, etc.), providing an unspoken assurance that the child is understood by her mother. It is obvious from the interaction that emotional communication is taking place and that it is pleasing to both infant and mother.

During the interaction, the mother is signaled to stop showing emotion. Her face, eyes, and body language become the means to communicate no emotional interest to her baby. The infant is observed to pick up on this difference immediately and begins trying everything she knows how to get her mother to respond in the manner she previously did. None of the baby's attempts are successful and you notice quickly the stress level going up in the baby. The infant girl contorts her body, she looks away in an attempt to decrease her stress, but when she looks back she is reminded that though mother is physically present, her mother is not attuned to her (the infant's) internal state. The baby becomes further distressed and loud screams, change in skin color, and finally complete loss of composure are observed as the baby collapses in tears.

At this point, mother re-engages with her young daughter, showing once again through *smiling eye* contact, facial expressions of happiness, body language which indicates a desire to be close to her baby, sweet tones of caring, and touches – all of which lead to an immediate recovery within the infant. The baby girl responds with reciprocal, non-verbal communication that aligns with mother's internal state. It is a powerful example of the importance of successful emotional communication and the influential impact emotional attunement has on our relationships.

While verbal communication is important, and we will talk more about that later, it appears that non-verbal communication has a greater capacity to create resonance between two people's internal state. This collaborative communication enriches our relationship with our children and leads to secure feelings between parent and child.

Knowing how important non-verbal cueing is to emotional bonding, listed below are the "*small things*" that if done correctly and repeatedly (you will find the most important is identified as the top suggestion) will create a healthy sense of self in us personally as well as our children with whom we are trying to attune with. The categories are the "*small things.*" These come from the work of Dan Siegel, while the application comes from the author's own experience.

Eye contact:	Smiling eyes produce automatically in another person a sense of being liked.
	Negative eyes send a message of unacceptability
Facial expression:	Positive expressions of happiness, interest, and funny expressions heighten attachment.
	Disapproving or judgmental expressions develop insecurity in the other person.
Tone of voice:	Calm, conversational tones, mildness and softness all provide the ability to better attunement (Helaman 5:30).
	Harshness, defensiveness, raising of one's voice activates threat modulating systems.
Posture:	Openness, signals to come closer, relaxed positioning signal safety and trust to the other person
	Rigidness, aggressive encroaching upon social space, turning away from the person, produces uncertainty responses in the other, including both shutting down or becoming aggressive
Gestures:	Acts of kindness, thoughtfulness, being happy for, expressions of gratitude are all gestures that produce a sense of importance in the other person.
	Forgetfulness, deriding others publicly, forms of humiliation, being competitive produces doubt in a person's confidence and importance.
Touching:	Softness, holding hands, rubbing a back, hugging and other appropriate forms of welcomed touch increase the flow of oxytocin thus increasing feelings of being bonded
	Touch that is unwelcomed, inappropriate, or hurtful increases disassociation in the other person.
Verbal Cues:	Talking about thoughts, feelings, perceptions, memories, sensations, attitudes, beliefs, and intentions – these are what help

develop compassion and leads to closeness.

Criticism, contempt, defensiveness and stonewalling (stonewalling would be listed under "Timing and Intensity of Response" but is mentioned here because of John Gottman's work) are toxic and will destroy attachment.

Timing and
Intensity
of Response: Emotional cueing is sensitive to responses. When we are available, when we are sensitive to an emotional cueing, when we respond in a caring and interested manner, when we can acknowledge to the other that we can relate to the emotional need being expressed, these send a message of support, safety and understanding.

When we withdraw, ignore, seem disgusted, hit back with anger, present with defensiveness or blame, then the other experiences doubt, shame, isolation, fear, and anger.

Verbal communication is also an important aspect of human design and allows the important process of securely attaching to heighten when coupled with the non-verbal aspects just discussed.

While language is a product of the processes of the neo-cortex and is uniquely specialized in humans, many of us have not developed the understanding of how our words can lead to either experiencing closeness or detachment.

When words are used accurately, and with the desire to lift others, relationships experience magic. Words are the means to accomplish what we desire to accomplish. Words can create emotional connections and intellectual alignment. Likewise, words can create dissatisfaction, misunderstanding and hurt.

Good communication is a manifestation of love as it develops respect between individuals, reduces conflict and opens the door of increasing levels of human intimacy. Every parent can learn to communicate effectively.

In reviewing briefly some of the work of John Gottman, he has identified four things we as humans do in our communication with others that will ultimately lead to insecure attachments and deepening resentments in our relationships:

Criticism – The most common negative verbal communication that emerges in long-term relationships is criticism. Frustrations, annoyances and resentment inevitably build up when people live or interact together — day in and day out. And criticism can be how these emotions manifest in the heat of an argument.

185

Note that criticism differs from complaining. Criticism focuses on the person. Complaining focuses on the behavior. This may seem like subtle nuance but research shows it is a distinction that makes a significant difference in the long term. For example, this is a critical statement: "You always are behind schedule. You are an awful organizer of your time and resources." These words are dripping with blame and accusation. They are a personal attack.

Unlike criticism, complaining has more to do with how the other person's behavior makes you feel. Complaining usually begins with an "I" instead of "You": "I get so frustrated when you get behind schedule." See the difference? The second statement is a negative comment about something you wish were otherwise. So though "I" statements can seem awkward, they really help keep the carnage manageable during explosive moments.

Contempt – You're an idiot. You can't do anything right. You make me sick. You're lazy. These contemptuous words have no place in any family relationship. They are meant to explicitly humiliate or wound. They are toxic and indefensible – period!

Contempt includes but is not limited to name-calling, hostility and sarcasm. Keep in mind that contempt can also be conveyed non-verbally. An excessively harsh tone or disgusted eye roll can escalate your garden-variety argument into WWIII in the blink of an eye. Avoid contempt in any of your communications at all cost. It is the basest, most childish tactic to resort to in a heated moment . Strive to respect your family members even when you disagree or feel upset with them. Contempt is like a poison. It will single-handedly erode trust and confidence in one another. It destroys a sense of security and mutual respect. It does real damage because it makes others feel belittled and unimportant.

Defensiveness – *Criticism+Contempt=Defensiveness*. Defensive statements become practically an involuntary reflex in workplaces where contempt and criticism are regular visitors. It is understandable. After all, who wouldn't put up their guard in response to an accusatory, belittling parent? Defensiveness is fundamentally a self-preserving tactic.

As understandable as this response can be, it is still hugely destructive. It builds walls. Rather than allow room for connectedness, the foundation for conflict resolution, it tends to breed emotional distance. Defensiveness blocks productivity.

Stonewalling – Stonewalling, is in effect, shutting down. It is being minimally invested. Because stonewalling is not explicitly aggressive, people often underestimate its destructive potential. But it can be just as devastating to relationships in its passiveness.

186

Stonewallers withdraw partly because they can feel overwhelmed with emotion. They may keep their faces expressionless, avoid eye contact, hold their posture rigid, avoid any signs of listening such as nodding or encouraging sounds. They radiate icy distance and disapproval to other individuals.

REPAIR ATTEMPTS – The Secret to Overcoming Contention

These four forms of communication will destroy the morale in the home. When we recognize that we are or have engaged in any of these styles with our children, we would do well to make a repair attempt. Repair attempts are any words or actions that prevent a conflict from escalating out of control. As simple as it sounds, repair attempts keep a home from becoming negative, hostile and distant.

Repair attempts can be as basic as changing the topic, giving a compliment, apologizing or saying, "I've had an overwhelming day, can we start over?" It can be as simple as saying, "Don't worry, we'll get through this" or cracking a joke to diffuse tension. Do whatever works for you when conflict rears its ugly head.

Remember, the more entrenched the negative patterns of behavior are in your way of being, the more difficult it becomes to break them. Don't become a victim of these negative cycles. When a parent can take ownership and be flexible, they will keep their relationship strong even though they may not always agree with their child.

Communication includes both verbal and non-verbal messages. It looks something like this:

Person 1 Communicates › Person 2 Receives Message ›

Person 2 Processes Information › Person 2 Responds

Secure connections will occur in this process when both individuals:

1. Remain open and explore what the meaning is behind the communication
2. Work toward experiencing the information from the other's point of view
3. Convey that understanding in a way that allows the other person to feel secure that he or she is indeed understood.

Insecure connections will occur in this process when both individuals:

1. Interrogate for the purpose of trying to control or manipulate the other person's perspective
2. Disagree with the other person's perspective, by judging it as inferior or wrong.
3. Telling the other person what they should do

187

THREE POINTS TO SOLIDIFY SECURE ATTACHMENT

1) If we go against the design (human design) we begin to experience some negative feedback. Human design includes thoughts, feelings and behaviors. While we have just discussed feelings and emotional awareness, we cannot neglect the other two. Several ideas on interacting with thoughts and behaviors will be addressed in upcoming chapters. Just understand that each of these must be utilized in order to influence better outcomes. The better we interact with human design, the closer our attachments become. *The closer our attachment, the more influence we have on our relationships.*

2) This next point may seem so obvious that it may be futile in mentioning it, but we are designed to be in relationships. In fact, of all of the animal kingdom, we are by far the most social. 75% of the human brain is dedicated to get us into relationships. In some remarkable, yet mysterious way, our brains are intuitively relational. Without much conscious effort our brains appear to be highly sensitive to other's internal experiences. This sensitivity, and depending upon our response to it, may lead to some of the richest experiences imagined or to some of the greatest disappointments ever experienced. For many (because of their unhealthy implicit memory), forming and/or maintaining relationships are stress inducing events and so many choose to minimize their efforts in connecting, some even choosing isolation, all going against human design (Genesis 2:18).

I bring this to the reader's attention because we may recognize our child has chosen this path. I am hoping that the idea of what I am trying to point out doesn't get overlooked, simply because it falls within the realm of common sense, but if our children are minimizing their efforts to develop friendships, my experience says that your child is not living within his or her design. When we are so wired to be in relationships and end up being more alone, it is not good (Moses 3:18) and produces many distortions in personal belief systems. Consider the following example:

> Penny is a 36 year old client that had gone through her teen years without one boy asking her out on a date. Penny questioned whether or not anyone would ever love her. Penny explains that she began to "feel" desperate about her opportunities. Penny likely had a couple of contributing factors that led to this outcome in her life, one being that she was overweight, and the other being that she presented with a measurable amount of insecurity. Her insecurity imprisoned any motivation to put forth effort in relationships and to take an honest look at her own contributions to the problem.

> Penny explains that her desperate feelings collided with her moral reasoning resulting in making several relationship choices that only ended up reinforcing her original belief. This is the typical "when the milk

is free, why buy the cow" scenarios. These selfish interactions would end up with the man not continuing any association after the sexual experience was over. With repeated rejection, Penny continued to withdraw. Her isolation tactics continued to severely impact her belief system of being acceptable and loveable. When directly asked the question, "Do you believe anyone can love you?" her reply was, "I don't know, probably not."

If your child is avoiding making connections, then it is most likely poisoning their implicit memory. If our relationships are poor or non-existent then we are not living life optimally and we end up with stress induced illnesses, physically, mentally, and relationally.

We have been talking about secure attachments and the influence secure connections have on our children. However, you may be a parent that questions whether or not your relationship is secure with your child. This next section will provide some assessment tools on determining the security or insecurity of that relationship.

What evidence do we have that begins to suggest to us that something is going wrong with our relationship or attachment with our children? Following are brief descriptions of three insecure attachment styles.

Avoidant – the child is observed to avoid sharing feelings or thoughts, presents with vagueness. Little eye contact, disengaged. Doesn't discriminate between parents and other adults.

Ambivalent – the child is observed to not demonstrate responsibility, is half-hearted in their approach to various facets of their life. At times it seems they want to connect but the attempt doesn't provide the relief they are looking for.

Disorganized – chaotic, doesn't make sense (their perception seems to be quite different than the majority), rapidly moving emotions, induced by fears directly related to their attaching process. Bottom line, the disorganized attachment is based in not mastering trust, something that should have occurred by 18 months.

All of these insecure attachment styles have spectrums. All of these can be healed. Number three (disorganized) is the most difficult.

To get a better look at insecure attachment, we must recognize that our parental style has contributed to its development. As we look at the parental styles and the descriptions that follow, I don't want parents to begin being filled with guilt. That is not the purpose. The purpose is to increase awareness about what leads to some of these *attaching patterns* so that we can create choice in our continued interaction, rather than remain stuck in a cycle of reactivity.

For the most part, insecure attachment is influenced by the parent's implicit memory, with maybe some exceptions in the case of adoptive parents. In a nutshell, when our internal experience (unresolved childhood experiences) keeps us from connecting with our children, their experience of our intense response (i.e., becoming critical and demanding, being unresponsive [numb], taking out our anger on our children, etc.), may trigger the arousal of a defensive emotional state in them. Repeated defensive emotional states develop insecure attaching patterns.

In essence, the authentic parent is difficult to be known by the child because the parent hides behind the walls of psychological defenses (i.e., the child does not obey, which then triggers the parent's own childhood experience of having little or no control, wherein the parent becomes angry to create distance between self and the perceived threat), so the child does not experience feeling connected or being understood.

The following chart and description of parent interactions will provide the basis to clarify our insecure relationships that we may be experiencing:

Relationship Type	Parental Style
Secure/Healthy	Responsive, Consistent
Avoidant	Rejecting, Distant
Ambivalent (internal sense of confusion and dread)	Inconsistent, Intrusive
Disorganized	Frightening, Confusing, Fearful

Avoidant Attachment - Insecure

Parents that lack the ability to feel comfortable in their own skin and tend to their own internal state are handicapped in being able to tend to the internal states of their children. The ability for a child to truly understand their thought processes, their feelings, their hopes and dreams develop because a parent is able to reflect back to the child, through attunement, that the child's internal state is real, and that it matters.

In a sense, the child interprets this relationship as the parent not having any intention on knowing the child. Therefore the next logical conclusion of the child is there is no one to know, creating a deep sense of emptiness.

Ambivalent Attachment – Insecure

A parent that presents with real doubt; uncertainty in his or her abilities; is anxious about whom they are and there effectiveness create a similar state in their children. This shows up in all aspects of the relationship between the parent and the child and therefore the child begins to integrate its normal needs with the anxiety and uncertainty being manifest by the parent.

190

When a child seeks for its caretaker in providing comfort when some sort of fear or need is being expressed and that parent's response has been inconsistent, the child has a complexing internal issue of finding the comfort they seek. They know they need someone to tune into their internal state to provide that calming influence, but if the reception of the caretaker is found to provide as much increase in anxiety as it does comfort, the child is in a bind.

Intrusiveness by parents can also lead to the development of this ambivalence, usually because the intrusiveness is not really intended to take interest in the child as much as it is to provide relief to the caretaker's anxiety or uncertainty.

Anxiety and uncertainty send the message that the person/parent has no personal resources to regulate the fears being felt, which translates into the child's ambivalence of whether the caretaker can provide any resources to the child.

Disorganized Attachment –Severely Insecure

If we experience terror in our lives, including seeing our parents terrified over and over again, our mirror neurons kick in and we like a sponge begin to attune to the anxiety, to the uncertainty and "I become confused, uncertain and anxious myself. My internal state is being molded by my parent's internal state."

One part of my brain says that because I feel frightened I should go toward my care-taker, but it is my care-taker that is the source of my fear, therefore a side of my brain tells me to get away. This internal chaos creates fragmentation, because there is no solution and therefore the child's internal resources collapse.

When a child's ability to regulate emotions is severely compromised, meaning they have difficulty in monitoring impulses. It produces a tendency to react and act out.

Fragmentation (Trauma Induced) – "You are coming at me with anger, therefore your intention is to hurt me. My adult provider is supposed to take care of me, to protect me, to want the best for me, but your whole demeanor goes against what you are supposed to be doing."

Fragmentation kicks in to provide a way of controlling our environment – Dissociative Identity Disorder (DID) in severe cases, Reactive Attachment in many cases, and Personality Disorders in adulthood if not treated. Each of the diagnosis is characterized by "black and white" thinking. Fragmentation does not allow a person to hold another person in a state of both good traits and bad traits. The fragmented mind intends on holding a person in only one state or the other.

If I offend, or try and show my independence from a disorganized attached parent, I likely would be seen as "all bad" or as "and enemy." On the other hand, if I support the disorganized attached parent, then I would likely be seen as "all good" or a "friend."

Dave Pelzer's book, "A Child Called It" provides a good example of this fragmentation or splitting. When Dave was a child, he challenged his mother's odd mannerisms and became the "all bad" child, while his siblings maintained the "good children" status. Disney's Rapunzel, also provides an example of this way of being. The movie did a wonderful job in showing how a disorganized attached adult can create emotional dependence in a child through manipulations displayed in the three roles mentioned below.

Being raised by such a parent manifests into adolescence and adulthood wherein the individual has great difficulty connecting because he or she has not developed the neurobiological capacity to attune. The underlying belief that develops in a disorganized attachment is that the world is not a safe place and their remains a constant fear of abandonment.

The disorganized attached parent develops roles that he or she expertly plays out. These roles allow for a sense of control in relationships. The three roles are 1) Abuser; 2) Victim; and 3) Rescuer.

Disorganized attached parents create an environment that pulls others into their chaos. Children have no capacity to understand or regulate the chaos, and usually turn the negative experiences inward, resulting in many negative implicit beliefs.

Effect of Attachment on Future Relationships – Generational Effects

Characteristics of Secure Attachment

As Child	As Adult
Able to separate from parent	Have trusting, lasting relationships
Seeks comfort from parents when frightened	Tend to have healthy esteem
Greets return of parent with positive emotions	Are comfortable sharing their feelings with those who are close
Prefers parents to strangers	Seeks out social relationships

Characteristics of Avoidant Attachment

As Child	As Adult
May avoid parents	Could have problems with intimacy
Does not seek much contact with parents	Invests little in social or romantic relationships
Shows no preference for parents over strangers	Unwilling or unable to share thoughts and feelings with others

Characteristics of Ambivalent Attachment

As Child	As Adult
Distrusting of strangers	Reluctant to be close to others
Becomes over distressed when parent leaves	Worry that they are not loved by their partner
Does not appear to be comforted on parent's return	Becomes distraught when relationship ends

Characteristics of Disorganized Attachment

As Child	As Adult
May seem dazed or confused	Tend to have a distorted view of others
They may see the world as an unsafe place	They may have trouble socially or struggle in using others to co-regulate their emotions

In the chapter entitled, "The Family Government," we reviewed Diane Baumrind's contribution to understanding parenting styles and their effects on children's belief systems. The following chart ties in attachment styles with parenting styles and the resulting adult characteristics of their children.

Tying Attachment to Parental Styles and Forecasting Adult Experience

Attachment Style	Parental Style	Resulting Adult Characteristics
Secure	Authoritative In tune with child's emotions	Able to create meaningful relationships, be empathic and set boundaries
Ambivalent	Permissive Inconsistent and intrusive	Anxious and insecure – tends to be blaming and controlling, although can act well – being charming. Can be unpredictable
Avoidant	Authoritarian Rejecting, critical, avoids listening	Avoids emotional connection. Can be critical, distant and intolerant
Disorganized	Uninvolved Ignored or does not respond to child's needs	Chaotic, insensitive, explosive, abusive, untrusting, even while craving security

	Parents are frightening and abusive	

IMPORTANT APPLICATIONS

1) So many issues naturally take care of themselves when attachments are healthy and secure. A known biological basis for children being incentivized to do well academically, to be less resistant to personal responsibilities, and to develop good peer relationships, is the presence of dopamine in the control and motivational systems of the brain. All the research demonstrates that children that are securely attached to their parents have the optimal states of this neurotransmitter in those regions.

2) ADHD – A child that experiences so many negative interactions and feedback due to their behavior associated with ADHD, likely form insecure attachments. If I am looking at a family whose child presents with ADHD, then I know that one of the parents likewise struggles with the same condition. Many aspects of ADHD prevent parents from interacting, both verbally and non-verbally, in a way that creates secure attachments.

If you will recall the section above that discussed the *small things* that lead to secure attachment, you will recognize that many of those are disrupted consistently or don't occur at all because of the condition. ADHD children and adults are typically poor eye-contact making people, for example, and yet that is the highest biological non-verbal communication that we as humans have in order to develop a sense of being included and feeling loved.

Next to diet and activity as a means to naturally get the ADHD brain to function better, this is the primary social intervention I teach parents to do and do well. I have had so many parents react with pleasant surprise when they begin to see the differences in their child's behavior, as a result of focusing on non-verbal, emotional communication.

THE BODY AND BRAIN ARE DESIGNED TO PROMOTE SECURE ATTACHMENTS

There are two major chemicals (hormones) that are involved with relationship building:

Vasopressin – I can feel friendly around you
Oxytocin – I can feel close to you (attaching, bonding, trust hormone)

When we have good experiences with peers, or perhaps a teacher or scout leader, there is a chemical (hormone) that is released in the body called Vasopressin. This chemical simply allows us to feel loosely connected and safe when we are with or see these individuals.

Let's say, for example, you are at the grocery store and you run into your neighbor. You smile and stop and chat for a moment. Your ability to do so is a result of Vasopressin.

However, the most important chemical (hormone) that allows us to feel deep security and experience connection in our relationships is Oxytocin. 13-14 years ago all we knew about Oxytocin is that it was associated with going into labor. Upon delivery, both mom's and baby's body are flooded with Oxytocin. So is dad's if he has not passed out. This is the cause for the overwhelming bonding feeling that is associated with this experience.

Oxytocin has many positive effects on our ability to bond and attach. Before I go into any depth of those benefits, I have often pondered on our human design and what the scriptures teach about the sanctity of life. My pondering has come from this apostolic teaching by Elder Jeffrey R. Holland, said he:

> "Clearly God's greatest concerns regarding mortality are how one gets into this world and how one gets out of it. These two most important issues in our very personal and carefully supervised progress are the two issues that he as our Creator and Father and Guide wishes most to reserve to himself. These are the two matters that he has repeatedly told us he wants us never to take illegally, illicitly, unfaithfully, without sanction." (Of Souls, Symbols and Sacraments, BYU Address, 1978)

As I have studied physiology, it became quite apparent that Elder Holland's comments are strikingly supported by the chemical reactions associated with both the preserving and giving of life.

The most powerful chemical in the body is adrenaline. Its presence is largely influenced by the biological drive of self-preservation. When we sense that our life is in danger physically, adrenaline begins to course through the body creating the body's ability to fight, flee, or freeze – all depending upon the circumstances that are presenting themselves.

Likewise, when our emotional state senses that it is being threatened, again, adrenaline is released and we experience the suppressing feeling of anger. Either physical or emotional threat is responded to by this modulating system, strictly for the purpose of saving life.

The second most powerful chemical in the body is oxytocin. This chemical is also associated with life – the giving and nurturing of it. It is what drives us into pairing off and creating families. It is the ongoing process by which we bond, experience security and trust. It provides the ability to resonate with each other's internal states. It is literally what seals us together!

195

Oxytocin works to develop secure attachments. It is a naturally occurring neuro-chemical that simultaneously acts like a hormone, meaning that it is not limited to the neural system, but it also courses through our blood and connects with every cell.

Everyday behavior signals the release of this attaching hormone. Our positive thoughts of another person, a soft touch, cuddling, and smiling eyes all release this neuro-transmitter. Mother's while breastfeeding experience this process, but so do all of us when we experience an orgasm. That intense feeling is the effect of oxytocin – yeah for oxytocin!

There are additional physiological benefits associated with oxytocin:

1. Reduces stress
2. Buffers against future stress
3. If stimulated consistently and appropriately in early development, the neuro-biological wiring emerges that allows for healthy connections throughout life. This is the science of Neuroplasticity. In essence, this healthy wiring literally allows us to feel accepted by and in turn accept others in a loving and trusting manner.
4. Oxytocin is involved in healing emotional wounds. When betrayal has occurred between two people, the positive experiences that produce oxytocin can act over time as a balm to heal the hurt of that betrayal. It does not occur in a moment, but consistent oxytocin producing experiences can lessen the memory and especially the negative feeling associated with that memory.
5. Oxytocin permits new learning about relationships and can alter or modify previous wiring (learning) related to stressful relationships. In essence, if we had a difficult time as a child feeling connected, if we enter a relationship with a healthy individual, that person's way of being can provide new information to our relationship wiring. As oxytocin begins to flow because of the healthy relationship, that oxytocin can "wash" old relationship wiring, creating a new sense of self as being important and wanted.

OXYTOCIN CONTINUES TO BE INFLUENCED THROUGH:

Looking in eye (smiling and accepting eyes)
Touch
Being attuned
Being together under uplifting experiences (especially outdoor experiences). This is likely why 'The Family, A Proclamation to the World states': "Successful marriages and families are established and maintained on [the] principle of...... wholesome recreational activities." The Manti Pageant is both outdoors and a driving powerful

uplifting experience. A family attending the pageant would naturally come away feeling closer to one another.

Behave in such a way with your children that will influence the flow of this chemical. When this chemical is activated, we feel closer to whoever we are with. Do not underestimate its ability to develop secure, emotional bonds.

Notice how this is related to *Erickson's Stages of Development* as it relates to TRUST. The tremendous amount of oxytocin being produced from birth through 18 months, as a result of our closeness and nurturing during that time is what is producing the sense of trust in our children. Oxytocin has been dubbed as the Trusting Hormone. Trust in relationships is what brings about emotional stability. You have the power to influence the flow of oxytocin in your children to create a greater sense of emotional stability by the way you interact with them.

INCREASING OUR INFLUENCE –
The Yes–Yes's of Parenting

In the next few sections we are going to discuss learning in association with brain development, creating an internal motivation engine within our children, and the nature and purpose of consequences. But, before we do, let's discuss some very practical ways of interacting with our children that will naturally increase your child's confidence.

Confidence is a word that best describes a sense of feeling good about one's self. It is associated with a sense of capability, of feeling like one matters and is included, and a healthy sense of one's body. The opposite of this quality of confidence is to feel helpless, unloved and having negative thoughts and feelings about one's body image.

Human performance is directly related to one's belief about him or herself. Parents have the greatest influence on the development of their child's internal sense of self. Healthy esteem is equated with confidence and unhealthy esteem is equated with doubt about one's effectiveness and social standing.

When a child believes that they are inadequate, they will stop trying to be successful in areas in which they think they cannot succeed. Here are things we want to avoid in our parenting approach:

- Teaching your child that his or her acceptance is based upon external things, i.e., popularity, what one wears, how much the family earns, etc.
- Sending the message that your child's worth is directly connected to his or her performance, i.e., perfectionism, being involved in every human activity to the point of exhaustion, demanding excellence in everything the child does, comparing your child to others
- Negative expectations, i.e., we have to appear a certain way in public; don't bring shame upon the family, what you do reflects my quality of parenting, etc.
- Coercion, intimidation, withholding of affection, isolating, harsh punishments, etc.

Increasing confidence or healthy esteem in our children occurs when we are encouraging (not saving), meaning we assist our children in recognizing the positive, including the child's strengths, their willingness to help, their ability to solve, their ability to create, etc. These types of interaction build a foundation for healthy support, mutual respect and a solid parent/child relationship.

I once had a young teenage client that displayed with great feelings of inadequacy. As I viewed the interaction between him and his mother, it was apparent that mother spent a significant amount of verbal energy telling her son what he had to do in order for her

198

acceptance to kick in. Oh, I don't think she understood what she was doing, but the message her boy was getting was loud and clear in his perspective:

> "Jack, if you would just do this," "Jack, you are to do it this way," "Jack, I don't want you to listen to Eminem," "Jack, I don't want to hear about it," "Oh Jack, if you would just change then your sister wouldn't do that."

On and on, Jack was criticized. Recall that criticism translates into rejection. Jack was so frustrated by the time he came to me, because he didn't believe he could do anything right. One way for him to combat this feeling of inadequacy was to be a straight "A" student. This approach to overcoming parent induced feelings of inadequacy is what we refer to as "Perfectionism." If a child can be perfect then the child can demonstrate that the parent's evaluation of the child is incorrect and may lead to the parent accepting the child. Perfectionism is an exhausting approach to feeling good about one's self and is subject to tremendous let downs. That is exactly the case of Jack.

One evening, Jack came into therapy upset and angry. "Well that was a *complete* waste of a semester!!" as he huffed while plopping down on the couch. I said, "It looks like something didn't go well." Jack replied, "Yes. I got an "A" in every class except one. I got an "A minus" in history!" Well not getting perfect A's was the same as not being perfect for Jack. Most of us would be happy with a semester that went that well, but for Jack it was evidence that he was not perfect, and if he was not perfect then his mother was right and he would have to go on proving his acceptability to her.

Better parenting creates positive beliefs in children. Your children need to know that:

1. You have faith and confidence in your child; that he or she can learn how to increasingly take responsibility for their life.
2. You trust that they will be able to learn through the experience of making choices.
3. You support their interests; recognize their natural talents, abilities, gifts, and strengths.
4. You can guide them by teaching them successful habits like setting goals and that you recognize their efforts as they improve.

Encouragement looks like this:

- Giving children responsibility
- Showing appreciation for their positive contributions to family and home life
- Inviting your children to offer their own opinions
- Asking for input on how to solve problems
- Handling childhood mistakes as a means of teaching
- Not harshly criticizing or punishing
- Teaching the importance of pro-social interaction

199

- Assisting your child to look for the positive (teaching positive, truthful thinking)
- Trusting your child's judgment
- Being straightforward about expectations and limits
- Helping your child to become a more critical thinker.

Encouragement is a pro-social skill that requires practice until it becomes second nature. Our language and the tones in our voice are what signal encouragement to our children. The following list will help you formulate your own encouraging language:

1. That was really cool the way you handled that situation.
2. What do you think we should do?
3. It looks like you had a really good time. I am so happy for you.
4. You've got good taste when it comes to clothing styles!
5. It looks like you are a little discouraged. What do you believe led to you feeling this way?
6. If you could do it over again, would you change anything?
7. I believe you have everything inside of yourself to do well in school.
8. Don't forget, I am always available to bounce things off of.
9. Wow, it is neat to see how much you have improved your game. Have you noticed it too?
10. What did your teacher say about solving quadratic equations? I think it is such a great quality that you are willing to take care of yourself by asking for help!
11. I love hearing you sing. You have a terrific voice!
12. Thank you for helping me this morning. It really made me feel good all day.
13. You know, it sounds like you have a few options. I trust your judgment and I will support your decision.
14. Hey, the backyard looks great! And you did it without being asked – I'm a lucky mom!
15. I am so glad to have you as my daughter! I am better for having you.
16. Thank you for being such a good example of serving and helping others.
17. Hey it was a hard lesson – that's kind of what life does for us – it creates opportunities to adjust our attitudes and behaviors, based upon negative outcomes. What did you gain or learn from this experience?
18. Our expectation is that you are never alone together in a home, either ours or hers, as it may make it more difficult to resist temptation.
19. It is unfortunate that so many kids are mean. I can tell that it really hurt your feelings. Let me teach you about a skill called "Kill them with kindness." We can practice it so you can try it out tomorrow, o.k.?
20. Sounds like a tough teacher. I have a friend at the bank that said getting a letter of recommendation from him to any of the local medical schools, is highly valued by those schools. They really respect him. I know you are interested in applying for medical school – can you see any good in being in his class?

While the list is not inclusive, it is a reference point on how encouragement is portrayed. You will notice that this list avoids many comments like:

1. You're pretty
2. You're smart
3. You're the best
4. You're so strong
5. You're so talented

These typical parenting phrases don't transmit the right kind or amount of correct information. Encouragement looks at the child's efforts, their experience, their ability to evaluate, their sense of direction. As we *notice* these attributes, then we are giving substantial feedback. When we tell our child that they are smart and yet they struggle with a math course, they may doubt your awareness and sincerity. On the other hand, if we recognize the gargantuan effort they put forth to prepare for the exam, then we are recognizing an attribute that is associated with the child's experience. Our noticing that effort brings greater awareness of the child's abilities and efforts – and the child experiences satisfaction for what the efforts brought.

THE SCIENCE OF HUMAN DESIGN
(The Power of Observing Our Children)

We have spoken about many things about what good parenting does up to this point in the book. Some of it may seem like common sense, some of it may have been experienced as brand new information, some of it may have produced some feelings of guilt; some of it may seem impossible to achieve.

To help us understand what is going on in the process of our purposeful parenting interventions, it is important that you understand some science concepts. What I am about to detail not only has application with the interventions we have discussed, but it will also provide the basis to understand how we ignite the engine of self-motivation.

Quantum Physics provides answers where Newtonian Physics falls short. Newtonian Physics translates into parenting skills that are more behavior modification based approaches, while Quantum Physics translates into parenting skills that change cellular activity, strengthen healthy neural associations, and results in increased respect and trust between parent and child. Which approach do you think will have the best results?

I would like to speak of three laws associated with Quantum Science as it is these laws that explain why our children are responding positively to our good parenting. The laws are:

1) The Law of Entanglement
2) All Matter has Potential
3) The Law of the Observer

Entanglement simply means that everything is connected. A couple of ways to understand this is by first, recognizing the life giving force that allows all things to live; by which all things are sustained and upheld. To help you reflect on what I am trying to describe, recall how many things you used today that required electricity. It may have been a computer, a toaster, or microwave – oh and don't forget the refrigerator! Each of these items works because they are connected to the same source of power.

Yet, we require much more energy than any of those appliances throughout our life and where is our power cord? How is it that we are able to move, and breathe, to exercise our mental faculties and so on? What is the flowing, renewing, replenishing source of our energy?

Researchers are finally catching up to what the scriptures already have pointed out. These intelligent observers and investigators are recognizing that the very power that provides life and organization within each of us is the same power that upholds, organizes and renews all life. It is the same power that maintains the universe and pushes it to greater expansion, all the while maintaining the systems of orbit, stellar creation, and movement among the galaxies. Following are some things you and I never think about but are an ongoing process within. These highlight the point I am intending on making:

#1

- Each eye has an auto-focusing lens.
- Nerves and muscles control two eyes to make one three-dimensional image
- The eyes are connected to the brain, which records the sights seen

#2

- If you were to lay out all of the alveoli of the lungs, it would take up an entire tennis court.

#3

- Your heart is an incredible pump
- It has four delicate valves that control the direction of blood flow
- These valves open and close more than 100,000 times a day – 36 million times a year
- Unless disease enters, these valves will last forever

#4

- The heart pumps two gallons of blood per minute, well over 100 gallons per hour
- The vascular system is about 60,000 miles in length – twice the circumference of the earth
- Yet the circulatory system makes up less than 3% of our body mass

#5

- Every 20-60 seconds each blood cell makes a complete circuit through the body
- If all of the red blood cells in our body were lined up it would reach 31,000 miles into the sky
- In the second it takes you to inhale, you lose three million red blood cells
- And in the next second the same number will be replaced.
- In one second, 100,000 chemical reactions occur in every cell of your body
- There are 70 to 100 trillion cells that make up our body

#6

- Just now, 10 million of your cells just died. And now 10 million more were just born
- The pancreas regenerates almost all of its cells in one day
- Around 40,000 new neuron cells are manufactured everyday
- Communication between cells happens faster than the speed of light

#7

- Something other than your conscious mind is causing the secretion of enzymes in exact amounts the food you consumed into its component nutrients
- Some mechanism of a higher order is filtering liters of blood through your kidneys every hour to make urine and eliminate waste.

#8

- This higher intelligence maintains the 66 functions of the liver, although most of us would have never guessed the liver does so many functions.
- Every cell contains your DNA. Stretching out the DNA in just one cell would create a 6 foot high tower of material.
- If we were to stretch out all of the DNA incorporated in every cell within our body, that material would reach to the sun and back 150 times

#9

- This greater intelligence which acts in us and through us orchestrates tiny protein enzymes that constantly zip through the 3.2 billion nucleic acid sequences that are the genes in every cell, checking for mutations.

#10

- The body's defense system is a wonder.
- To protect it from harm, it perceives pain.
- In response to infection, it generates anti-bodies
- Nutrition, exercise and thoughts all impact the body's defense system

#11

- Our own inner version of Homeland Security knows how to fight off thousands of bacteria and viruses without our ever needing to realize that we are under attack.

#12

- The skin provides protection
- It warns against injury that excessive heat or cold might cause

#13

- The body renews its own outdated cells and regulates the levels of its own vital ingredients
- The body heals its cuts, bruises, and broken bones.
- With correct thinking, the brain can be renewed

#14

- Most marvelous of all, this life force knows how to start from just two cells, a sperm and an egg, and create our almost 100 trillion specialized cells.
- Having given us life, it then continually regenerates that life and regulates an incredible number of processes.

#15

- The power that made the body is the power that maintains and heals the body.
- This power of intelligence animates our trillions of daily chemical reactions within the body, without thought. This light, which lighteth every man... (John 1:9; D&C 93:9), is expressing itself through us, it orders all things, and directs all things, and governs all things, and regenerates all things. Each descriptive word just used identifies the processes of biological survival we experience every second of our life.

#16

- In the midst of all of this life giving power is the gift of agency – the gift to believe or disbelieve what has been revealed about us.

Again, these are things that we never think about but are being supported in all living organisms by the same power. What allows your biological survival is the exact same thing or power that allows for my daily survival and your children's. This is certainly one way we are all entangled or connected.

A second way to think about the *Law of Entanglement* is to understand how one simple thing impacts another thing. This coordinated and correlated process can be as simple as a thought. What if our thought is filled with assumption? Would we likely interact with another person differently because we believe we know their motives? Does that interaction then resonate negatively in the person we are making conclusions about?

Or what if our thoughts are filled with distortions and untruthful judgments about our own worth, capacity, and importance? Would such thinking, due to being entangled with the rest of our physiology, create genetic mutations, abnormal rates of stress hormones within our blood stream, or immune system abreactions that may lead to deteriorating health? Is the mind and body entangled with each other?

What if I decide to refrain from watering my houseplants? How does that one simple choice begin to impact the health of the plant, the beauty of the room, and the content of fresh air? In essence, the Law of Entanglement says that there is nothing we do that doesn't have a ripple effect throughout our environment and even further, the entire universe. The closer or more secure we are connected to someone else, the greater the influence we will have on their experience, learning and understanding. We are going to highlight several aspects of this law when we speak about learning, and our interactions with our children. For now, I just wanted to introduce the idea of what this law is saying.

Next is the *Law that All Matter has Potential*. The basic building blocks of the universe are found formed in many different ways, yet essentially the chemical compounds are the same. The basic components of dirt are Carbon, Hydrogen, Oxygen, and Nitrogen, yet so is our human body (Ecclesiastes 12:7). In fact, many things are composed of these basic elements, yet are expressed so differently. What allows matter to take on so many forms? The answer to that question is found in the *Law of the Observer*.

If you have ever created anything, you took of materials (all materials are made up of the basic building blocks found throughout the universe) and combined, fastened, and formed them in a way that your mind conceived it could. This ability to picture an end result is the difference between the details of the finished product. When we stop long enough and observe something, that observation has the power to change the outcome. A simple example of this process is how our children act when they are in our presence, and how they act when they are not. There is something about our observing them that creates a different outcome. Likewise, when we choose to observe a situation positively instead of negatively, we too will get a different outcome. This law is what we want to utilize in order to get the outcome we picture in our children.

It is important to understand these three laws as we now get further into human design. We will begin by looking at the child's developing neural system. It should become evident quickly that these processes are not just coming together due to some genetic blueprint, no, it should be clear that the environment we are providing is acting on the development, sequencing, and strong associations being formed.

After we look at the developmental neural changes that are occurring in our young children, we will look at the power of "signaling" that each of us is so sensitive to. Signaling is that process either genetically or environmentally that continues to impose itself on us throughout life and in doing so strengthens our self-concept or weakens it.

A good portion of that signaling also comes from the internal responses we experience when our environment shapes the opportunities to either have reoccurring positive or negative intrapersonal feedback. In all of my dealing with the host of issues mental health counselors deal with on a regular basis, it has been unequivocally my experience that most symptoms of the various diagnosis have a magical way of disappearing as individuals begin taking greater responsibility for their circumstances, especially their thoughts. That greater individual effort to work on the etiology and formation of these negative symptoms and be personally responsible for the outcome someone is seeking is the KEY to living more abundantly. It is certainly our role as parents to teach children how to take increasingly more responsibility for their lives as they mature. There is much learning going on when our children accept greater responsibility.

LEARNING – TYING IT ALL TOGETHER

If it hasn't become evident enough to this point, let me just clearly say that there is nothing more important in a child's life than a quality parent. What we do as parents with our children, especially from the very beginning (in utero through six years old), will be more predictive of their outcome than any other single factor. The main reason for this is because of brain development and growth.

There are so many neural connections that are occurring during this time that we have only so long to stimulate and influence those connections in such a way to produce the foundation that provides the basis for a positive life. Essential to this foundation is the development of a self-concept that includes certain beliefs and attitudes that will act as buffers against stress and challenges that are surely to come their way.

Following are a collection of over 70 points in relation to our interaction with our children and the impact it has on healthy brain development. Also included are some interesting facts about brain development, which simply reinforce the importance of everything we have discussed to this point on the importance of our positive and healthy interaction with our children.

Literally, it is us as the parents that are developing and training a belief system in our children by the way we engage with or disengage from them. I hear so many parents, especially as their children are approaching or are in their adolescent years express confusion as to why their child s struggling. Much of what we have already considered to this point likely plays a significant role in those struggles. What you are about to read likely plays even a bigger role.

Brain Neuroplasticity and Brain Development in Children
(The following facts are attributable to among others, Bruce Lipton, Ph.D., Joe Dispenza, D.C., Allen Schore, Ph.D., and Dan Siegel, M.D.)

1. Did you know that 90% of a child's brain develops during the first 5 years of life? Baby brain development sets the stage for the child's intelligence, emotional stability and personality.

2. Research also shows that parental involvement with a child during these early years is directly related to the child's vocabulary development, reading readiness and eventual academic achievement.

3. In fact, a baby's brain begins development in the early embryo when cell division proliferates into millions of neurons in the brain. At some time in the third trimester, this neuron cell division produces 20.000 new cells per second!

207

4. Soon after birth, billions of neurons begin making connections with each other to create neural pathways within the nervous system. This is in large measure due to stimulation provided in the child's environment. Failure to stimulate critical pathways will lead to the brain "clipping off" that which is not being used. There are critical pathways and time-frames associated with this early development. Sight, for example, is stimulated by presenting light to the child. Light acts on the sight pathway to stimulate and activate the system of being able to see, focus, and discriminate. The muscles of the eye are already beginning to constrict or dilate based upon light waves. These in turn activate other sight oriented neurons that sharpen this whole process. If we fail to stimulate this system, then the brain will "clip off" the neurons, believing that they are not necessary and the child will not ever be able to see.

While this is a pretty drastic example, yet it demonstrates the need for enough stimulation so that the child's brain can begin making more and more neural connections. These early processes are vital in developing important connections that lead to greater capacity to read, write, comprehend, spell, analyze, solve and regulate.

Singing to our children, reading to our children, playing with our children, holding our children, taking our children outside to touch, see, smell, hear and sometimes taste of the earth, all stimulate the brain to form greater amounts of and stronger neural circuits.

5. Each neuron has the ability to make as many as 15,000 new connections. In a strong healthy brain, these connections become the wiring or circuitry that defines the child's experiences and capabilities.

6. An infant's brain at birth has 100 billion neurons. If the brain is not stimulated from birth, these neurons wither and die, impeding the child's ability to learn and develop properly.

7. The brain of a 6 month old infant is at least 25% the size of an adult brain.

8. By 3 years, a child's brain is about the size of an adult brain.

9. It is during these early years of neuronal growth and proliferation that the brain is most Neuroplastic. This means the brain is most malleable and formative during these early years.

10. The Role the Environment Plays in Brain Development in Children - Environmental factors such as nurture, love, stimulation, and proper nutrition have a direct impact on the psychological, physiological and cognitive development of the child.

11. Emerging research shows the importance of essential fatty acids like DHA in promoting the cognitive functions and development of children.

12. Their intelligence and mental stability can be enhanced with brain food.

13. Negative environmental factors such as alcohol or secondhand smoke can have a deleterious influence on the unborn child.

14. In fact the environment can change gene function and determine how the brain develops. Social and emotional factors like nurturing and love can also alter genetic expression. This is the science of Epi-genetics.

15. That's why early stimulation is crucial for brain development in children.

16. The brain grows like a sponge as it absorbs input from the world around it. The larger the brain, the greater the resources available to master the environment.

17. Animals in the wild have much greater brain volumes than animals raised in captivity. Why? Animals in the wild are exposed to greater stimulation.

18. Similarly, children exposed to opportunities for stimulation in early life make more synaptic connections in the brain.

19. Stimulation provides opportunities for these connections to occur. And the more these connections are made, the greater the cognitive and social intelligence of the child.

20. Music, for example, stimulates the cognitive, verbal and emotional centers of the brain. Music is vital to brain development in children.

21. Social interaction is critical to brain development in children.

What Kind of Activities Promote Cognitive Stimulation?

22. Music, Art, Exercise, Books, Play-- all these activities stimulate the child's mind. Babies should also be encouraged to explore and play safely. They should be able to do these things without experiencing ongoing negative feedback.

23. Allowing an 8 month old baby to crawl safely around a room nurtures the development of his brain. Toys are also means for safe exploration. Coloring and other types of art work provide optimal types of stimulation.

24. By the same token, a toxic environment can kill brain cells. Alcohol, drugs, anger, stress, abuse produce high levels of cortisol (stress hormones) in the child's brain.

26. Cortisol can cause brain cells to wither, thus reducing the connections between cells in the brain. When stress impacts the hippocampus, it can create difficulty in creating memories. We also know that in the case of the hippocampus, that when stress is reduced, the hippocampus revitalizes.

27. New research suggests that loss of brain connectivity is the cause of aging. Do we want our children's brains to age even before they have a chance at life?

28. Babies who grow up in a loving, nurturing environment develop strong emotional bonds with their nurturers. These emotional bonds can become buffers protecting them from the negative impact of stress. This was covered when we talked about oxytocin.

29. I cannot emphasize enough how much the early environment of a baby's experience is critical to brain development in children.

30. Because of brain Neuroplasticity, our direct impact on the child's development is critical. Everything we are doing in the child's environment is shaping the neurological wiring of that child.

31. A new study done by a team of researchers at McGill University shows that traumatic experiences in childhood can alter the genetic profile of the brain. Known as "epigenetic alterations," these changes in DNA can occur even before birth--during gestation.

32. Researchers also found epigenetic alterations in the stress response genes of suicide victims who had suffered abuse or neglect during childhood. These alterations had compromised their ability to deal with stress.

33. Research also shows that the expression of "violent" genes in youth can be moderated through family and social interventions.

34. Something as simple as having a daily meal with parents can alter the way a child with the genetic DNA for violence actually behaves. (Remember the quote from Ronald Reagan that was found at the beginning of the discussion on Family Government?)

35. As parents and grandparents, we have a responsibility for the well-being of our children. This well-being goes beyond food and shelter. It is important that we are aware of our influence on our child's developing belief system.

36. This well-being is the security that allows them to grow into independent, confident human beings who participate in the Light of Christ and who will in turn pass on the reflection of this Light to their children.

37. We must make it a priority to leave them a Legacy where the Light of Christ is experienced and understood.

Why is Gamma Wave Activity Important During Brain Development in Children?

38. Gamma wave activity in brains of infants provides a window into their cognitive development and language skills.

39. The first 36 months of a child's life are crucial for laying the groundwork of a healthy, intelligent, curious and creative mind.

40. From 16 to 36 months, the child experiences a tremendous growth spurt in language, increasing vocabulary to more than 1000 words.

41. Dr. April Benasich, Professor of Neuroscience at Rutgers University in Newark and her colleagues have recently identified the role gamma wave activity in the frontal cortex plays in the brain development in children during the first 3 years of life.

What Are Gamma Waves?

42. Gamma waves are fast, high-frequency rhythm brain waves associated with higher level mental activity when higher cognitive functions are engaged.

43. In general, gamma waves are associated with insight and consciousness, when the brain comes to a higher form of information such as the "aha moment", precognition or intuition. It would not surprise me if these Gamma Waves are influenced when the Holy Ghost provides spiritual insights to those that are seeking truth.

44. The gamma brain wave state corresponds to frequencies of 40 Hz or higher.

45. Studies have found that seasoned mediators' (like Tibetan monks) produce high-frequency gamma waves during their meditative state.

46. Many researchers account for this unusual level of gamma waves to the mental training of the monks.

What Do Gamma Wave Activity Mean For Brain Development in Children?

47. In her study of children 16, 24 and 36 months old, Dr. Benasich found that those with higher language and cognitive abilities showed higher gamma power than those with poorer cognitive and language scores. She also found that high gamma power was evident in children with better attention and executive functions control.

48. These children had the ability to moderate their behavior when told to do so.

211

49. By contrast, infants with low cognition and language skills showed below average gamma activity. Through her research, Dr. Benasich has identified a window during which dramatic linguistic and mental growth can be seen to correlate with gamma wave activity.

50. This window can be used to identify children at risk of language problems. By measuring gamma activity in the frontal cortex, doctors will be able to evaluate the status of brain development in children; they will also be able to make necessary interventions at critical points to ensure proper mental functioning.

For more information on Gamma Brain Waves and Brain Development, please visit:

http://mary-desaulniers.suite101.com/what-are-gamma-brainwaves-a172656

What are the Effects of Trauma and Stress on Brain Development in Children?

51. Early brain development sets the stage for the child's physical, emotional and mental health in later life.

52. In the past 15 years, we have discovered much about the brain's plastic and malleable nature, specifically its ability to develop new circuitry in response to experience.

Stress Creates a Maladaptive Response

53. Animal studies show that rat pups subjected to stress and neglect developed an over compensating stress response that usually lasted into adulthood.

54. Laboratory rats raised in shoebox cages with little or no stimulation have been compared with rats raised in an enriched environment of grooming and play. The privileged rats consistently developed a thicker cerebral cortex and denser neural networks than the deprived rats.

55. The same situation is found in children. Persistent stress in early brain development have resulted in children with a smaller corpus callosum than their normal counterparts. The corpus callosum is essential because it connects both hemispheres allowing needed communication that assists in all areas of brain function. The smaller the corpus callosum the more difficult for necessary communication to take place.

56. Persistent stress and abuse not only increases the release of cortisol and dopamine, promoting the body's fight or flight response, it rewires the brain for a chronic state of fear, depression and anxiety.

212

57. This maladaptive response creates a brain on hyper alert for danger.

58. The result is the child's inability to function normally in the world, even when he is placed in a nurturing and empathetic setting. Just ask parents that have adopted children diagnosed with fetal alcohol syndrome, or other addictive scenarios. Reactive Attachment is due to the increase of cortisol in these children.

59. With his brain stuck in the danger zone, this child will have difficulty developing higher thinking skills or wiring for experiences of trust and love.

60. The child remains trapped in hostility and aggression.

Subconscious Programming and Early Brain Development

61. This entrapment, says Bruce Lipton Ph.D. is often caused by well-meaning but unconscious parents who are not aware of the impact their words, criticisms, outbursts can have on their children.

62. In his book, The Biology of Belief: Unleashing the Power of Consciousness, Matter and Miracles (Santa Rosa, CA:Mountain of Love/Elite Books, 2005), Lipton claims that the parents' response to their offspring can program the child's brain for success or failure.

63. The reason is that between birth and 6 years of age, the human brain operates mainly at the EEG brain frequencies of delta and theta waves. These are slow, low frequency brain waves associated with a highly suggestible and programmable state.

64. What this means is that all information and experiences encountered by a child between birth and 6 become instantly "downloaded" into the child's subconscious mind. There is no buffer between these experiences or beliefs and the internal reception of the child.

65. Once programmed into the subconscious mind (i.e., implicit memory), these beliefs control the child's biology for the rest of his life unless he works consciously to free himself from their influence. "A child who is told he "will never amount to anything" will become that which he has heard and internalized; by the same token, a child who is told he can do whatever he sets his mind to will experience a stronger sense of benevolent destiny.

Intervention Can Reverse Negative Programming

66. Does that mean we are forever doomed by a traumatic or not so magical childhood?

67. Not so, says J.F. Mustard who refers to research that shows even children stunted at birth can "approach the performance of control children after 24 months" of intervention provided they are given proper nutrition and stimulation at birth.

68. Studies of Romanian orphans also indicate that the earlier these orphans are adopted, the more normal their cognitive functioning will be when they get older.

69. Orphans adopted at four months fared much better than those adopted at 8 months or older. When these children were tested at 11 years of age, those adopted at 8 months or older showed a greater incidence of abnormal brain development and abnormal behavior (i.e., ADHD, aggression, etc.) than the younger group.

70. The earlier the intervention, the stronger the likelihood that the negative programming these children internalized during their early brain development can be rewired and reversed.

71. No one is trapped by his early programming. Adults, even seniors, have the ability to reverse brain circuitry. In his book, The Brain that Changes Itself (Toronto:Viking Penguin, 2007), Norman Doidge relates the case of a young woman diagnosed from childhood as learning disabled. Yet this young woman was able to retrain her brain with specific exercises designed to compensate for her mental deficits. She is now an educator and Principal of the world renowned Arrowsmith School in Toronto.

72. In the same vein, Psychiatrist Jeffrey Schwartz was able to help his adult OCD patients change their obsessive compulsive behavior by teaching them how to actively rewire their brains through mental power, *the power of Neuroplasticity through observation.*

73. Given the neuroplastic nature of our brain, we can no longer see ourselves as victims of the programming we received during our early brain development. Lipton urges us to use our conscious mind that offers us free will.

74. Our conscious mind (The Law of the Observer) can stop the undesired behavior and create a new response.

75. Contrary to the well-used adage that you can't teach an old dog new tricks, neuroscientists are discovering that the immense formative power of the brain is infinite; it can change, even in old age, if it is given proper encouragement and stimulation.

76. A child's brain is even more malleable, which means that every experience in early life has a significant impact on brain development.

214

77. Even breast feeding makes a significant impact on the infant's brain development.

78. Growth in the brain is predicated on neural connections that create neural pathways within the nervous system. Connections evolve into wiring or circuitry that define the experiences and potential of a child.

Sources:
Gunnar M.R., A. Herrera and C.E. Hostinar. "Stress and Early Brain Development." Encyclopedia on Early Childhood Development. Centre of Excellence for Early childhood Development. Published online June 10 2009. Accessed October 26 2010.

Mustard, J. Fraser. "Early Brain Development and Human Development." Encyclopedia on Early Childhood Development. Centre of Excellence for Early childhood Development. Published online February 17, 2010. Accessed October 26 2010.

Schwartz, Jeffrey M. and Sharon Begley. The Mind and the Brain: Neuroplasticity and the Power of Mental Force. New York: HarperCollins, 2003.

APPLICATION OF THE ABOVE INFORMATION IN A SPECIFIC SETTING

A short explanation is necessary in order to understand the application I am going to make relative to the above facts and negative interactions with our children. When we hear the word "TRAUMA" most of us think about significant events that fall out of the average relational interactions we experience. A car accident, an extensive injury, being threatened, watching someone be killed, experiencing life threatening situations, being raped, molested, and a host of other "big events" that stimulate our threat modulating systems for survival.

Such events create a systemic rise in chemical, cortical and brain stem activity. It is this rise in activity that defines what trauma is. However, research has closely monitored the rise of this activity in experiences that are not necessarily life threatening. It is now clear that children that experience hostile (being spanked out of anger), angry, rejecting, emotionally manipulative, distancing parents experience chronic rises of activity related to the threat modulating system and thereby experience the same effects of someone that may has experienced a "big" trauma.

Because of the sequential development of the brain and it tremendous malleability early in life, early life experiences play a remarkable role in shaping how the brain functions and on developing belief systems. Early experiences create a cascade, or sequential set of cognitive, emotional, social, and physiological templates (implicit memory; mental model) that the child carries around with them and use as they go through life.

Children raised in a home where there is a consistent environment of anger/abuse will often have their Neural Systems associated with threat activated for days and weeks and years. This literally changes how their brain is organized – how their neural systems mediating threat are organized, and how they function. This child will learn very differently than a child that is raised in a nurturing environment. Anger, yelling, emotional targeting disrupts self-worth!

The brain has the capacity to absorb experience; and it absorbs experiences in multiple ways and at multiple levels. One level is how it absorbs the accumulated experience, beliefs and attitudes of previous biological generations (i.e., that of parents and grandparents). This process alone develops or invents a basis of one's identity.

But likewise, the brain has the remarkable capability to take experiences – patterned, repetitive experiences, and internalize them, and change our brains in ways that allows us to make internal representations based upon our meaning of those external experiences.

One of the most important things to recognize about the brain is that it is not one big mass of billions of neurons in some disorganized array. The brain is not simply a big lump of fat. It is organized in a sensible, hierarchical fashion. The neural systems we use to respond to a threatening situation and the neural systems that are activated during trauma originate in the brain stem, and then they send out neurons that connect with other neuronal connections all throughout the brain. When our children experience negative tones, raised voices, negative facial expressions, their threat modulating systems are being activated. If these interactions are the consistent pattern of a parent-child relationship, a chain of neural networks is developed across brain regions, which become easily triggered through patterned experience and creates many difficulties in regulating emotions and behaviors.

These negative patterned, repetitive interactions change the nature and function of neural cells and activity. These chronic negative interactions become stored as memory, which provides the basis to generalize a child's experience with critical, harsh parents to others that the child comes into contact with. In other words, the child not sensing acceptance from their parents may generalize that no one will accept or think well of them.

Children's primary relationships are critical because during the process of explosive growth in the first years of life, the brain is creating template memories that will be used throughout life. Primary relationships create the relational template against which all subsequent human interaction will be compared. If this template makes an association between an intimate connection with another human being and fear, unpredictability and threat, it's going to have significant consequences in the child's ability to form and maintain healthy relationships. On the other hand, if a child has a care giver who is loving, nurturing and attentive, one who has met the child's needs, the child's internal template for what human beings are like will be positive. In short, the sequential acquisition of memory is what development is. This means that the early experiences that first shape these organizing systems have a disproportionate power, because they become the filter against which all subsequent input is compared.

HOW DO WE LEARN?

It is now time to quit brushing at the concept of SIGNALING as has been done in a couple of previous places in this book and set the format for how learning is structured through SIGNALING.

So much of what goes on in the development and workings of the neural system and in the chemical processes found at the cellular level occurs in absence of high consciousness or awareness. We do know that all learning (conscious or unconscious) is associated with neural connectivity, but the formation of how neurons connect is in direct relation to the signals the *mind* receives. Likewise, cellular functioning is directly related to the information our cells receive. In this *signaling*, we are not robots of destiny, meaning that our experiences do not cement our outcomes because there is something that is very real, yet elusive to researchers in this process, which allows us to shape our experiences *based upon our observation of them*.

Neither, the mortal physical brain; or the physiology associated with cellular activity is operating independent of the real experience that each of us share – that of being able to be reflective of our thoughts, feelings, and behaviors. The reflective part is not a product of neural anatomy, it is something operating at some master level of the physical experiences we are having.

One way to conceptualize this concept is to reflect upon the teachings of prophets concerning our true identity:

> "You are not a human being having a spiritual experience; you are a spiritual being having a human experience."

The constant pleadings of prophets to remember who we really are provides a pervasive, synchronistic message over thousands of years, millions upon millions of droplets of revealed truth from the Holy Ghost as a witness of our divine heritage. Our identities are indeed unique and eternal. They did not form during the process of mitosis. Long before having a physical, mortal neuro-anatomy and physical cellular functioning, we were, we existed. William Wordsworth's "Ode: Intimations of Immortality from Recollections of Early Childhood," provides a glimpse of this innate experience we each have:

Our birth is but a sleep and a forgetting:
The Soul that rises with us, our life's Star,
Hath had elsewhere its setting,
And cometh from afar:
Not in entire forgetfulness,
And not in utter nakedness,
But trailing clouds of glory do we come
From God, who is our home:
Heaven lies about us in our infancy!

Our identity (life's Star), which came from "afar" is the very thing that we experience when we are able to observe what our thoughts are saying; what feelings we recognize, and what behaviors we choose. This eternal identity is the core self. It operates on the physical aspects of our learning, our knowing; our being. It too, among other things we are about to discuss, sends *signals* to our physical experience and has the power to shape, influence, interact and support our sense of self.

Perhaps to a Latter Day Saint this, innate, reflective part may be referred to as "intelligence" though even in our modern revelations, this concept is still not fully revealed. From the Topical Guide to the scriptures we find the following:

> Intelligence has several meanings, three of which are: (1) It is the light of truth which gives life and light to all things in the universe. It has always existed. (2) The word *intelligences* may also refer to spirit children of God. (3) The scriptures also may speak of intelligence as referring to the spirit element that existed before we were begotten as spirit children.

Important scriptures that highlight these concepts:

- Intelligence cleaveth unto intelligence:D&C 88:40;
- Intelligence was not created or made:D&C 93:29;
- All intelligence is independent in that sphere in which God has placed it:D&C 93:30;
- The glory of God is intelligence:D&C 93:36–37;
- Intelligence acquired in this life rises with us in the resurrection:D&C 130:18–19;
- The Lord rules over all the intelligences:Abr. 3:21;
- The Lord showed Abraham the intelligences that were organized before the world was:Abr. 3:22;

(The above references appear in order in the Topical Guide)

Our pre-existent character, our true identity acts upon the anatomy of humanness in order to shape the structures that provide scaffolding of self concept. The spiritual DNA we each received from our Heavenly Father has encoded on it the eternal nature and potential to become as He is. All of his experience, all of his knowledge, all of his character is encoded within this spiritual DNA and it too sends *signals* that lift us above the fray if we attune to these subtle promptings. It is this DNA, currently expressing itself in limited levels that can magnify its expression if we are willing to Come Follow Him (Luke 18:22). As we do so, we experience greater light, greater capacity to create and govern; greater capacity to learn and change, and greater capacity to love. This increasing capacity to become is modifying the expression of that eternal information so that greater amounts of that information becomes available to us. In the language of the Savior:

> "For intelligence cleaveth unto intelligence; wisdom receiveth wisdom; truth embraceth truth; virtue loveth virtue; light cleaveth unto light; mercy hath compassion on mercy and claimeth her own; justice continueth its course and claimeth its own; judgment goeth before the face of him who sitteth upon the throne and governeth and executeth all things." (D&C 88:40)

Each of us receives from our earthly parents their DNA. Physical features take shape based upon the coding stored within their genetics. But this is not all we receive through the blue-prints of their mapping. Stored on their genes is their experiences, their attitudes; their way of being, their strengths and limitations. We inherit all of this information and it contributes to our neural mapping and the functioning of cellular activity. Genes provide the storage of many characteristics that can be manifest or expressed in different ways. As said before, if I am an anxious parent, that anxiety is encoded within my genes and its expression is passed on to my children. An anxious brain looks and functions differently that a non-anxious brain, but the development of wiring with an anxiety ridden neural system is being activated and developed through the genetic expression of the anxiously wired parent.

The parent's genetics are too sending *signals* to their children's physiological experience (cellular activity) and self concept. A child that has received the neural blue-print to form an anxiously wired brain will automatically (unconsciously) receive such *signaling* as a sense of doubt and fear. When that child operates from this existence, that child will develop a sense of incapability and helplessness. On the other hand, if a parent has developed a strong testimony of spiritual realities, that too can send powerful *signals* of testimony to their children. Such children experience greater feelings of hope and are motivated due to the purpose that engenders that hope.

The other area that contributes to *signals* we receive is our environment. If genetics were the only apparatus of *signaling*, we would all be doomed. Perhaps the most important source of *signaling* is our environment. Many of the negative, genetically driven *signals* can be overcome by environmental *signaling* or stimuli.

Chronic, negative parenting is an environmental *signal* received by a child, with an ongoing message that the child does not rise to the standard that would allow the parent to be happy. Such a negative parent has already predisposed their child to this message for the simple fact that the negativity is written or encoded upon the parent's DNA, which is shared with the offspring. But the environment of ongoing hostile, negative, unhappy interactions of this parent with his or her child simply reinforces the already *implanted sense* of not being acceptable, due to the DNA *signaling.*

Many times I meet parents that are struggling with stressful relationships with their children. As I review their parenting interactions, I ALWAYS find that the interaction with their own parents while growing up was less than superb. Having a poor example of parenting would be an indicator why their current struggles with their own children is being experienced. Poor parenting, however, is not a deterministic attribute. A parent can change their style of interaction through learning and practice, thus changing the *signals* they send to their children.

Though we are not at the end of the book quite yet, already you are connecting the dots with how our interactions develop within our children a sense of "I" or "Identity." Their identity is what they believe about themselves and we are constantly sending the *signals* that are either strengthening their core identity or weakening it.

Here is some more science behind human design. Approximately every 60 days, we replace most of the cells of our body. Every cell contains hundreds, even thousands of receptor sites. The purpose of the vastness of receptor sites is to maximize availability to *signals*. Some receptor sites will not allow negatively encoded signals to dock, while others are designed specifically for one type of signaling, like "I am worthless." If our environment *signals* that we are worthless, (i.e., a child being ridiculed, a child not having a parent spend time with them; a child that experiences a lot of negative feedback), the thoughts associated with such interactions become encoded upon protein carriers (polypeptides), which then dock with these established receptor sites on our cells. The encoded information then informs the cell how to act. This information could have a cell lose energy (slowing metabolism), or send off chemicals that tell the body to release stress chemicals, or opening or closing ion channels, and even instruct THE CELL IN HOW IT SHOULD DIVIDE. Cell division is part of the mechanism and process of how our cells are replaced.

Here in lies the problem. Because DNA is housed in every cell, the signals received in the cell set-off a biochemical process that is telling how the DNA should express itself during the creation of the next cell as it divides. DNA is not a static product. DNA is altered continually, due to ongoing or differentiated *signaling*. Typically what we discover is that cells that predominately receive environmental signals of worthlessness, alter DNA to create new cells that reduce positive signaling receptor sites and increase negative signaling receptor sites. This is important stuff – because we are conditioning cells to become more prone to negative signals as positive environmental signals have less chance to find sites to dock to. This can lead to a cascade of ongoing biochemical processes that leads to a sense of helplessness, hopelessness, and insignificance. A child that develops that sense of self is going to be presenting with all types of behavioral and emotional problems.

However, if through our intentional, purposeful interactions we signal the cellular activities, including the DNA, to give our child a sense of their acceptance, worth, importance and capability, then we develop cells and DNA that promote more positive receptor sites in future cell division. The greater capacity to receive positive signals leads to emotional stability, a sense of profound worth, and motivation to care for one's self.

Again I ask, what do you want your child to believe?

The power of observance, that core pre-existent character of intelligence which is separate from the physical brain, has the capacity to filter all of the incoming and internal *signals* we receive daily. Correct observance alters or disempowers negative, untruthful thoughts of our identity, while amplifying or strengthening the signals that are realistic and congruent with revealed truth of our identity and purpose. This is the concept of mind over matter, or the mind being the master of the body in the mind-body connect.

That capacity however can be stunted. It becomes stunted when we have childhoods filled with *signaling* that develops physiology of inferior, struggling identities. In this scenario, the power of observance has not had the nurturing it needs to intervene. The child becomes victim to the shaping of limiting ability to negotiate its experiences. The negative, physiological functioning has now taken control of the child and the child is sure that he or she is worthless because of the feelings that have had such a long run of convincing the child of this distortion. Emotions have a powerful effect on an untrained observer, to convince them of all types of inferiority complexes.

One other way we receive *signals* through our environment is through how we take care of our health. Nutrition alone has the capacity to change our DNA structures and expressions. Exercise has profound positive effects at the cellular level as well. I don't want to spend any time discussing these last two points, (i.e., nutrition and exercise as signals form our environment), but I will point out that our discovery of all of these processes are fairly recent. If you are reading this book, you are receiving some incredible and exciting insight as to how the human organism operates. Because we are discovering these truths, it changes how one looks at mental health and how to recover if our *signals* have been consistently negative. One of the sciences that explains some of these processes is called Epi-genetics. However, for the sake of further discovery I would recommend Molecules of Emotion: The Science Behind Body-Mind Medicine, by Candace Pert. It is one of several books that puts this new information into perspective. My intent is just to explain enough of the science of human design to invite parents to consider their interactions with their children due to the profound effect it has on developing a belief system.

With the foregoing information, we can now appreciate the process of learning, understanding that there are billions of mind-body impulses or *signals* that we experience every second. We have no ability to consciously deal with that vast amount of information. That is why it is important to become excellent observers of what we do notice, whether that is within our own experience or the observing we do of our children's experiences. Observing slows these *signals* down so that we might have the opportunity to intervene, checking metaphorical passports, determining what thoughts we will allow to pass on to the body. What thoughts we act on purposely become the building blocks of belief.

MOVING FORWARD

All Learning is:

1. Cumulative – We never unlearn anything that is truly learned– we only modify earlier learning based upon continuing information and experience. Learning is closely associated with memory. We have several types of memory, but as previously explained, we are just focusing on two:

    a. Explicit – Recalling details from our memory – data and autobiographical recall
    b. Implicit (things that get stored without full conscious awareness) – Reacting to wiring that took place under the conditions of our early years, or highly charged emotional experiences – the personally held beliefs that we developed due to our parents style of interaction or other significant events occurring during our lifetime.

2. Associative – The brain is compartmentalized yet has a vast network of wiring that speaks to each other.

I don't intend on being too simplimatic in these definitions, because certainly, on a daily basis, some learning is reinforced more than other learning. We take in so much information on a daily basis that it is impossible to consciously integrate it all. The dreaming sequence at night somehow involves itself with the process of determining what is important to keep and what is not. I don't think it is clear yet about what does or does not get stored or how much, but the definitions above provide the accurate framework to understand the general process of learning.

Research has clearly defined that learning does get stored, not just in neural circuits, but also at the cellular level. It is our cells that store learning as physical memories. This makes sense as it has been shown that massages can release memories. Crazy, I know, but true. But, perhaps not so crazy! When one acquaints themselves with certain scriptures it is interesting to correlate the research with the doctrine being conveyed. Some scriptures speak of felt pain or joy based upon some life-learning experiences. For example, Alma, in using memory recall, describes some pretty intense feelings based upon choices he had made during his lifetime:

"Nevertheless, after wading through much tribulation, repenting nigh unto death, the Lord in mercy hath seen fit to snatch me out of an everlasting *burning*, and I am born of God."

"My soul hath been redeemed from the *gall of bitterness* and bonds of iniquity. I was in the *darkest abyss*; but now I behold the *marvelous light* of God. My soul was racked with eternal *torment*; but I am snatched, and my soul is *pained no more......*"

"But I was racked with eternal torment, for my soul was *harrowed* up to the greatest degree and racked with all my sins."

"Yea, *I did remember* all my sins and iniquities, for which I was tormented with the pains of hell; yea, I saw that I had rebelled against my God, and that I had not kept his holy commandments."

"Yea, and I had murdered many of his children, or rather led them away unto destruction; yea, and in fine so great had been my iniquities, that the very thought of coming into the presence of my God *did rack my soul with inexpressible horror.*"

"Oh, thought I, that I could be banished and become extinct both soul and body, that I might not be brought to stand in the presence of my God, to be judged of my deeds."

"And now, for three days and for three nights was I racked, even with *the pains* of a damned soul."

"And it came to pass that as I was thus racked with *torment*, while I was harrowed up by *the memory of my many sins*, behold, *I remembered* also to have heard my father prophesy unto the people concerning the coming of one Jesus Christ, a Son of God, to atone for the sins of the world."

"*Now, as my mind caught hold upon this thought*, I cried within my heart: O Jesus, thou Son of God, have mercy on me, who am in the gall of bitterness, and am encircled about by the everlasting chains of death."

"And now, behold, *when I thought this, I could remember my pains no more*; yea, I was harrowed up by the memory of my sins no more."

"And oh, what *joy*, and what marvelous light I did behold; yea, my soul was *filled with joy* as exceeding as was my pain!"

"Yea, I say unto you, my son, that *there could be nothing so exquisite and so bitter as were my pains.* Yea, and again I say unto you, my son, that on the other hand, *there can be nothing so exquisite and sweet as was my joy."* (Mosiah 27:28-29; Alma 36:12-21; **Italics added to emphasize stored memory being utilized**)

Other scriptures are very clear on the power of retrieval of a flood of memories when placed in a position to account for one's life:

"The spirit and the body shall be reunited again in its perfect form; both limb and joint shall be restored to its proper frame, even as we now are at this time; and we shall be brought to stand before God, *knowing even as we know now, and have a bright recollection of all our guilt."* (Alma 11:43; Italics for emphasis)

Of this certainty, Elder D. Kelly Ogden taught:

"Each of us will stand before our Father and look into His divine eyes and report on what we have done with this brief moment of time. We will all have photographic memories (and instant recall!), a perfect recollection of all we've done on earth—and that perfect awareness will either send us into deep despair and remorse or fill us with happiness and gratitude. It is up to us. We will all live forever—no exceptions." (BYU Devotional, June 25, 2013)

Many thousands of people that have had near-death experiences speak candidly about "their lives flashing before their eyes." These scriptures and anecdotal experiences all speak to the truth of our learning being cumulative and associative.

We Learn Through:

1. Association – Learning cannot take place unless associations are occurring in our neural networks (Recall: The definition of learning is when two neurons connect). There are several regions of the brain that do different tasks, which without much conscious effort, work together to interpret our environment. Depending on what regions are being stimulated will directly influence how that event is interpreted. For example, when we yell at our children we activate their "fight and flight" system, which is directly wired for survival. Therefore if we are

trying to teach a child to change his or her behavior, it will be less effective when we turn on their survival instincts. A child that is consistently yelled at, lectured to, abused, threatened and harshly punished will be wired to learn completely differently than a child that is being corrected through gentleness, patience and firmness. It is substantially more likely that the former child will have a difficult time concentrating and will believe that the he or she is to a degree worthless.

Another example of associative learning may occur when a child takes the personal responsibility to complete a task (i.e., academic assignment, chore, creative design, etc.). The associations of positive feedback, self-pride, the joy of completing a difficult project, and increasing confidence in one's ability, become associated in the child's learning that he or she will have the increased capacity to complete future tasks. Much of that feedback is being associated through the limbic – prefrontal cortex circuitry.

2. Repetition – (Is this why parents nag?) The more we observe a particular subject, concept, experience, principle or interaction, the stronger the association of that experience becomes. This process reinforces and reintegrates the same circuitry, therefore we strengthen that circuitry. The stronger the circuits become the easier it is to recall information. But what most do not realize is that "the moment of forgetting" and then being reintroduced to the same experience, the same problem, etc.; that type of learning becomes much more entrenched. All of the neurological underpinnings of learning and memory consist of cellular networks that grow stronger every time a memory is recalled; every time we have to think about something again. Therefore, forgetting (giving yourself a break) is actually a useful mechanism in developing greater memory. So take a break, go daydream, go for a walk, take a quick nap, and when you come back to look at that material again, it will be easier to store and recall.

3. Observation – We can learn by simply observing. Other's mistakes or successes help us understand how the world works. We also can observe our own experiences and learn from them. The brain also has the unique quality to observe itself. This quality can lead to ongoing adjustments in brainwave activity to assist in experiencing life more abundantly.

4. Pain – Pain is a very effective teacher. Pain is not limited to physical sensations. Pain is felt when we lose something important, or it may be as simple as embarrassment. As we go through life we each experience pain and most of us then work hard to avoid future pain by changing our behavioral choices. Sin is pain!

5. Reward – Getting something desirable is also an effective teacher. External rewards are usually what we think of in this category, however, it is the internal rewards that lead to the development of confidence, self-motivation, etc.

6. Study and Faith (It is good to be human!) – Unique to us as humans is the ability to learn through symbolic reasoning. Symbolic reasoning develops as we get older and it is the very means by which we both communicate and translate information. I have always said to my own children, if you can read, you can do anything. It is through the process of being read to, and later, reading ourselves that we learn. What we fill our heads with has a great deal to do with what our circumstances end up being. It is through acquired (correct) knowledge that we obtain the power to act and not be acted upon. We then use the principle and power of faith to act based upon our acquired learning. The counsel THAT SAYS:

> "And as all have not faith, seek ye diligently and teach one another words of wisdom; yea, seek ye out of the best books words of wisdom; seek learning, even by study and also by faith.... Study and learn and become acquainted with all good books, and with languages, tongues and people... And as all have not faith, seek ye diligently and teach one another words of wisdom; yea, seek ye out of the best books words of wisdom, seek learning even by study and also by faith." (D&C 88:118; 90:15; 109:7) is dead-on accurate.

Our experiences with reading, our viewing of someone else's experience through literature, our observation of other's responses to varying circumstances, contribute to shaping our own reactions and our own experiences in real life. The best books provide the basis to develop rationally and emotionally. What we fill our head with become the resources we utilize when meeting life's challenges.

A Few Thoughts on Using the Less Than Optimal Mode of Learning Too Much

When I was in college, I had the opportunity to teach rats how to run a maze. I worked with fellow students using two methods to achieve the goal. These two methods were then compared to determine which was most effective. The two methods were REWARD and PAIN as highlighted in # 4 and #5 above.

The design of any maze is to provide options of which way to turn. In a general sense, and certainly in the case of the mazes we were operating with, there was only one way to get from the start to the finish. Any wrong turn in that process would have had the rat end up in a dead end.

By using a desired food reward, we conditioned the first group of rats to make correct choices until they were able to run the maze from beginning to end without any mistakes. Likewise, by using pain (electrical shocks) the other group of rats also learned to run the maze correctly in order to avoid pain.

One way of measuring the effectiveness of our design was to compare time trials between the two interventions. I am happy to say that the rats that were trained by reward were quicker in their time trial as compared to their counterparts that ran the maze in order to avoid pain. Hopefully that says something about focusing on the positive in our children rather than the negative in order to get the desired results. I believe that the rats that were trained by avoiding pain likely experienced greater stress and therefore impacted their ability to focus – that is just my theory, after all, I didn't speak rat!

Another finding of these two groups was to determine extinction rates, in other words, over a period of time, how permanent had the learning become. We removed the rats from the maze for three weeks. Every rat, both the reward trained rats and the pain avoidance trained rats made mistakes when reintroduced to the mazes. Between the two groups, there were more rats that were able to complete the maze, with fewer mistakes that had been trained through reward rather than pain.

Now I know these are rats and that they do not possess the impressive neo-cortex of a human, yet I still think there are some applications here, 1st) while reward and pain approaches are effective, they appear to have limited effectiveness in long term recall; and 2nd) the positive approach appears to be the better of the two.

Many of us as parents focus on either REWARD or PAIN approaches to having our children learn. I hope that the findings of the experiment might impress upon your mind that such approaches used exclusively will have limitations in trying to achieve what we are trying to influence in our children's personal belief systems.

RESPONSIBILITY – WHO'S IS IT?

As a parent, you are in the business of training a belief system. It is important to ask the question, "What do I want my child to believe about him or herself?" The *'what'* does not have much purpose unless you can also answer effectively, "Why do I want my child to believe that about him or herself?" May I caution here, that if the *'why'* is not big enough, the *'how'* to get to the *'what'* doesn't really matter. May I also add, the only thing preventing the desired outcome is what is in ours and our children's heads!

The starting point of developing this healthy, truthful belief system is demonstrating that what you want your child to believe in is what you already believe about them. For those of us that have an eternal perspective, this should already be in place. The notion that we are children of the Highest (Psalm 82:1,6; John 10:34-35; Romans 8:16), imprints upon our mind the potential invested in each of our children.

In large measure, our children will learn of their capacity because of our long term view of them. That long term view assists us as parents in organizing our daily thoughts and behaviors to bring about that eternal view into full realization. In this regard, I am reminded of the hymn, "We are Sowing Daily Sowing," wherein the lyricist has us look closely at the impact of our daily interactions:

"We are sowing, daily sowing
Countless seeds of good and ill....."

"Seeds that lie unchanged , unquickened,
Lifeless on the teeming mold;
Seeds that live and grow and flourish
when the sower's hand is cold."

"By a whisper sow we blessings, by a breath we scatter strife. In our
words and thoughts and actions lie the seeds of death and life."
(LDS Hymn Book, Hymn # 216)

As we sow daily we should do so with the long view in mind. For example, developing early on - spiritual habits that become an anchor to our children such as family prayer and scripture study. Too many times we decide to forego these consistent behaviors early in our children's lives because we may not see any real benefit when our children are so young. Sometimes, the hassle of occupying attention may convince us that this part of family development is better suited when children are more mature.

Far-off seeing parents make decisions on what is best for their children later in life, not what may be the easiest for the family now. Such prophetic parenting prepares the

228

foundation of what is best to do now so that later their children will have access to firm assistance later.

Unseeing parents can easily get trapped in what will make the family appear better now or what may be easiest in the short term. Parents getting caught in the trap of doing the child's projects or homework is an example of short-sighted parenting. Children's ability to plan, execute, problem solve and creating a mind of learning develop due to their being responsible, not due to the parent's taking over.

Children have the capacity to detect our motivation for doing things. If the motivation is other than helping the child in developing his or her potential, children begin to manipulate the unproductive motive in order to avoid responsibility. The most powerful way to get our children to see the long view is by being an example of what we want them to become.

Learning is the responsibility of the child. This truth ties in with previous concepts of child development and task mastery. The growing belief that one is capable develops from mastering the demands of industry, for example.

I met with a mother one evening who pleaded for my help regarding her son. I inquired what the matter was and she informed me that her son was suspended from playing football due to his grades falling below the required GPA. Not understanding her concern (as the consequence seemed reasonable), I came to find out that this mother had done everything for her son, e.g., provided money for dating, bought his Jeep, paid for his cell phone and even allowed him to sleep-over with his girlfriend. According to mom, the only thing that her son was responsible for was to maintain the minimum GPA so that he could play sports.

Her motive was to ensure that her son, upon making it as a professional athlete, would in turn take care of her the rest of her life. Her 'why' was not big enough, thus preventing the 'what' she wanted her child to believe about himself, and her son manipulated this unproductive motive..

Well, I would say that about the only thing that son learned about himself, was that he could manipulate his mother, that he was entitled and that he had no real sense of confidence as he had everything provided for him.

As parents, we are in the business of training. Love and Reason are not enough! I have met many parents that spend countless hours trying to reason with their children. They will spend an hour or two talking with them about why they should do something a certain way. Sometimes I will ask these parents in a funny way, "After having this long discussion, did you hear your child stand up, place their hands on their hips and declare – 'Wow mom, wow dad, I am so lucky to have you as parents. You are both so wise. I am now going to go out and do it differently?" They just look at me and smile!

229

Learning comes from the struggles and successes. That's what builds character, integrity, desire, self-confidence, a sense of responsibility and endurance. Our wisdom is our own – our children need to gain theirs. So, our responsibility in our children's learning is to allow our children to make choices and experience the outcomes of those choices. We should not be in the business of saving or removing our children too early from the impact of their choices. By doing so impedes learning. We as parents are also responsible for teaching our children principles that will assist them in gaining wisdom; social skills (good manners included) that will allow them to develop and maintain healthy relationships; and emotional regulation so they can make good decisions, focus and not become overwhelmed.

Their responsibility is to be accountable to their choices, and make better decisions based upon that learning. Theirs is the responsibility to recognize the connection between choices and outcomes. Theirs is the responsibility to learn how to earn, to learn that 'stick-to-it-ness' mentality that will result in favorable outcomes. Theirs is to learn to ask for help when needed and develop a healthy support system that provides emotional support during the struggle. Theirs is to learn the appropriate social skills that enable the development of true intimacy. Theirs is to learn that things do not make much of us. We are not happy because of what we possess, but because of who we are.

Our children's environment needs to be rich with opportunity – Garden of Eden – What good did it serve? It was not until the expulsion that Adam and Eve began to acquire the confidence, skills, etc. that allowed them to teach their children correctly and acquire the skills to provide for themselves. It was through their work ethic and experience that their identity was maturely formed.

EMOTIONAL TIME WARPING

Emotional growth occurs with learning responsibility. When we do too much for our children their emotional development stops. So, while they may end up looking like mature teenagers, in reality they are stuck emotionally at a much younger age – in essence we have time warped them.

Problems are directly related to age. The problems become increasingly difficult as we get older. What a child is supposed to learn at age two directly assists him or her at three years old; and so on. However, if we begin to rescue our child we impede aspects of their development. This is what is meant by sending them into a time warp.

An easy example of what this may look like is when our child loses something, or our child does not take proper care of things. Many parents would just choose to replace the item. This approach impedes the child in understanding of the invested effort that was required to trade for the value of the possession. Such a child cannot develop a healthy sense of caring for things, because things just simply get replaced. The same with chores or home responsibilities - if not learned, children will not learn basic life skills and find themselves at a disadvantage when it is time to be on their own. This will feel like a time warp as they grapple with learning how to manage things that should have been developed long before. Military or other real life experiences (i.e., going away to college; getting married, etc.) become a culture shock for kids that have never learned personal responsibility.

Addictions, especially those related to substance use are incredibly devastating on a child's emotional development. I once had a client that grew up in an environment of wealth. There was nothing that Brandon asked for that he did not get. Brandon never had to work for anything. His free time became a time to begin experimenting with drugs and alcohol. At the young age of 13, Brandon was already a regular consumer of these mind altering substances. Because he was never required to do anything and because his parents would continually bail him out, Brandon never emotionally developed beyond that of a seven year old. Though 16, he never learned to apply himself in school, therefore when he should have been trying to "master industry" he was still doing what 3-6 year olds do – play, play, play. It made complete sense to me that Brandon acted more like a seven year old.

I believe this is one of the reasons why addiction was so difficult for him. Brandon recognized that he did not share the same abilities as other children his age – he did not feel as accomplished or capable. Addiction numbed these uncomfortable feelings, but simultaneously kept him stuck emotionally. Drugs interfere with emotional development. His environment was replete with opportunity to not try, to not experience challenges; to not learn.

If we are the type of parent that loves too much, reasons too much, does too much and saves too much in relation to our children, we are not sending the right messages and are interfering with developing a healthy belief system. If we wait too long, it gets more difficult. Our power to influence becomes greatly diminished.

RESPONSIBILITY – CREATING THE NEED

> Children have to be educated, but they have also to be left to educate themselves. ~Abbé Dimnet, *Art of Thinking*, 1928

When I was younger, I wandered into my sister's room. I didn't have any objective, but in my tinkering, I opened her top desk drawer and inside was some money. I took five dollars from the stash, headed to "Stop & Go" and proceeded to buy myself some candy – lots of candy. When my supply had dwindled, I thought to myself how easy it was the first time to get the money and since no one seemed to have missed the original amount, I ventured into my sister's room again. Some time had passed and my stash was getting low; again no mention of the missing money was being spoken about, so I invested in my system again.

That night at the dinner table, my luck had run out. My parents questioned if anyone knew about the missing $15. My non-verbal language gave me away and soon I was facing the firing squad. After my parents taught me about the principle of honesty, which included not stealing, they told me that I was going to have to go out and earn the money to repay my sister. They also stated that things like watching college football, Gilligan's Island or other T.V. shows was suspended, as well as any extra-curricular activities until I had paid back the money.

The next day I went to the shed, pulled out our push mower and some edging shears and started knocking on neighbor's doors. There is no way to verify this, but I strongly suspect that my mother called ahead to each of the neighbors, because it was really difficult to negotiate any good financial arrangement (and sometimes not at all), in order to get this ball rolling and get my life back to normal.

At the Long's door I asked if I could cut their yard to earn some money. Mr. Long asked how much I charged. I thought to myself – let's make this process easy, "15 dollars," I answered. Mr. Long replied, "I think it is worth $2 dollars. Do you want to do it?" What choice did I have, I had no negotiating power. I needed money because I *needed* my life back.

As I went around the neighborhood, I was mostly met with "No's," and it took me close to three weeks to earn that money back. Obviously a lot of life lessons learned in the process, but the purpose of the story was to highlight that my personal responsibility kicked into higher gear because of the *need* my parent's created in my life.

As has been indicated before, we are a wealthy society and "things" are much easier to come by. It seems as if the only thing the child needs to do nowadays, to put forth any effort in taking care of individual needs and wants is to just ask and we parents get busy saving, solving and buying. I know families where children don't even have to ask, they just hint, i.e., "I'm hungry," and the parents start ordering pizza.

Well it is time to look at the messages that are sent by that type of parenting along with the corresponding belief systems being developed. It doesn't look pretty. My suggestion is that we begin to look at the requests our children are making of us and begin to give them part ownership in obtaining what they want.

When my children hint of things that they want – I tell them what I did when I was their age. I told them that I began by having a neighborhood paper route and then graduated to assisting with a very large car route. I also washed cars, mowed lawns, did some landscaping and other small jobs – all for the purpose of having money. I bought most of my clothes from 8th grade on. I want my children to have ownership in what they want to buy and what they want to do. Sometimes I pay a percentage, especially if it is a bigger ticket item, but for the most part I tell them "If you want it bad enough you can earn it," I then let go. Most of the time children get busy working because their need is not being met by the parent's resources.

In this approach, I also take the time to listen to what they are experiencing as a result of working for something. I have yet to hear any complaints about the joy and sense of accomplishment they express as part of the process. In other words, they like themselves and believe that they are capable of doing much for themselves.

A FEW EFFECTIVE SKILLS IN CREATING THE NEED

There are some things we can do to get the environment of need revved up in our children. Here are a few effective skills in doing so:

1) Reframing to have children buy in – What do they want? What do you want? Set up token economy, needs to be fun, needs to be doable.

   If my intention as a parent is to instill the belief of capability within my child, then I myself have to have a clear portrait of how such a belief is developed. So many of us sell ourselves short of what we can or cannot do. In large measure, the interfering mechanism of developing greater capacity is our unwillingness to try. Usually some level of fear and doubt is telling us "don't try" and obviously I am going to point out once again that such fears are related to our implicit memories. Even if a child demonstrates that their inability is related to a character flaw, like laziness, such character flaws are still part of one's core belief.

   As children develop, we teach capability by showing our children how to do things. Working alongside our children provides some level of motivation for them and allows us the opportunity to provide feedback on how well they are doing. As time proceeds and the child demonstrates competency, the parent can expect the child to perform the tasks without close supervision. In time, our children learn that everyone in the family works alongside one another in sharing household duties, and fulfilling their responsibilities to the family.

   When mom and dad model this concept, by themselves taking care of their personal responsibilities, it provides an example and expectation for the rest of the family.

   For some reason, there are those children who have a hard time making connections between having their needs met and the prerequisite work in order to do so. The calculations we consider in teaching capability are as follows:

- If "it" is simply given = ENTITLEMENT
- If we create a need = DEVELOPS OWNERSHIP
- When a child develops ownership = CAPABILITY

If we find our children are presenting with a sense of entitlement, then reframing their attitude through a token economy can be very useful. A token economy can be used for:

- Changing attitude and family culture
- Single behaviors we are trying to encourage or extinguish
- When a child does not demonstrate personal responsibility
- When we are trying to teach and prepare our children for the real world

CHANGING ATTITUDE AND FAMILY CULTURE

Sometime families will find themselves in a funk. Maybe there is too much negativity, complaining when asked to do something, sibling rivalry, and responsibilities being completed in a less than stellar manner.

This is a good time to call the family together and announce that mom and dad want to take the family to (let's say) Disneyland. As the children begin to express their excitement and begin to ask when – dad chimes in and says, "As soon as we are ready to be at the happiest place on earth" (for those that did not know 'the happiest place on earth' is the slogan for Disneyland)! Dad continues:

Dad: "You know, I'm not sure any of us would really enjoy Disneyland right at this moment because we are not the happiest people. I want to make sure that when we are there, that we have the right frame of mind and attitude to make it enjoyable for everyone."

Mom: Yes, we have noticed that when you are asked to do something that your attitude sours, or you complain, or become critical with one another. Would you say those are examples of happiness?

Children (in unison): No.

Mom: I have also noticed that your regular responsibilities around the house have been done in such a way that has had me call you back to do it correctly. Is that right also?

Children: Yeah, sometimes.

Dad: Well that is what mom and I have discussed and we think it is time to get away as a family to refresh and renew ourselves, but if we are going to go to Disneyland, we can't go with our current family culture.

Mom: So let's lay it out for you. In order for us to go to Disneyland, the family has to earn 50,000 points. Here is how we are going to earn them.

Sample Chart – Disneyland Trip (50,000 Points)

Desired Behavior	Point Value	S	M	T	W	TH	F	S
Doing things without complaining	200	II			II	I		III
Doing chores correctly	100		II	I	I	II		I
Positive sibling interaction	300	III	I				I	
Doing things without being asked	200		I		II		I	
	1st Week Totals	1600	600	100	900	400	500	700
After the first week, erase the chicken scratch and start again	2nd Week Totals	1200	700	600	400			200
Repeat	3rd Week Totals	1000	300		300	600		900
Repeat	4th Week Totals	800	1000	400			400	
First Month's Totals	13,600	4600	2600	1100	1600	1000	900	1800
Points to Go	36400							
At This Rate It Will Take Us (In Weeks) To Go To Disneyland	10 More Weeks							

When the children see the bottom line, you can expect that they will pick up the pace from the first four weeks. They will recognize that the speed it takes to get their faster lies in their power.

Just some brief counsel on the sample chart. 1) Try to frame the behaviors you are trying to encourage and shape in a positive manner. In other words, focus on the behaviors you want, instead of the behaviors you do not want. 2) You don't want to make it too easy and so you will have to consider the size of your family when assigning points to the desired behaviors. This process will be less effective if the children can earn the reward too quickly. Remember, we are having them practice the behaviors we want them to use. The more practice, the more likely they will stick. 3) Never take points away as this will become discouraging. If they do not do well one day, it will simply take at least one more day to obtain the desired outcome. 4) Parents are in control of recording the progress. If a child would like to report a desired behavior that the parents did not see, that is allowed. 5) Keep the record on a white board. It makes it easier when it is time to erase the previous week's totals. 6) Place the higher points on the most desired behaviors.

Your children will become highly attuned to this chart. The older children who are able to calculate will likely mentor the younger children. You will see a whole new buzz within your children's attitudes.

Now, this process is not very effective if we are not observing for our children their emotions in relation to their experiences. We have already spoken about this concept in the Chapter – Functional vs. Dysfunctional, under Item #1. It is going to be addressed again in greater depth when we discuss Emotions in a few short pages from now. Just recall, that when our children are able to connect their experiences (i.e. behaviors) with their emotions, they are far more likely to retain the behaviors that bring positive feelings. It is our job as the parent to help observe this for our children otherwise the lesson may be lost.

As we draw near to the date of going to Disneyland, it would be helpful to sit down together as a family and have a discussion similar to the following:

Dad: Mom and I want each of you to know that we have noticed your tremendous efforts to prepare our family attitudes to go to Disneyland. Just a short 2-1/2 months ago, we didn't think we were ready to go to the happiest place on earth because we were not the happiest people on earth.

Mom: Yes, dad and I have noticed how much more positive and happy everyone is feeling. Do you like these feelings of happiness?

Children (in unison): Yes – (with a bit of laughter)

Mom: How did we get to feeling so happy?

Child: We did things without complaining, we did our chores correctly, we were nicer to each other and every once and a while we did things that we saw needing to be done without being asked.

Dad: That's correct. Do you really believe that by doing those things will continue to bring happiness?

Children: Yes!

Dad: Well mom and I have another surprise, an added bonus. For every time you did something without being asked, we kept track. We are going to give $10 to whoever did this behavior for every time they did it.

Children (smiling and squirming with excitement): OOOHH!

Mom: Yes, and the other bonus is, if you are able to continue practicing these new behaviors while we are at Disneyland, then we would also like to take you to Sea World, instead of coming back home after our three days at Disneyland.

Children (some excited screams being heard): Yeah! Alright: I'm so excited!

Dad: We hope that we never go back to the old ways. I know that I feel happier and I like this feeling. Hopefully you feel the same way.

Mom and the Children: We do!

SINGLE BEHAVIORS WE ARE TRYING TO ENCOURAGE OR EXTINGUISH

One complaint I hear frequently from mothers is in relation to their daughter's clothing being left all over the place. My advice to such mom's is to sit down with their daughter and have a conversation like the following:

Mom: Natalie, I am going to present something to you that may on its appearances seem as an idle threat. After all, I have nagged and bugged you and then have given in time and time again. But I am determined this time to follow through.

I am no longer going to nag or threaten you about your clothes. But before I proceed, I want to make sure that you are clear on the expectations. What have you been told about your clothes?

Natalie: Dirty clothes are to be in the laundry room, divided into whites, colors and darks and put in those respective baskets. Clean clothes are supposed to be either hanging or folded and put into drawers.

Mom: Sounds like you got it.

Natalie: Well now what?

Mom: Nothing else, I just wanted to make sure that you understood the expectation.

At this point, I instruct mom, whenever she sees any of Natalie's clothes out of place to simply remove those items and place them somewhere out of Natalie's awareness. In time, Natalie is going to be looking for something she wants to wear that she can't find. When she asks mom about it, I simply have mom reply with a question, "Where did you last place it?"

This places the responsibility back onto Natalie. It becomes an observing moment for mom, so that Natalie increases her own awareness of the behaviors that lead to the frustration of not finding things. Natalie may suspect that mom has taken the item, but is not likely to make a big deal about it. Perhaps she will begin to take greater interest in keeping her clothing so as to avoid having anything else go missing. That interest is likely to wane however, because of Natalie's poorly formed habit of not being responsible for her clothing.

As time goes on, and this may be four months down the road (depending upon the amount of clothes Natalie has), Natalie will recognize that she is running out of clothes. The telling moment is when Natalie recognizes that her underclothing is down to just a few items. It will be at this point that Natalie will come to talk about her dilemma. At this point, mom informs Natalie that she can earn her clothes back. It may look something like this:

Sample Chart – Clothes Buying

Desired Behavior	Point Value	S	M	T	W	TH	F	S
Clothes sorted in laundry room daily	15	I	I	I	I	I	I	I
Closets neat and tidy	30			I	I	I		
Fold laundry and put clothes away on laundry day	50		I			I		
Drawers are neat and orderly	30	I	I	I	I		I	I
At the end of each week she may buy her clothes back	Daily Totals	45	95	75	75	95	45	45
Weekly Total	475							
Clothing Item	**Cost**							
Underwear	25	3						
Bra	50	1						
Socks	35	1						
T-Shirt	15							
Blouse	45							
Other Shirts	50							
Belt	35							
Jeans	85	1						

Other Pants	65								
Accessories (i.e. ear rings)	25								
Dress	75								
Skirt	45								
Undershirt	10								
Pajamas	15								
Purse	75								
Hair Accessory (i.e., hat)	20	1							
Shorts	50	2							
Shoes/Sandals	100	1							
Sweater	50								
Coat	75								
Jacket	75								
Sweatshirt	50								
Gym Clothes (this can be a set)	50								

Based upon the example, Natalie was able to spend $465 of the $475 she earned that week. By her seeing the cost of the clothes she is likely step-it-up in the coming week in order to get more of her clothes back.

This approach should have her more invested in her responsibility toward her clothes in the future. Knowing how hard it is to earn the clothes should help her remember to do the right thing daily.

One of the caveats I would put into place is that she is required to earn all of her clothes back before any new shopping takes place. In addition, I would inform Natalie that she has to keep her clothes out of hawk for a period of six months and if she does then she has earned a shopping spree.

WHEN A CHILD DOES NOT DEMONSTRATE PERSONAL RESPONSIBILITY

Don't forget the formula for developing the need - Reframing to have children buy in – What do they want? What do you want? Set up token economy, needs to be fun, needs to be doable.

FIRST EXAMPLE

Let's say that our teen son wants to go to basketball camp in the summer, but is resistant in keeping his room up to expected standards:

239

Sample Chart – Basketball Camp (20,000 Points)

Desired Behavior	Point Value	S	M	T	W	TH	F	S
Laundry folded and put away	50		I			I		
Drawers neat and tidy	150		I			I		I
Bed made	25	I	I	I	I	I	I	
Floor clear	50		I	I	I		I	
Dusted weekly	250				I			
Vacuumed weekly	250				I			
Dirty laundry in the hamper	100	I		I	I			I
Window opened to air out room	75	I		I	I	I		I
	1st Week Totals	200	275	250	750	300	75	325
After the first week, erase the chicken scratch and start again	2nd Week Totals	200	250	350	750	200	125	0
Repeat	3rd Week Totals	200	250	0	750	250	250	100
Repeat	4th Week Totals	300	300	125	750	100	100	100
First Month's Totals	7,625	900	1075	725	3000	850	550	525
Points to Go	12,375							
At This Rate It Will Take You (In Weeks) To Earn Basketball Camp	10-1/2 More Weeks							

Because your teen son really wants to attend camp, he may recognize that he needs to do more each week to make sure he earns enough in time.

Again, just like the Disneyland example, we want to notice the feelings associated with his behaviors. What might someone feel that has a tidy room compared to an untidy room? Would they find by doing just a little bit each day makes their life easier?

SECOND EXAMPLE

Perhaps your child is struggling in doing her best academically. One way to get her to be more responsible is to have her carry a "Daily Progress Note" (DPN) with her to school. The DPN provides for almost real time updates (at least daily) for your child. It is another form of "observing" that comes directly from the teachers – not you as the parents.

I would recommend that there be a 3-ring binder kept at the side kitchen counter. Every school day, your child is responsible for taking a blank form with her to school. If there are any classes that are left blank and not signed by the teacher's initials, then the child forfeits all of the point for the week. At the end of the week, the sheet(s) are to be placed back in the 3-ring binder in chronological order, so that it is easy for the parent to review the child's recording. This may be what it looks like:

Daily Progress Note (DPN)

Name: _____ Date(s): _____
Please rate this child/teen in each of the areas listed below according to how he/she performed in school today, using ratings of 1 to 5. (1=Excellent; 2=Good; 3=Fair; 4=Poor, 5=Unsatisfactory). If any of the areas did not pertain to the day's reporting, then please place a / in that box. For example, maybe there is no homework due on the day you are filling out the report – just put a / in that box for that day. Some helps:

Homework – We are not providing points based upon the quality of the homework. Points are awarded based upon having the assignment done and turned in on the correct day. If the homework is late, then you will likely choose a number other than 1.

Class Participation – Was the child involved in discussions, group work, or demonstrations

Class Work – Working on assignments during class period as opposed to wasting time.

Asks For Help – This is a skill that every child should learn. Did this child ask for help today?

Peer Interactions – Positive/Negative spectrum.

	Class Period					
	1	2	3	4	5	6
Subjects	History		Science	Math		Language Arts
Homework						
Class Participation						
Class Work						
Asks For Help						
Peer Interactions						
Teacher's Initials						
Point Total						

Spending Points:			Example of Activities
1 = 5 Points			2 = ½ hour of television
2 = 2 Points			2 = 1 hour playing outside
3 = 1 Point			3 = Being w/ a friend for an hour
4 and 5 = 0 Points			2 = ½ hour of gaming
			4 = IPOD on Saturday
Points Used (#)/Activity:			10 = Sporting Events
1.	4.	7.	10 = Night Games
2.	5.	8.	15 = Staying Out late
3	6.	9.	300 = Magic Mountain

On the bottom are activities that your child has stated that she wants to be able to do. As you can see, there are points attached to the activities and therefore your daughter now has options of what is most important to her and provides her with the challenge of prioritizing.

There is also a place to record the activities she decides to do and a record of how many points she has used in comparison to points earned. You will notice that there is one big activity listed on the sheet. That is there because your daughter chose that as something she would really like to do. The DPN allows for points to be rolled over every week, meaning that any unused points accumulate. While she may use some of the points to do activities during the week, she is also keeping her eye on the big event and will likely learn how to save for that day.

As with all of the token economy approaches, remember, we are not striving to motivate our child through external rewards. We are using the external rewards in order to produce conversations where the child becomes aware of his or her internal experience. As we assist our child through the process of observation to recognize the benefits with newly learned principles or behaviors, he or she will begin valuing the feelings associated with such and more likely choose the better part more consistently.

WHEN WE ARE TRYING TO TEACH AND PREPARE OUR CHILDREN FOR THE REAL WORLD

I think one very important area to focus on in preparing your children for the real world is having them learn how to handle money, including learning how to delay gratification, living well within his or her means, rendering to Caesar, that which is Caesar's and to God, that which is God's (Mark 12:17), saving for important events, and saving for a rainy day. Here are just a few comments on each:

Delaying Gratification – Credit is easy to get and difficult to pay-off. I want my children to obtain credit and even use a credit card, but to do so in a manner that doesn't extend them beyond 30 days. If I use my credit card to purchase gas, pay my cell phone, buy groceries, etc, it is important that I also pay off that credit card bill each month. I would recommend that a credit card that earns points for air miles or some other benefit be utilized.

If my child desires something that may take a month or more of saving and he or she does so, I may be interested in providing for some of the cost to reward the wise handling of resources.

Living Well Within Means – I want my children to learn to avoid living pay check-to-paycheck. I want them to learn about compound interest and how living simply can provide for great future financial rewards. In a moment I will talk about rendering to the government and God, but surely the idea that I want to pay an honest tithe and be in a position to contribute to offerings is to be considered in deciding what it means to live within one's means. Let's say that I want to contribute 15% of my income to church, 10% to me (personal savings), and 50% to living requirements. That means I have kept in reserve 25% that can go into rainy day and important events savings.

This approach provides for peace of mind and will lead to greater happiness in the homes they will establish.

Rendering To Caesar – If there is any way that my child can form a business, which allows for the possibility of tax deductions, I believe this is a good vehicle for keeping more of what we make. My daughter had a window washing business, which allowed her to write-off supplies, marketing, mileage/gas, work clothes, etc. While she had a regular paying job, where taxes were deducted from each check, her side business allowed her to receive more back in refunds than if she had just had W4 employment.

Rendering To God – All that we have is His. All that He asks is that we pay an honest tithe, no matter what and a generous offering as we are able. It is unwise to deal with God other than on His terms. He has promised an increase if we are willing (Malachi 3:10-12).

Of this financial wisdom, President Spencer W. Kimball once said:

> "The Lord herein makes clear that tithing is his law and is required of all his followers. It is our honor and privilege, our safety and promise, our great blessing to live this law of God. To fail to meet this obligation in full is to deny ourselves the promises and is to omit a weighty matter. It is a transgression, not an inconsequential oversight." ("President Kimball Speaks Out on Tithing," *New Era*, Apr. 1981, 6)

Saving For Important Events – Missions, schooling, and vacations all fall within this category.

Saving For A Rainy Day – Putting something away for the unexpected can make the difference between being destitute and stranded, or still at financial peace and a way to get home.

As my child demonstrates their willingness to learn and apply these financial strategies, I may take the opportunity to match some of what they did for themselves. And while my gesture may excite them, that excitement will not be as important as their own feelings associated with such wise management.

There is a big difference in the feelings associated with financial stress as compared to financial security. There will be no difficulty in having your children internalize the value of this real world lesson.

3 ASPECTS REQUIRED FOR CHANGE TO OCCUR

When anybody approaches the subject of change, there are three steps that we go through in order to have the outcomes we desire. These are as follows:

Awareness – We must have some understanding that our current way of doing things is not bringing the level of satisfaction we hope for. This could be in the form of bad habits, reacting to our implicit memory, lack of achievement, or even our negative way of looking at things. Awareness is largely an intellectual observation.

Commitment – If any change is going to occur, we must be committed to the interventions necessary in order to have change occur. As we consider what needs to take place, we are using mental affirmation of those needed changes in order to prepare ourselves for the place real change occurs.

Action – Awareness and commitment are not enough. Action is what internalizes change. We each possess the remarkable ability to change – but what prevents us into action is usually the very thing we are trying to overcome, e.g., fear, character defects such as laziness, etc. Action makes the difference between success and failure. "The secret of getting things done is to act." Dante Aligheri

AS SOON AS

Too many parents grapple at how to get their children to be involved in upkeep, like keeping their rooms cleaned, or their bathroom, being more organized, etc. If you didn't start your children early in teaching them the skills of personal responsibility of such things, and now are resorting to nagging or throwing the towel in and doing it yourself, this simple phrase, "As soon as" will work wonders.

Your children want to do things. When a child comes and asks their parent if they can go to the football game Friday night, far too many parents look at the situation as an opportunity to punish (i.e., "No you can't go because you have not kept your room clean). Such parents miss the grand opportunity to leverage the child's wishes.

In the case of the football game, a couple of approaches come to mind. 1) The parent may on the spot reply, "Yes, you may go to the game *as soon as* your room is completely in order" or 2) "I know how much you look forward to being with your friends on Friday night, going to the football games and such and I want you to go as well. However, your ability to have that occur is dependent upon your personal responsibility in keeping your room up. *As long as* (a form of "as soon as") you have kept your room fairly organized and clean each day, then that privilege is yours.

Please parents, recognize the grand opportunity your children are passing to you when they announce they want something. You can tie almost anything to that desire. Think about all of the possibilities, "As soon as you paint the house you can go," "As soon as you finish the laundry you can go," "As soon as you wash my car you can go." The opportunities are limitless.

EMPOWERING YOUR CHILDREN THROUGH

REFLECTIVE LISTENING – This method simply reflects back to the child what was heard; it does not engage in further connection or provide solutions.

Human design creates the ability for any of us to be aware of someone else's brains. Our brains and our children's brains are constructed to be directly influenced by each other, which is the reason why our children don't have to hardly ask for anything. Our sense of their needs or wants, in some mysterious way, becomes known to us and we begin to act to meet those needs and wants.

The problem develops when this becomes the consistent pattern, especially as children mature. Our children become so used to our mind reading and nurturing behavior that they come to expect that to be the norm. Unfortunately, it likely does not prepare them for the real world and stifles other relational skills that lead to our children obtaining what they want or need.

For example, a child may say, "These shoes are wearing out." The parent responds by saying, "Well, let's hop in the car and go get some new ones." You'll notice in this dialogue that the child really never expresses what they want because the parent is so programmed to take care of the child.

What we are teaching our children is to rely on someone else to meet their needs and wants without fully asking. I have watched many children sit in class, confused, lost, and uncertain. So many of these children never learn to take care of themselves by *asking for help* because they are so programmed to have someone respond to their quietness, their withdrawal; and their non-verbal distress. These children send the signals out hoping that someone will notice and then get busy helping them. I am not sure that is an effective means of getting through tough challenges.

By being merely reflective will cause confusion and perhaps frustration in your child. That is because their relational brain is hoping (based upon past experience) that the parent's relational brain will get busy supplying the needs or wants being hinted at. When we don't, it will finally have the child perform the task of "asking." Following is an example:

Child: Mom, I'm starved

Mom: It sounds like your hungry honey? (Mom then doesn't say anything else; while the child pauses waiting for mother to get busy getting something to eat for the child. When mother does not respond beyond the reflective statement, the child continues);

Child: Mom, didn't you hear me?

Mother: Of course dear, did you not hear what I said?

Child: Yes, you said that "I sounded hungry."

Mother: That's right dear. (Mother then becomes quiet again; again the child anxiously waits for mother to do what she normally does – but mother does not respond)

Child: What's up with you mom? How come you are not responding?

Mother: What do you mean?

Child: I said that I am hungry.

Mother: I heard you dear, now a couple of times.

Child: Well, aren't you going to get me something to eat?

Mother: Well first of all, I am glad that you finally helped me understand what you wanted. It works so much better when you are clear on what you need or want. Unfortunately, honey, I have other things that I am trying to get done right now.

Child: Well, what is there to eat?

Mother: Last time I checked there were some nice peaches in the fruit drawer.

Child: I don't want peaches.

Mother: Well, I am sure that if you get busy looking you will find something you like. (The child at this point leaves the kitchen because he doesn't want to invest the energy)

Empowering our children means taking the opportunity to let the child develop the skill of asking for help. A wise parent recognizes when the child really needs some help, or when the child is simply trying to get the parent to do something that the child is capable of doing for him or herself. When children do ask for help or assistance, praise them for using such a high social skill.

HITTING THE BALL BACK – This is the strategy that transfers the responsibility back on the child.

Have you noticed how good your children are at taking their responsibility and placing it on you? As if you didn't have enough on your plate, now each of your children want you to fight their battles, support their view of their having a bad teacher as the reason why they have a poor grade, make them feel better when they are having a negative feeling, you taking ownership for their rooms of chaos, you recognizing that you're the evil parent that won't allow them to play video games for 10 hours a day, and taking their side against the other parent. Exhausting and depressing!

Your children come to you to solve their problems, to have you give them permission not to do the hard or right thing, to take the emotional beating of their own upset feelings, and to provide for them all of their immediate gratification demands. And they will continue to do so until you learn how to hit the ball back.

If you have played any of the games that require a net between the opponents (i.e., volleyball, ping pong, pickleball, or tennis), then you realize that the strategy is to hit the ball back into the opponent's court and let them deal with it. The more the ball is in the opponent's court; the more they are taking responsibility for what is on their side. The more it is on their side, the better they get at managing it and taking care of it. That is a little bit like what parent's do when they want to empower their children.

You will notice the reflective listening exercise is "hitting the ball back" until your child decides what they really want to do with the responsibility. If you are not going to take it for them then their options are:

1) Don't take any responsibility and experience the outcome of that choice; or
2) Take some degree (partial or full) of responsibility and experience the outcome of that choice.

In the case of #1, the child doesn't eat, and in the case of #2, the child does eat something. Each experience has an outcome and either one had nothing to do with your own personal experience or performance as a parent. They owned the problem either way. That is the pathway of teaching about the real world!

As you allow them to work it out you are strengthening your child to take stock in their own resources in being able to meet the greater demands of personal responsibility. Parents become amazed at their child's resources when they are finally willing to let go and let their children find their own solutions, regulate their own emotions, and develop the effort to get things accomplished.

The next section on learning is going to bring the granddaddy skill of what good parents do and do well. This next section is what all of the parenting books seem to miss or not fully realize the power of. A book like Love and Logic stops with the idea that a child will learn from the consequences of their choices. Yes, there will be some degree of learning that results from that approach and many children are able to internalize the lessons, but for a great deal more, the consequences simply seem to reinforce the child's negative implicit memory. The next section will now pull together Quantum Science in demonstrating why good, intentional parenting, provides the positive outcomes we desire.

But before we go there, let's please understand the practicality of empowering your children. 1st) Stop rescuing your children. Why do we do it? So that our children don't have to suffer or experience negative things (2 Nephi 2:11)? Do we do it because of some insecurity in ourselves? The message it sends is that the child is not capable. That becomes internalized. On the other hand, if we will support the truth that opposition is a necessary component of development and growth, we can then help our children grow to understand that it is not the trial or test that measures us, it is our response to the test or trial. Children are perfectly capable of learning that good outcomes derive from good approaches to problems. 2nd) Let go of the power struggle. Trying to control your children only builds resentment. It also solidifies the child's belief that he or she is only acceptable when doing things your way. Research shows that most children that grow up under a system of control choose a different path than their parent's desire. Trust in your children. Believe in them; they will come to respond to those positive influences.

An example of hitting the ball back:

Child: I just can't do this homework. I don't get it. It's stupid. (The normal response to these kind of distress signals is to start providing help or solutions – let's stop doing that)

Parent: Honey, it sounds like you are not happy.

Child: I'm not. This teacher is so lame. No one gets what he is talking about. I wish I could just switch classes to Mr. Turley. (Many parents would be inclined to call the school to either complain or request the classroom change – let's stop doing that)

Parent: Well, what do you think you will do?

Child: Will you go down to the school and talk to the counselor? (Many parents would follow the suggestion of their child – let's stop doing that)

Parent: Honey, if it is that important to you and if you see it as a realistic solution, you don't need me to intervene. It sounds like you've got some legitimate reasons for wanting to change. What do you think you might do?

Child: Please mom, can't you just do it for me? (Many parents would be triggered (manipulated) by the emotion seen in their child's face and expression – Let's stop doing that)

Parent: Honey, I believe that you have all the resources to go and take care of this yourself. I will support you whatever you decide to do.

This mother just played an excellent game of "personal responsibility tennis" with her child. Four times the child tried to get her mother to do what she could have done for herself, but mother hit the ball back each time.

EMOTIONS – THE FEEDBACK SYSTEM

Emotions are part of human design. Sometimes they can get the best of us, other times we learn to rely on their message in order to evaluate our current experience or functioning. Emotions do not occur in a vacuum, though many have come to believe they do. Current social issues are being driven by emotions that are being claimed as the only reason for changing social mores. The selling point of such approaches consist of emotional reasoning like, "If I feel it then it must be true," or its twin, "Emotions are neither right nor wrong, they are just emotions," justifying the reason for certain choices or behaviors.

If only it were that simple, then we could make all laws and rules relative to what we are feeling in the moment, "Honey, you shouldn't be mad at me because I flirted with her, it was how I was feeling," or, "Your honor, I shouldn't have to spend any time in prison. I was mad and therefore I simply acted on my feeling. You can't condemn me for a feeling and the natural outcome such a feeling produces?" Yet, such is the reasoning that is leading to increasing social chaos.

As clear as I can possibly be here is that human design requires that a thought precede emotion. Some might argue that a feeling produces thoughts – and they would not be wrong, because all that is going on physiologically (in the body) and neurologically (in the brain) is connected (law of entanglement) and interacts with each other. But when an emotion is felt, be assured that a thought preceded it, even if we are unaware of it.

Here is the problem, but it should not be too big of a problem by this point. Many of our thoughts are so engrained in our implicit memory (you know that memory that is stored in a place below the threshold of awareness or consciousness) that they occur quickly and under the radar. When I say quickly, I mean at the speed of light quickly. In other words, we have said to ourselves so many times the same thoughts that consciousness does not have to pay any special attention to them. They are on automatic drive and when we experience something during the day, these automatic thoughts act as the guardians of already well formed core beliefs or templates. Since they are managing our interpretation of the environment, we simply become aware of their existence only because we are having an emotion. Becoming aware of the emotion then elicits more thoughts, either reinforcing the emotion (Reactive - this is how unaware people function) or challenging the emotion (Responsive - this is how highly conscious people function) to determine its efficacy.

Human design is established in a hierarchy. The mind is supposed to be the master of the physiology (or body). A mind that is highly aware and attuned maintains this hierarchy. A mind that has developed distorted core beliefs or templates ends up training the physiology (or body) to become the master of the mind. These are the people that are so highly attuned to their emotions (the body's response) that they reason from those emotions – or in kind of a straightforward way of saying it – they are run by their emotions, not their minds. Such a person experiences many, many complications when they have gotten to this point.

When I was the Executive Director for a youth residential program, I would require the parents to attend a parent weekend within the first six weeks of their child's stay. The purpose of the parent weekend was to provide greater information on the process of change and begin to provide enough information so that the parents could wrap their minds around why their child had struggled so much; more than perhaps their children's peers.

One of the questions that I would ask right off the bat was – "What do you think your child believes about him or herself?" I would say that most parents never considered this question. It was obvious from many of their answers that there was a real disconnect from what the parents offered and from what their children were observed to be saying. After the parent's responses, I would go to the next frame in the Power Point presentation, and on that frame would be direct quotes from their children. Here are samples of what these children believed about themselves:

1. I don't feel like my parents want me around
2. I feel lower than a worthless piece of crap
3. I don't fit in
4. I only feel like I am acceptable when I do what my parents want me to do
5. I'm stupid
6. When I look in the mirror all I see is smallness and insignificance.
7. No one would like me if they really knew me
8. I'm not worth knowing
9. I'm worthless

I then asked the parents how they might *act* if they held any of these same core beliefs. The "Aha" moment was beginning. Naturally, parents would question how such beliefs formed and wanted to quickly address the issue by telling their children that they shouldn't think or feel that way. Surely, if they just knew how wrong their beliefs were they would be alright, these parents surmised. Unfortunately, implicit memories are formed over long periods of time and cannot be dismantled with a simple "stop thinking that way" request.

The main reason for the difficulty is in the emotional experience humans have as their long-time circuits of inferiority are triggered. When someone has trained their physiology (the body) to become the master of the mind, the emotions become the single most important evidence that what is being felt is simply a confirmation of the inferiority. So let's look in greater depth at this process that creates the physiology (the body) to rule over the mind.

Going back to the Chapter, "Setting the Stage," we discovered that learning gets stored as physical memory in the cells (this is physical memory being stored in the body). The reason for this phenomenon is due to the process of protein synthesis occurring within the hypothalamus, as simple amino acids are converted into polypeptides, which transmit information (one's thoughts, attitudes [a collection of our thoughts], and beliefs) throughout the body – connecting to cells and then releasing that information within the cells. A cell that has had repeated information of "I'm not good enough" becomes the master of producing cells that react with the same response, over and over again. The more times the cell learns to react to such negative thinking, the more powerful the reaction becomes.

Now recall, the nervous system is interacting with the cells in that it is taking the chemical reactions occurring at the cellular level, due to the information we supplied them through our thoughts, and translating these chemical reactions into a coherent feeling, perhaps depression or anxiety. This translating cellular activity is the major responsibility of the limbic system. As the cellular reaction increases in intensity, so does the limbic system's decoding of the feeling. In laymen's terms, depression and anxiety grow to be more burdensome, more intense, and more out of control. As these negative feelings increase our power to regulate them decreases. Anxiety turns into panic attacks, and depression grows progressively worse until one feels hopeless, meaningless, and exhausted. The immediate response of someone that is experiencing such negative feelings is to produce more negative thoughts. These are the thoughts that the individual becomes aware of, not the original negative thoughts that started the whole process.

As the person reinforces the negative feelings with more negative thoughts, the same process of protein synthesis, transporting negative thoughts to the cells continues. This becomes a vicious cycle, a seemingly unending loop. At this point, the body has become the master of the mind. When someone becomes so emotionally burdened; when the cellular activity is so negatively pronounced, other chemicals are then produced by the body to try and combat the toxic environment. Cortisol and adrenaline levels rise, adding to the increased stress levels and physiological reactions in all systems of the body; including hyper tension, memory loss, genetic mutations, onset of diseases like cancer, attacks on the immune system, or even physical collapse. Truly the intense physiological response reinforces the body master concept.

Learning in its simplest definition is when two neurons connect. The repeated experience of feeling the same emotions, day after day, is evidence that no new learning is taking place. In the process just described, a person simply continues to reinforce the same neuronal connections over and over again, thus strengthening the incorrect learning. The individual (maybe your child) continues to experience the same thoughts, the same emotions day after day. The associations become so strong that it speeds up the reaction time. The child experiences it as rapid shifts in emotional states.

My analogy to this is when it snows, we find children outside with their inner tubes or sleds, going down hills. It isn't long before distinct pathways are cut into the snow that begins to freeze over and the track becomes slicker and faster. Such is the case when we are unaware of the negative thoughts associated with our implicit memory. They become triggered over and over again so that our whole physiological response quickly triggers our emotions. It speeds the whole process up. When emotions are experienced, these act on our belief system and we begin to internalize distortions as reality.

The key to undoing this process or to imbed correct information in the first place is to slow the whole mechanism down. As parents, we do this by observing for our children when they are experiencing emotions. Since emotions play such an impactful role on internalizing our belief systems, then we should be alert to the opportunities that will occur in the natural flow of our child's experience.

When correct learning becomes internalized through the process of connecting our child's emotions with their experiences, it produces:

1) A sense of control
2) *Motivation*
3) Extinguishing
4) Self Confidence
5) Improved judgment
6) Moral compass

This is important because we can get caught in the trap of gauging our children's internal attributions by their behaviors. Behavior alone is not an indicator of motivation or belief. Many times children behave well because they can manipulate their parents by doing so. That manipulation is focused on an external process. Children make better choices behaviorally when their motivation is internalized.

What undermines all of this influence? – SAVING OUR CHILDREN.
1) What a two year old learns directly affects what it will be like when he or she turns three and so forth.
2) Saving sends the message that our children are incapable – which directly impacts their sense of control, motivation and self-esteem.
3) It cuts off our children emotionally – time warping (What have we learned about the importance of emotions in developing internalization?)
4) The longer it goes on the harder it is to turn around. *Sense of entitlement vs. gratitude*

CONNECTING OUR CHILD'S EXPERIENCE WITH THEIR FEELINGS

In the following article I wrote for a newspaper column, I combine some of what we learned about task mastery and demonstrate a parenting technique that assists in creating children that can stand on their own. The parenting technique is found near the end of the article and introduces some phrases or questions we can ask our children to assist them in understanding the connection between their experiences and the feelings they have.

George Washington advised:

> "Labor to keep alive in your breast that little spark of celestial fire, called conscience."

Every person is born with an inherent sense of right and wrong. While good parenting can diminish or enhance that flame of distinction, nonetheless, it is very real and every part of our human design. Feelings and emotions are directly related to our interaction to this thing we call conscience. Feelings and emotions, more than intellectual reasoning assists us in making choices. Therefore, it is essential that we tie our child's experience to the emotions that result from their choices.

By doing so begins to create a greater sense of control of one's feelings. If done effectively, the child will likely value the experiences that bring greater satisfaction and positive feelings to his or her life. He or she begins to value the positive and beneficial feelings and begins to act in such a way to make them a constant in his or her life.

This is called the development of a moral compass, and our taking the time to talk to our children about their feelings in connection with their choices and experience will assist in developing a good moral compass. That moral compass then is INTERNALIZED resulting in our children becoming SELF-MOTIVATED to maintain the benefits of positive emotions, like happiness, peace, calmness, achievement, courage, hope and faith. Obviously, the reverse is also true. Our children will be internally motivated to extinguish those choices, behaviors, and attitudes that lead to negative feelings.

THE ARTICLE

HELPING OUR CHILDREN STAND ON THEIR OWN
(DEVELOPING AUTONOMY IN OUR CHILDREN)

A mother comes to see me because "her 13 year old son is shy and doesn't want to try anything for fear that someone will notice him," asking me what she should do. In the coming weeks, it was discovered that her son's struggles had less to do with shyness

255

and more to do with the young man's sense of doubt in his abilities and the fear that someone would find out he wasn't capable. This young man's doubt and shame were interfering with living a more positive life.

Erik Erickson, a prominent American Developmental Psychologist, pointed out that there are things (he called them tasks) each of us must master if we are going to handle life in a positive manner. If we did not master these things at the age when such mastery should take place, then we would continue experiencing difficulty until we did – even into adulthood. One of those things is a sense that we can do things on our own. He referenced this as the skill or task of autonomy. He further suggested that those that struggle in mastering autonomy would instead approach life filled with shame and doubt.

This article is about how to assist our children in developing the skills that lead to autonomy. Autonomy, in its very definition, provides an intellectual understanding that every human is capable of standing on their own, learning how to master their physical environment, to regulate their emotions appropriately, to navigate and strive to live in healthy relationships, and to develop a sense of confidence that in spite of life's challenges, a person has faith in their capacity to meet those challenges.

Truly autonomous children face the world knowing that from their own experience they are capable, that with faith and effort, being consistent with true principles, that life is good. Children that have not attained to true autonomy live their life and make decisions based upon fear that they cannot do it on their own.

The quest for autonomy begins early in our development and then becomes a process of learning how to separate in a healthy degree from mother and father and take responsibility for life in a positive manner. Ironically, true and healthy autonomy is the product of good parenting. Unfortunately, many parents are unaware of this important process, and even though they instinctively know that one day their child will leave the nest, they have never learned the way to interact with their child that sends them out of the nest with confidence.

Always wanting to make sure their child doesn't fail, or experience embarrassment, or hurt feelings, too many parents do too much with or for their children that they should be doing for themselves. Some intervene at higher rates because they themselves don't want to be seen as a bad or poor parent. Therefore some parents invest a lot of energy in helping their child succeed rather than have their child internalize lessons that can be taught from the outcomes of their own efforts. I have found that children that have had too much done for them have parents that then do not know what to do with their children. That is because parents have spent their effort in having their child look good, rather than expending effort in teaching their children about principles.

Autonomy, as defined in human development can only be achieved through internalization of principles. Self-motivation becomes the product of internalization of principles, because the child has discovered truths that inspire personal effort and exploration. I will get to the process of how to assist with internalization later. What I want to say is that limited parenting always has a way of being manifested by the parent's limited way of trying to get their child to do things. Usually it is through external rewards or deficits. Such parenting emphasizes the importance of those things outside of us, the externals, rather than on developing the child from the inside or internally. In other words, such parenting develops children who begin to measure their worth and importance by what they have or don't have rather than who they are.

I once had a client, a 16 year old male that had been sent to the program I was working at. His family was affluent and could afford to buy many things. His father had purchased a classic Pontiac GTO and this young man loved to cruise Miami Beach in it as it drew the attention of many young ladies. The young man however was being treated for drug addiction. When I asked him what he believed the reason for the continued use of drugs was, he replied,

> "At first it was just about having fun and fitting in. It was the thing to do. But I realized that there was an added benefit, I recognized that I didn't have to deal with unpleasant feelings and I enjoyed how quickly drugs would take those negative feelings away."

This young man's father interacted with his son more on what he could buy his son, rather than developing a sense of who is son had the potential of becoming internally. Therefore, this young man's negative feelings about himself, i.e., being dependent on his father, not learning a good work ethic, etc. produced feelings of inferiority, shame and doubt in his own abilities (The drugs interacted with and numbed these negative, internal feelings).

Near the end of his program, in a large group setting of about sixty peers, this young man spoke about his growing excitement to return home. To reinforce what he had learned about himself, I questioned him about that Pontiac GTO. I said:

> "You used to talk about the fun and joy you experienced in cruising in your dad's GTO. Can I ask you a question? If you had the choice to drive your dad's GTO down the strip in Miami or a car that you worked and paid for, which one would you actually feel better being in?

The young man responded in the way I had hoped he would, he stated, "Definitely the car I worked to pay for." I further asked, "What is it that you notice that leads you to say that?" He replied, "Knowing that I did something for myself, instead of my parents doing it for me creates such a wonderful feeling inside. A feeling of, 'yeah, I did this' is so much better than 'look what my dad gave me!" He further quipped, "I just hope I can afford to buy a hot car." I suggested that with his finding how to be self-motivated that he likely would not have to worry about that.

Parenting is serious business. It is by far the most important responsibility we have in life, other than the responsibility to our spouse. It is more important than any position of rank, power, prestige or occupation. What we do with our children will have far more repercussions in future generations than anything we did with the other roles we play.

Our children need our attention, they need our presence, they need our input and to hear about our own experiences. When we are unavailable to them, either through our busyness, or because of our inability to connect with them due to our walls, our addictions, our mood disorders, our low self-esteem, or our fear, such children will have a difficult time achieving autonomy as they will always be working on getting our approval. As parents, we may sense their effort as being needy or dependent, but in reality, no one has ever modeled for them how to become autonomous.

Becoming autonomous requires significant effort in both personal development and interpersonal development. There are no substitutes or shortcuts. When through our limited parenting we emphasize external things as the way in developing autonomy, we will end up creating dependency in its stead. Again, autonomy is an internal quest of discovering principles that bring value to the individual. When our children begin to value how abiding by correct principles brings about greater happiness, better management of one's emotions, and an energy to go and take greater responsibility for their lives, we have likely witnessed our children suffer a little, experienced some disappointments, and faced some opposition, all without dying! Positive parenting allowed for such children to learn from those experiences and that learning became internalized.

I stated that becoming autonomous requires interpersonal development. What I am about to say may fall on deaf or not understanding ears. Possessions are not as meaningful or as important as our relationships. If you had a difficult time understanding that then you are likely a parent with limits. Autonomy fully recognizes the need for relationships and healthy relationships allow for true autonomy. Stuff is great, what money can buy is fun, but when stuff and money become our object of affection rather than our relationships, we are in trouble personally and the message that our children receive is not good. As with other substitutes, i.e. addictions, substituting our affection for our children with things, creates a disconnect emotionally with our children. That emotional disconnect is what prevents autonomy from occurring. It impairs self-development, including the development of authentic expression, of empathy for others, of purpose in relationships, of personal management, and of belief of personal worth and capability.

Stuff will never resolve underlying issues related to stress, anxiety, uncertainty, etc. Human intimacy and connectedness, especially from parents as children are growing, will create far better mechanisms that lead to resolve of such issues as they arise. Healthy attachments provide the resiliency within our children to pick themselves up when meeting the challenges of mastering their environment.

Each of us is designed to experience feelings. Feelings are a core part in developing autonomy. How we as parents interact with the feelings our children experience is how we assist in the process of developing true autonomy in our children. *By connecting our children's feelings with their experiences, assists our children in taking greater ownership in creating more positive feelings.* Following are a few phrases that will enable us to promote this connection:

1. That sounds like something hard to deal with. I sense that you are not happy right now. Help me understand what led to you being so unhappy.

2. It seems that you are experiencing some negative emotions. Can I ask you a simple question? Do you like what you are feeling right now? If you could change that feeling out for any other feeling, what would you replace it with? Do you have any idea how to create the feelings you want?

3. The other day I recognized that you were a bit down, but now I see that you are doing well. Help me understand, do you know what led to both of the feelings? What feeling do you like better?

Such interactions are manifestations of positive parenting. One last point about helping our children develop autonomy, when we engage with our children in a way that devalues their thoughts, perceptions and opinions, when we minimize their expressed feelings, we can end up creating a lot of doubt in our children's ability to manage life in a good way.

Their thoughts, perceptions and opinions may be different than ours and we may not necessarily respond emotionally to a similar situation, but remember they are practicing how to become autonomous and it is important that they know that we understand them. When someone has that type of support they can continue to practice and learn from their experiences until they have gained the internal fortitude to stand on their own.

THE FOLLOWING ADDRESS IS A GOOD REINFORCEMENT OF THE CONCEPTS ABOUT LEARNING

The following address by Cheryl Esplin provides real examples of how to put into action this very concept I am trying to pound into parent's toolboxes. If you are not spiritual, I

259

am asking you to set aside judgments and not tune out about what is being taught. I have 'bolded' certain references that support or reinforce the skill of connecting our children's experiences with their feelings in order to produce self-value to true principles (Again, what is a principle? A natural human law that provides structure to living our life in a good and meaningful way).

As parents we spend a lot of time asking "WHY" our children did so and so, e.g., Why did you hit your brother, Why did you not do your homework, Why did you lie to me, Why were you late, etc. There is not a lot of benefit from this approach, and you likely recognize the amount of frustration that you feel with the million "I don't know" replies you get to your 'Why' questions.

Your frustration is recognized by your children when you approach them this way. While your intentions are to teach and correct, the messages that your children are receiving can be quite different than the ones you are sending. For example, your frustration can be interpreted by the child as:

1. I can never make my mom (or dad) happy.
2. My mom (or dad) does not like me or anything I do.
3. I am only acceptable when I do things a certain way.
4. My mom (or dad) is trying to control me.
5. It seems my mom (or dad) is more invested in this than I am, e.g. meaning it is more important to mom or dad than the child.
6. A way to control mom (or dad).

If the child continues to believe any of the above messages, then the process breaks down and what we are trying to achieve does not come into fruition. Our "Why's" become the signal that triggers the negative messages and therefore the child is not incentivized to accept responsibility for his or her actions.

Good parents understand that they are in the business of training a belief system that if healthy, will have the child learn to take greater responsibility for his or her choices. The ONLY way to get that healthy belief system internalized is to connect the child's experiences with his or her emotional response to the choices he or she made. If we use this approach instead of the "Why" approach, our children will begin to take greater responsibility because they learn (through our help in making those connections) that they are the ones that are producing the outcomes and therefore have a greater sense of control.

"Teaching Our Children to Understand"
By Cheryl A. Esplin
Second Counselor in the Primary General Presidency

Teaching our children to understand is more than just imparting information. It's helping our children get the doctrine into their hearts.

As years pass, many details in my life are becoming more and more dim, but some of the memories that remain most clear are the births of each of our children. Heaven seemed so near, and if I try, I can almost feel those same feelings of reverence and wonder I experienced each time one of those precious infants was placed in my arms.

Our "children are an heritage of the Lord" (Psalm 127:3). He knows and loves each one with perfect love (see Moroni 8:17). What a sacred responsibility Heavenly Father places upon us as parents to partner with Him in helping His choice spirits become what He knows they can become.

This divine privilege of raising our children is a much greater responsibility than we can do alone, without the Lord's help. He knows exactly what our children need to know, what they need to do, and what they need to be to come back into His presence. He gives mothers and fathers specific instruction and guidance through the scriptures, His prophets, and the Holy Ghost.

In a latter-day revelation through the Prophet Joseph Smith, the Lord instructs parents to teach their children to *understand* the doctrine of repentance, faith in Christ, baptism, and the gift of the Holy Ghost. Notice the Lord doesn't just say we are to "teach the doctrine"; His instructions are to teach our children to "*understand* the doctrine." (See D&C 68:25, 28; emphasis added.)

In Psalms we read, "Give me understanding, and I shall keep thy law; yea, I shall observe it with my whole heart" (Psalm 119:34).

Teaching our children to understand is more than just imparting information. It's helping our children get the doctrine into their hearts in a way that it becomes part of their very being and is reflected in their attitudes and behavior throughout their lives.

Nephi taught that the role of the Holy Ghost is to carry the truth "unto the hearts of the children of men" (2 Nephi 33:1). Our role as parents is to do all we can to create an atmosphere where our children can *feel* the influence of the Spirit and then help them recognize what they are feeling.

I'm reminded of a phone call I received several years ago from our daughter, Michelle. With tender emotion she said, "Mom, I just had the most incredible experience with Ashley." Ashley is her daughter who was five years old at the time. Michelle described the morning as being one of constant squabbling between Ashley and three-year-old Andrew—one wouldn't share and the other would hit. After helping them work things out, Michelle went to check the baby.

Soon, Ashley came running in, angry that Andrew wasn't sharing. Michelle reminded Ashley of the commitment they had made in home evening to be more kind to each other.

She asked Ashley if she wanted to pray and ask for Heavenly Father's help, but Ashley, still very angry, responded, "No." When asked if she believed Heavenly Father would answer her prayer, Ashley said she didn't know. Her mother asked her to try and gently took her hands and knelt down with her.

Michelle suggested that Ashley could ask Heavenly Father to help Andrew share—and help her be kind. The thought of Heavenly Father helping her little brother share must have piqued Ashley's interest, and she began to pray, first asking Heavenly Father to help Andrew share. As she asked Him to help her be kind, she began to cry. Ashley ended her prayer and buried her head on her mother's shoulder. Michelle held her and asked why she was crying. Ashley said she didn't know.

Her mother said, "I think I know why you're crying. **Do you feel good inside?**" Ashley nodded, and her mother continued, "This is the Spirit helping you feel this way. It's Heavenly Father's way of telling you He loves you and will help you."

She asked Ashley if she believed this, if she believed Heavenly Father could help her. With her little eyes full of tears, Ashley said she did.

Sometimes the most powerful way to teach our children to understand a doctrine is to teach in the context of what they are experiencing right at that moment. These moments are spontaneous and unplanned and happen in the normal flow of family life. They come and go quickly, so we need to be alert and recognize a teaching moment when our children come to us with a question or worry, when they have problems getting along with siblings or friends, when they need to control their anger, when they make a mistake, or when they need to make a decision. (See *Teaching, No Greater Call: A Resource Guide for Gospel Teaching* [1999], 140–41; *Marriage and Family Relations Instructor's Manual* [2000], 61.)

If we are ready and will let the Spirit guide in these situations, our children will be taught with greater effect and understanding.

Just as important are the teaching moments that come as we thoughtfully plan regular occasions such as family prayer, family scripture study, family home evening, and other family activities.

In every teaching situation all learning and all understanding are best nurtured in an atmosphere of warmth and love where the Spirit is present.

About two months before his children turned eight years old, one father would set aside time each week to prepare them for baptism. His daughter said that when it was her turn, he gave her a journal and they sat together, just the two of them, and discussed and shared feelings about gospel principles. He had her draw a visual aid as they went along. It showed the premortal existence, this earth life, and each step she needed to take to return to live with Heavenly Father. He bore his testimony about each step of the plan of salvation as he taught it to her.

When his daughter recalled this experience after she was grown, she said: "I will never forget the love I felt from my dad as he spent that time with me. ... I believe that this experience was a major reason I had a testimony of the gospel when I was baptized." (See *Teaching, No Greater Call,* 129.)

Teaching for understanding takes determined and consistent effort. It requires teaching by precept and by example **and especially by helping our children live what they learn**.

President Harold B. Lee taught, "Without experiencing a gospel principle in action, it is ... more difficult to believe in that principle" (*Teachings of Presidents of the Church: Harold B. Lee* [2000], 121).

I first learned to pray by kneeling with my family in family prayer. I was taught the language of prayer as I listened to my parents pray and as they helped me say my first prayers. I learned that I could talk to Heavenly Father and ask for guidance.

Every morning without fail, my mother and father gathered us around the kitchen table before breakfast, and we knelt in family prayer. We prayed at every meal. In the evening before bed, we knelt together in the living room and closed the day with family prayer.

Although there was much I didn't understand about prayer as a child, it became such a part of my life that it stayed with me. I still continue to learn, and my understanding of the power of prayer still continues to grow.

Elder Jeffrey R. Holland said, "We all understand that the success of the gospel message depends upon its being taught and then understood and then lived in such a way that its promise of happiness and salvation can be realized" ("Teaching and Learning in the Church" [worldwide leadership training meeting, Feb. 10, 2007], *Liahona,* June 2007, 57; *Ensign,* June 2007, 89).

Learning to fully understand the doctrines of the gospel is a process of a lifetime and comes "line upon line, precept upon precept, here a little and there a little" (2 Nephi 28:30). **As children learn and act upon what they learn, their understanding is expanded, which leads to more learning, more action, and an even greater and more enduring understanding.**

We can know our children are beginning to understand the doctrine when we see it revealed in their attitudes and actions *without external threats or rewards*. As our children learn to understand gospel doctrines, they become more self-reliant and more responsible. They become part of the solution to our family challenges and make a positive contribution to the environment of our home and the success of our family.

We will teach our children to understand as we take advantage of every teaching situation, invite the Spirit, set the example, and help them live what they learn.

When we look into the eyes of a tiny infant, we are reminded of the song:

I am a child of God,
And so my needs are great;
Help me to understand his words
Before it grows too late.
Lead me, guide me, walk beside me,
Help me find the way.
Teach me all that I must do
To live with him someday.
("I Am a Child of God," *Hymns,* no. 301; emphasis added)

May we do so. In the name of Jesus Christ, amen. (April General Conference, 2012)

Michelle's interaction with her daughter Ashley was impactful. Her *observing* for her daughter her internal experience helped Ashley to make sense of what she was experiencing.

This is where Quantum Science and our intentional interventions meet in such a meaningful way. Because of the Law of Entanglement (i.e., meaning that all things are connected), Michelle's relationship with Ashley provides the basis of influence. Likewise, Ashley being a daughter of Heavenly Father is connected to the influence that comes from the Godhead, meaning through the Spirit. Ashley felt of that influence, and because all things are connected, Michelle also detected what was going on in, as she too felt the Spirit.

This was a tender moment and whether Michelle recognized what she was doing or not as it relates to Quantum Science, the experience that Ashley was having was interacting with Ashley's thoughts and emotions. Thoughts and emotions are electro/chemical processes that are made of matter. They are measurable, weighable and can actually be seen. They are made of some of the same building blocks found throughout the universe. Because all matter has potential and because that potential is profoundly influenced through observation, Michelle's observation was able to assist Ashley by increasing her understanding of what she was experiencing. Had Michelle let that moment pass by, likely Ashley would not have had the same outcome. It is obvious that Sister Esplin's daughter, whether coming from an educated framework, or simply being intuitive, her recognition that,

> **"Sometimes the most powerful way to teach our children to understand .... is to teach in the context of what they are experiencing right at that moment. These moments are spontaneous and unplanned and happen in the normal flow of family life. They come and go quickly, so we need to be alert and recognize a teaching moment..."**

May I now share one of my own personal experiences to continue to enforce this mostly neglected approach to purposeful and intentional parenting?

At the end of 6th grade, one of my sons began to demonstrate greater care and skill with his friends than with his studies. In our day, we have almost immediate access to our children's grades because of the internet. As the year end approached, I noticed that the feelings between my wife and my son began to grow contentious.

As my son would come in through the door, he was met with questions as to why a particular assignment was missing or why a grade was so low. This pattern persisted and it appeared that my wife was taking greater responsibility for our son's grades rather than my son.

As with all children, my son was expert at providing reasons why the internet record appeared as it did. "My teacher has not posted the grade yet," or "The next test is where most of the points are going to come from," etc. Eventually, as most parents do, my son was approached with the reward or pain model of motivation to inspire him to get his grades up. Sometimes this approached worked, sometimes it did not – it all depended upon whether my son really wanted something or didn't want to lose something. As it turned out, the last half of 6th grade was the worst my son had ever done academically.

Now, I want you to know something about my son. He is very capable academically. He is bright, resourceful, and a hard worker. But he has that socialization gene or as the experts call it, social intelligence.

When 7th grade began, the first two weeks went well. Our son was getting worked turned in and by his own report, seemed to be on track. Shortly thereafter, the internet reporting site (Power School) was indicating the same pattern of missed assignments and the like as was occurring at the end of his 6th grade year.

Following is the discussion that took place between him and his parents:

Dad: Son, your mother and I would like to sit with you for a moment to have a discussion about your habits at school and what we believe will be supportive of you taking responsibility for your own stuff.

Dad: Let me ask you a question. When it comes to your grades, who seems to be the one most invested? Who is acting like it is most important to them?

Son: Mom

Dad: Yeah, how do you know that?

Son: She is the one constantly looking at the grades and making issues about them.

Dad: Yes, I agree. Her involvement does send the message that your grades are more important to her rather than to you. Well, part of our discussion today is to clearly shift that responsibility to whom it rightly belongs – namely you. Before we do that, mom and I want to remind you of an upcoming reality.

Mom: Son, in six short years you will be leaving our home. That transition is a reality – there is no stopping it. Sometimes it is hard when you are 12 years old to look down the corridors of time and even consider what you need to do to make that transition with as little problems as possible.

What we want you to think about right now is "options."

Dad: If you do well academically, there may be many more options available to you, including college choices and perhaps scholarships. If you decide to not make academics a priority, then your options decrease. There is always McDonald's! Either way, you are leaving our home – it is in your power what options you want to make available to yourself.

If you choose McDonald's (I kiddingly added), I understand that they have made it relatively easy. All you have to do is memorize numbers because they have pictures on the cash register of all of the food items. So if you know what a Big Mac looks like then all you have to do is press a number and a picture when a customer orders.

Son: Knock it off dad! (Said with an understanding that he was being teased a bit)

Dad: One thing you have learned about dad is that because of his education, it has provided for many more options. Have you noticed that?

Son: Yes. I can remember before your Master's Degree, your options were more limited.

Dad: Good, I'm glad you have noticed. The same is true of anyone. The more and better our education, the more marketable we become.

Mom: Son, it is now time for us to turn over your grades to you. They are your grades, not mine, not dad's. We will no longer nag you about them. If you decide that you would like to slide through school without much effort, one day it will catch-up to you and we are OK with that outcome.

Dad: Yes, your choices will not have any bearing on us as parents. It is your life that will likely struggle as a result. It is our duty to simply warn you and then leave the choice up to you.

Mom: What do you think about what we are saying?

Son: It sounds like it is all up to me. This is a pretty serious discussion for a 7th Grader.

Dad: Well, we believe in you and it is never too early to prepare your children for the real world. Right now, you are a bit protected from the real world's demands because we shelter you from it. But if we do not allow you to take greater ownership for your life, then you will be shocked and dismayed when you are out on your own. We don't want that for you.

Mom: Son, it seems to me that when you are not up on your game that you become more stressed. Am I noticing that correctly?

Son: Yes. I don't like the way I feel when I get behind.

Dad: I can recall when I was in high school I would do the same thing. I always told myself, I will do it later. As I got behind, I would become overwhelmed and spent way too many late nights trying to get work done. I did not like it. Sometimes I would shoot myself in the foot and not leave myself enough time to complete all of my work.

Son: Yeah, I do the same thing.

Dad: You know son, sometimes I wonder what you believe about yourself when you see some of your grades.

Son: Sometimes I think I am stupid or not as smart as others.

Dad: Yeah, I was wondering if that might have been your experience. Well, can I ask you a question?

Son: Sure.

Dad: These "getting behind" feelings, or "I think I am stupid" thoughts – Do you enjoy these?

Son: No, I don't.

Dad: Do you have an understanding of what leads to these negative feelings and thoughts?

Son: Yes, it is when I procrastinate. I then begin to worry about getting it done. Because I don't do my homework when I should, I am not as prepared as I should be for class the next time. I don't understand what the teacher is teaching because I didn't do my homework. Because I don't get it, I just tune out and the pressure mounts.

Mom: Well, it sounds like you see how your choices are connected with the negative outcomes. But you say you don't like the negative feelings and negative thoughts.

Son: That's right.

Mom: Well, if you could replace those feelings and thoughts with something else, what would you change them to?

Son: I like the feeling that comes with getting it and being prepared.

Mom: Do you have any idea how to produce those feelings?

Son: When I stay on top of things, I have those feelings.

Mom: Well, again, you sound like you have some good insight. Do you trust yourself?

Son: What do you mean?

Mom: Do you believe that you have the ability and capacity to stay on top of things?

Son: Yes.

Mom: Well that's half the battle. Like dad just said – we both believe in you as well.

268

Dad: I just want to make sure that what you are saying is clear to you. Between the two feelings discussed which one do you like better?

Son: The positive feelings that come from staying up with my work.

Dad: OK. Well, like we said – your grades are now your own. We are always here to help you when you need some support. One of the greatest habits you can form is the habit of asking for help when you need it. Some people don't ask for help because they become concerned what someone else may think of them. There is no shame in asking for assistance when we need it.

Mom: Now, while your grades are your own and we no longer are going to pester you about them, there is something parents have the right to do and that is provide some external motivation. Starting today, your "extra friend time" privileges are suspended until your grades come out November 4th. You can still attend young men's, scouts, be on the school teams, etc. but things like talking to your friends after school for 45 minutes, or night games and the like are suspended.

On November 4th, if you have at a least a "B" in each class, your suspension is immediately lifted. Our hope is that you will practice from now until then the good habits that will bring about the good feelings and thoughts you desire.

Dad: So, what is it that you just heard us say?

Son: That my "extra friend time" is suspended until my grades come out in November. If I have at least a "B" in each class those privileges are restored immediately.

Dad: Sounds like you got it. I wonder what you might do?

This was an actual conversation we had with our son. Our tones were conversational, meaning they were not harsh or raised in any manner. Our demeanor was "kind but firm." You will take notice how many times we observed for our son what he was likely experiencing and even took the time to be transparent with him, letting him know that we too, when younger, experienced many of the same thoughts and feelings.

You will also recognize how intentional we were in having our son connect his feelings with his experience and making a conscious declaration of what feelings he enjoyed more. This is the very process that allows "emotions" to become our friends and our helpers instead of our enemy whom we fear.

Our son was learning how important emotions are in creating internal states. If we are filled with doubt, shame or other negative beliefs, emotions act in a way to cement those beliefs in us, but the same is true when we experience positive emotions and we are able to determine what in our experience led to those positive emotions. Children,

269

in and of themselves are unable to discern these processes and they need us to observe for them so they learn to make sense of how they are contributing to these emotional outcomes.

If that was all my wife and I did to encourage our son's personal development, it likely would not have produced much. Our observing is an ongoing parental skill that is necessary to have our children learn about self-control, thinking beyond the immediate moment, and growing in confidence in how to manage life.

A couple of weeks later, I noticed that my son was feeling lighter, less stressed. I said to him:

Dad: Son, is it me or do you seem a bit happier lately?

Son: No, you did not miss anything – I am feeling a lot happier.

Dad: Well I have grown intensely interested. Help me understand, how is it that you have come to feeling so positive?

Son: Well, dad – after our discussion, I made the choice to do the work in school so that I wouldn't feel so stressed out. And that is exactly what I have been doing. I am getting my work turned in, I prepare for my classes and I understand what's going on.

Dad: And you're saying that your current happiness is connected with that activity?

Son: Yes

Dad: Well, I am happy for you. Now son, look at my hair – what color is it?

Son: Gray – very gray!

Dad: (With a smile on my face) Son, this gray hair represents my wisdom. I have earned it through my many experiences. Today, you have gained your own. Here, let me take a look (I grabbed him to get a close look at his hair). Yup, here are a couple of gray hairs now in your head. Congratulations – your wisdom is increasing.

Son: (Laughing) Thanks dad for believing in me.

Dad: I'm glad you noticed. I think you are terrific and I am impressed with your work ethic. I wonder if your recent experience will motivate you to meet the goal laid out in November?

Son: I am going to do it!

These purposeful interactions (observations) continued through the Fall. Now, I am going to tell you the truth about what happened, and you are going to think I am making this up – but I am not.

Our son had one teacher that in my estimation had personal problems. She had students who she treated like they could do no wrong and she had students who she treated like they could do no right. I believe she preyed upon those students that were more sensitive to negative interactions – and my son fell into that category. This was a difficult class for him because he would rather do nothing in those situations (not cooperate) rather than feel controlled. Without going into a lot of detail, my son was able to decide that his freedom (extra friend privileges) was more important than his attitude toward her.

Well, November 4th came. My son, upon getting home went into the office and pulled up Power School so that he could show us his grades. It wasn't long before we heard a very upset son and words coming from the office:

Son: There is no way. I know that I got a B+ in her class. She must have done something wrong. This must be someone else's grade.

My wife and I entered the office to see a very angry young man. Many of his decrees sounded so familiar – many were fashioned after the same comments he would give when we would question him about grades. This was a terribly emotional experience, not just for him, but also for us as his parents. There was no doubt that he had put in consistent effort throughout the trimester. Shouldn't that be rewarded? Could we possibly add insult to injury at this point by being firm in our expectation? I said to him:

Dad: Son, it is obvious how disappointed you are. There is no doubt in our minds that you really turned things around.

Son: I am so mad at her. I just want to go down to the school and yell at her. I know I had a B+ in her class. How could I possibly have a D?

Just then, an email came across to our parent account. It was from this teacher. It read, "I am sorry, but I recorded the wrong grade for your son. His final grade for the class is a B+."

You should have seen the immediate change in our son. He let out a victorious yell, leaped into the air and became so happy.

Son: I told you I got a B+, I told you!

It was then that I noticed a most profound teaching moment. I said:

271

Dad: Son, it wasn't but a moment ago that you were extremely angry and bitter and in just a split second have changed your entire reaction. You jumped off the ground, let out a yell of relief and are now crying, with what I think are tears of joy!

Tell me, which of the two experiences do you like the most?

Son: This one. This is the greatest feeling.

Mom: And well deserved. We hope that you have learned something about yourself through all of this.

Son: I have, I have. I have much greater confidence in myself. I know that with effort, I can do the work.

With that, our son high-tailed out of our house and we did not see him for about 3-1/2 hours – he went and joined up with his friends.

This power of observing for our children appears to have support from Elder Russell M. Ballard, as he taught:

> "Perhaps that is one reason why the Savior tearfully urged his Nephite followers to "behold your little ones" (3 Ne. 17:23). Notice that He didn't say "glance at them" or "casually observe them" or "occasionally take a look in their general direction." He said to behold them. To me that means that we should embrace them with our eyes and with our hearts; we should see and appreciate them for who they really are: spirit children of our Heavenly Father, with divine attributes."

> "When we truly behold our little ones, we behold the glory, wonder, and majesty of God, our Eternal Father. All children are His spirit offspring. We have no more eloquent testimony that our Heavenly Father lives and that He loves us than the first raspy cry of a newborn child. All babies have faith in their eyes and purity in their hearts. They are receptive to the truth because they have no preconceived notions; everything is real to children. Regardless of physical limitations or the challenge of circumstance, their souls are endowed naturally with divine potential that is infinite and eternal."

> "Clearly, those of us who have been entrusted with precious children have been given a sacred, noble stewardship, for we are the ones God has appointed to encircle today's children with love and the fire of faith and an understanding of who they are." (Elder Russell M. Ballard, Great Shall Be The Peace of Thy Children, General Conference, April, 1994)

I would like to think and suggest that our intentional and purposeful observing for our son worked because it fell within the boundaries of truth – especially the truth about who he really is and the eternal potential he possesses to become.

Let me once again present the benefits of correctly tying emotions to your children's experiences and go look back in this story and observe how these benefits *naturally* arose because of this process and intentional parenting skill.

- A sense of control
- *Motivation*
- Extinguishing
- Self Confidence
- Improved judgment
- Moral compass

Our son experienced each of these and so will yours when you begin this process of observing for your children the connection between experiences and emotions. Our observing of our son provided a completely different outcome than would have occurred if we had not done so.

Because our child is made of matter, and especially his thoughts and emotions, our observations of that matter is what provided for the outcome we desired. Our watching and observing of his thoughts, his actions, feelings and his words led to living a better life. I believe that is what King Benjamin is trying to help us understand when he counseled:

> "But this much I can tell you, that if ye do not watch yourselves, and your thoughts, and your words, and your deeds, and observe the commandments of God, and continue in the faith of what ye have heard concerning the coming of our Lord, even unto the end of your lives, ye must perish. And now, O man, remember, and perish not." (Mosiah 4:30)

While King Benjamin's theme is to invite people to live faithfully, much of the reason why people do not is because of their implicit thoughts, and reactive (addictive) behaviors. Until one is able to become highly conscious of such, thoughts and behaviors associated with untruthful self-perceptions will lead to people dying spiritually, intellectually and emotionally.

Consider this often overlooked interaction of God during the creative process:

> "And the Gods watched (observed) those things (the matter of which this world was created) they had ordered until they (the matter) obeyed." (Abraham 4:18)

273

How long did God watch or observe? Until the matter had obeyed. There is a reason why we have our children for 18 years. It is the time of their creative process and we are simply watching and observing so they can get it right. Again, it is not something they can get on their own

Now, is this a more purposeful, intentional method of parenting? Yes it is. But it is this type of parenting that develops healthy implicit memories in our children. We are not simply conditioning our children to obey to avoid pain or gain a reward. We are literally creating neural networks of profound worth that lead to rational and emotional regulation. At the very cellular and genetic levels we are engineering DNA and cellular activity to be filled with positive, truthful information that promotes belief of acceptability, importance and capability. Because we are teaching truth to our children, heaven's assistance will confirm these truths through the power of the Holy Ghost. These are sown in the very sinews (stored in the body) providing strength not just for our children, but for generations to come. Yes, that last line was filled with temple language. Elder Joseph Fielding Smith taught:

> "The Spirit of God speaking to the spirit of man has power to impart truth with greater effect and understanding than the truth can be imparted by personal contact even with heavenly beings. Through the Holy Ghost the truth is woven into the very fibre and sinews of the body so that it cannot be forgotten." ("The Sin against the Holy Ghost," Instructor, Oct. 1935, p. 431.)

CREATIVE CONSEQUENCING

We live in a real world and the real world has an environment that provides a constant education. If you were to think about each of your children, you may recognize that some will more naturally do well in the real world, while others you have some concern for. That ability to discern is based in your own experience of what the real world is like.

To some degree, our children grow up protected from the demands of the real world. They exist in more of a classroom setting, where mistakes are not treated as abruptly as they would in the real world. Likewise, our children's achievements may be recognized more in the home setting than they ever would be in the real world environment.

Regardless, real life places important needs before us and our ability to meet those needs is largely developed within the walls of our homes. Children that come out of a family that has done well in establishing healthy implicit memories will fare much better than those that have not. The reason is due to the power and faith that comes to an individual's mind that believes they are capable, that believe they are likeable, that recognize their strengths are needed in this life, who have a purpose, and who have a healthy, truthful awareness of inherent worth.

Some people face this life realistically, recognizing that personal choices have the ability to unlock greater happiness and freedom, while others try to cheat reality by developing strategies that forego the negative consequences attached to poor decision making. As stated earlier in this book, teaching correct principles to our children through the duration of their stay with us plays a pivotal role in developing the resources and habits of choosing well. This is not simply rhetoric, as I am a living witness to the benefits that come to children that meet together often with their parents in scripture study, prayer, designated family time, and those opportunities that come from the flow of everyday experience to teach and reinforce correct principles and re-energize relationships.

To the youth of the church have come these apostolic words of warning and advice:

> "While you are free to choose your course of action, you are not free to choose the consequences. Whether for good or bad, consequences follow as a natural result of the choices you make. Some sinful behavior may bring temporary, worldly pleasure, but such choices delay your progress and lead to heartache and misery. Righteous choices lead to lasting happiness and eternal life. Remember, true freedom comes from using your agency to choose obedience; loss of freedom comes from choosing disobedience." (For the Strength of Youth, Agency and Accountability)

Within the same section is the reminder that parents and children are not alone in developing the implicit memory that leads to making better choices, as is stated, "God is mindful of you and will help you make good choices."

In the Introduction of this book I briefly mentioned the challenges that mortal, imperfect parents face in childrearing and said, It has been my experience that many, many parents don't trust revealed truth and instead rely upon their own wisdom to raise their children, having the opposite result of what they were intending. Their wisdom forgets to take into account about how God designed us. Understanding and utilizing *human design* is crucial if we want to influence better outcomes. I don't know if I am being too simple minded, but it seems that if there is revealed truth regarding us as individuals and revealed truth about correct principles that guide our personal development and relationships then the closer we adhere to those truths, the better outcomes we can expect.

Our test of faith seems to be in believing the revelations, including that our children are related to God and that they *each are able to have spiritual awakenings and live according to what the Holy Ghost teaches them* (Jacob 4:8, 10; Proverbs 3:5-6). The question every faithful parent should repeatedly ask themselves is, "Does God ever vary from that which He has said" (Mosiah 2:22)? The correct answer to that question produces faith, the incorrect answer, fear and doubt.

Our design includes an internal compass. It is given to every man so that we might know instinctively right from wrong (D&C 84:46; 88:11, 13; Moroni 7:16). The strengthening of our children's moorings is directly related to their development of character, which derives from understanding and acting well in true principles. Parents that *observe* well for their children during this process are vital in making principles become values within their children.

But we are not acting alone. Our Father in Heaven is right along side of us encouraging our children through experiences that strengthen faith and understanding. As our children put into practice those things that are revealed, Father in Heaven reinforces those choices by adding a measure of His good spirit. This added measure is experienced through the gift and operations of the Holy Ghost. Of this process, President Spencer W. Kimball taught:

> "The Holy Ghost "comes a little at a time as you merit it. And as your life is in harmony, you gradually receive the Holy Ghost in a great measure" (*The Teachings of Spencer W. Kimball*, ed. Edward L. Kimball [1982], 114).

Our children are created with the capacity to feel, to discern, and to experience strength and enlightenment through both the Light of Christ and through the workings of the Holy Ghost. Children that have parents, who highly regard and establish an environment where the Spirit can dwell, are children that are more likely to begin to experience these manifestations and recognize their value and worth as *whisperings* (heavenly hugs) from the Father of their spirits (Hebrews 12:9; Numbers 16:22). We call these "spiritual experiences" and those that prepare themselves will continue to have such *whisperings*, all of which act on solidifying healthy, internal templates.

So let's get down to the "Nuts and Bolts" – How do we influence all of this that makes so much sense? What is our role? What processes do we use so that the child stays engaged in this process?

Let's end where we began. The revelations to us indicate that belief is the driving force of personal strength or weakness, our ability to handle life's challenges or fold under its pressure. Healthy belief promotes healthy relationships, while unhealthy beliefs interfere with developing and maintaining rewarding relationships. Our personal belief system will either have us experience acceptability and capability, or inferiority and helplessness. What we believe about ourselves has ongoing and serious ramifications.

Since a good portion of our belief is stored as implicit memory, it is important to make that implicit memory align with the truths that have been revealed about us. Again, as Elder Bruce R. McConkie so well taught:

Belief is antecedent to performance – We are *training* their belief system

1) Belief is the beginning of spiritual (internal) discovery and progression.
2) Belief is a gift bestowed upon all mankind, including your children.
3) Beliefs are born of thoughts, they are then expressed in words; are reinforced by feelings, and finally are manifest in one's actions.
4) Every normal and accountable person believes something.
5) If we believe that we are God's children, endowed with the capacity to fill the measure of our creation, then we will act in accordance with that belief.
   (A New Witness for the Articles of Faith, Chapter 3, Pgs 21-32)

Question: How do we influence healthy belief?

Answer:

1. By teaching – Make things clear (Correct principles)

2. By listening – Seek 1st to understand (Sending the message of value and importance)

3. By consistency – Structure provides security (Children rely on consistency in order to develop faith in themselves)

277

4. By involvement – Creating positive feelings (Nothing says importance more than our time)

5. By giving responsibility – Learning control (Capability comes from having mastered our environment)

6. By being highly charactered and principled (In order to exercise faith in our counsel and direction, children must sense that our way of being is desirable)

7. By connecting our child's experience with their emotions – (Following Heavenly Father's magical way of observing. It works for Him, it will work for us)

8. By example – The #1 indicator for influencing belief

Question: What is our role as a parent?

Answer: Coach	Limit Setter	Nurturer
Trainer	Example	Regulator
Adviser	Teacher	Mediator
Cheerleader	Trusted Adult	Sufferer
Confidant	Caregiver	Savior

None of these roles indicate any type of control or coercion. These are roles that maintain the stance of influence. Please notice the two roles listed in the third column at the bottom, "Sufferer" and "Savior" They are there to remind us that we will act as saviors for our children throughout their life experience (Obadiah 1:17,21). The reason we are able to do so is because of our own mortal experience, which has brought to us the capacity to feel of others burdens due to our own suffering. There is very little your children will experience that you are not acquainted with already. This experience provides the wisdom on how to succor your children. Remember, only those that have suffered can become saviors. Recall experiences when you were young that you can draw upon and be transparent so that your children know that you understand what they are experiencing.

Question: What principles do we use so that the child stays engaged in this process?

Answer:

1. Firm but Kind
2. Keeping the Responsibility Where it Rightly Belongs
3. Spending Time
4. Willingness To Listen
5. Noticing The Positive
6. Validating The Child's Emotions and Thoughts
7. Connecting The Child's Emotions With Their Experience

CONSEQUENCES – TWO TYPES

As we have spoken of the coming day, when our children will venture out on their own (hooray!), they will meet the world for what it really is – an environment where *every* choice will bring with it an outcome. Whether outcomes are immediate to choices or some how add up over a period of time before we experience their full impact, the outcomes will surely come. If some of these natural outcomes hurt, remember such experiences are intended to teach, not punish, though there may be some pain and suffering involved. Natural consequences occur because of law, as laws govern all things (D&C 88:42-43). The source of natural human law that governs all things is God. These laws are largely discerned through the light of Christ (D&C 88:13). It will be to Him that one day we will have to give an accounting for the things done in the flesh (Alma 12:14). If we have learned from the consequences that come from our choices then that day will be great. For those that continued to act in their own understanding that day will be dreadful (Malachi 4:5).

So that we might desire happiness, rather than emptiness and misery, Heavenly Father allows experience to interact with both our spirit and our physiology. Obedience to law brings peace, happiness and safety. Disobedience brings, regret, heartache, and misery (Alma 42:18). In large measure, the meting out of these "felt" experiences is found in what we call "Natural Consequences." Natural consequences are by far the best instructors. When natural consequences are seemingly absent or when we as parents observe that such will create greater harm than good, we mercifully step-in and provide what are known as "Logical Consequences." Do you trust this design or are you afraid that your child can not learn this way?

In Summary:

- **Natural consequences** are those that would follow an action without any outside intervention.
- Natural consequences are usually the best teachers because they are direct result of the behavior and happen as part of everyday life.

- **Logical consequences** are the result of an outside intervention.
- The key to formulating logical consequences is tying them to the behavior in a way that makes sense to the young person.
- Logical consequences are the tools we use when natural consequences are too harsh or seemingly absent.

CONSEQUENCES – TEACHING BELIEF vs. PUNISHMENT

Traditionally, what we call consequences actually have been punishments, i.e.:
a. Losing privileges
b. Being isolated
c. Losing allowance
d. Having things taken away

These consequences are based on deficit model thinking and ARE LESS EFFECTIVE in *teaching* belief. This is one of the paradigm shifts that I want parents to make in relation to consequences. Consequences are not punishments, they are teaching moments. Our most vital role as parents is to be teachers. When we approach consequences from this position, we will tend to become more creative so as to have an experience that provides correct information while maintaining the child's sense of worth and value.

Deficit model parenting usually just sends the unending message of – you are bad, your feelings are unimportant and you are only acceptable when you are doing it the parent's way! What an implicit memory to have – uuggh! Many of these children begin to fill the role they believe their parents are emphasizing they are, i.e., "a bad kid."

WHAT IS BEING COMMUNICATED

To be effective, we must try to understand the need being expressed through their behavior, rather than focusing on the behavior itself. It may seem odd to you, but

280

children many times purposely choose behaviors instead of words to communicate a need or want. In our home, my wife is keenly attuned to this type of communication and has been a good example of focusing on the need being expressed rather than focusing on the behavior.

WHEN BEHAVIOR NEEDS TO BE ADDRESSED

When behaviors do need to be addressed, and their appears to be a natural consequence absent from the scenario that might teach, then we look to formulating Logical Consequences. In doing so, there are some important questions to ask ourselves in order to produce more effective outcomes:

- *What do I want my child to learn?*
- *What might I teach from what I do?*
- *What will my child learn about me?*
- *What will my child learn about the world?*
- *Will I change, or reconfirm, my child's view of how things work?*

Maintaining focus on the *why* (training their belief system) we are doing *what* we are doing and the intent of our intervention will assist us in developing consequences that are more likely to bring about desired change.

1st Example of this Process: "Jesus with the woman caught in adultery." (John 8:1-11)

This story finds a woman "caught in the very act of adultery," who then is taken by force by the religious zealots of the community to Jesus. Though this is aside from the point I am trying to make, the intent of these religious leaders was to trap Jesus into saying something that would go against the Law of Moses, thus creating an opportunity to smear Jesus' reputation.

As the story unfolds, it is obvious that Jesus is not focused on the purpose of these religious leaders, but on the needs of the woman. I would like to think that Jesus had in mind the questions listed above. He being such a prolific teacher now has the opportunity to teach her things about herself that perhaps she has never known or had stopped believing. This was His opportunity to perhaps have her see herself and her circumstances differently – thus encouraging her to live a more optimistic life.

281

One of the details of the story, which has me think that Jesus was focused on being responsive to this woman's needs, was the fact that he did not answer the religious leaders immediately. Perhaps this was time that He was taking to answer the type of questions above in his mind.

I usually do not like to read too much into sacred text, but if you will allow me to make some of my personal observations. It appears that the woman is feeling and experiencing both fear and shame. I do not know how long this woman had been engaging in being sexually active with others that were married or perhaps cheating on her own husband, but the feelings associated with the event would certainly produce many negative emotions, including many self-rejecting feelings of being a bad person.

So what is it that Jesus wants this woman to know about herself? Perhaps He doesn't want her to get caught-up into being judged as a person of no worth. Maybe He senses that she is getting stuck in her own self-critical judgments and He wants to have her get out of these inaccurate portrayals.

What might Jesus teach from what He does? Does He want her to know that not everyone sees her as those religious leaders did? Will this woman begin to experience the joy of someone extending mercy to her? If she follows Jesus' advice, might she experience the good feelings associated with renewal and living more positively?

What would this woman learn about Jesus? Would she sense His great love and wisdom? Would she walk away knowing how much He cares for her? Would she learn more about the compassionate attributes of Godhood, as opposed to the rigid, punishing God of the Old Law as formed by these religious fanatics? Would this interaction have her begin seeing Jesus as her personal Savior?

What would this woman learn about the world? Because of Jesus' kindness, might she have begun learning greater discernment between men that were truly godly and others that were simply worried about their position of prominence and power? Would Jesus' counsel to avoid behaviors that bring negative feelings have produced greater understanding within her that wickedness never leads to happiness?

Did Jesus' interaction with this woman change, or simply reconfirm this woman's view of how things really work? Did this woman walk away feeling respected? Did she experience condemnation of herself as a person by the way Jesus interacted with her? I suspect that the kind interaction led this woman to change what she believed about herself, that she mattered more than what she previously held to believe about herself.

The account in the scriptures about this woman is very brief, but it is obvious that Jesus wanted to interact with her in a way that led to her feeling better about herself; providing hope that she could live happier, and that she experienced in Him the effects of pure love. The point being is that this story illustrates the process of Creative Consequencing for the purpose of teaching, not punishing.

2nd Example of this Process: I had a client that was frustrated that his oldest daughter did not help keep the house tidy by cleaning up after herself. By going through each of the questions above, my client was able to provide an opportunity of learning for his daughter, without the need to yell, coerce, punish, or any other negative interaction.

It was discovered that the daughter's laundry was done by her mother. It was suggested that mother not do her daughter's laundry until it began having an impact on the daughter's experience (that would be an example of a natural consequence).

It wasn't long before this young lady began to run out of clean clothes and she approached her mother about why her laundry hadn't been done. Keeping the *questions* in mind, it was the desires of the parents to have their daughter understand the benefit of every member of the family being responsible for the ongoing upkeep of the home.

When her father asked her what thoughts or feelings she was experiencing by not having her laundry kept up, the daughter replied that she was upset that there were no clean clothes to wear. She also expressed that it would be disgusting to have to wear dirty clothes to school. Her father asked her if it made her happy knowing that her mom had not done her laundry. The daughter replied, "No, and in fact it had made her a bit mad and annoyed." Dad asked her, if she liked those feelings, and she replied that she did not. Dad then asked her what would lead to his daughter having more positive feelings and the daughter replied, that if mom would have kept her laundry up that she would not have experienced those feelings.

Keeping a kind, conversational tone, this father took the opportunity to express to his daughter similar feelings they have had as parents as she neglected her own responsibility of picking up after herself. With gentleness, this father invited his daughter to enlarge her awareness about the roles and responsibilities that were hers and how those impacted the family. He continued by enlisting his daughter's greater cooperation, as she could now better understand the importance and impact of each family member's interaction within the family.

What did this young lady learn about herself during this experience? What principle was reinforced or taught during this time? What did this daughter learn about her father and mother? What, if anything did she learn about how the world operates? And, did anything in this experience change how the daughter saw herself?

With some conjecture, I suppose that this young lady recognized that she is needed and is a valuable member of her household, as she developed a greater awareness of how her actions impact her family members. The value of personal responsibility was a principle that was reinforced here and the importance of not taking each other for granted. The manner in which these parents spoke with their daughter certainly would have suggested to her mind that she has great worth and that her parents think well of her. When her mother stopped doing her laundry, it certainly would have had this young lady think about the real world – who would do her laundry once she left home? I believe that the whole approach allowed this young lady to change her sense of entitlement, to one of gratitude for how others make her life better.

3rd Example of this Process: My children could easily get in the habit of doing their chores "half-way," meaning that though they could check off their list, the manner in which the chores were completed were not fully up to the standards established.

What I chose to do was fix a nice pancake and sausage breakfast for them Saturday morning. Now the thing about sausage and pancakes is that you can create a nice brown exterior without the insides being fully cooked. As my children cut into the sausage they saw the pinkness and as they put their forks into the pancakes, the batter oozed out. Their response was that of disappointment, as they questioned me on why I hadn't done a better job.

I said to them (with love in my eyes and a smile on my face), "I don't understand, I thought for sure you would have really liked it this way. After all, it seems that you like lots of things half-way done!" My children smiled and got the point. I encouraged them to do their chores and academics more fully, rather than just looking like they were working. A phrase that my mother used, which signals in our family the importance of doing things well is, "Dust it, don't just dust at it." This is the signal, now passed onto our children, when their efforts need to improve.

284

Hopefully, as the reader of this book, you can see how principles are being taught and reinforced; the creativity being used to teach these lessons and the kindness being exhibited, while teaching, allows the lessons to become internalized, while the children's positive self-concept stays intact.

4th **Example of this Process:** Rock Duty – I had a client that wanted to assist her children in fighting less. She called her children together and told them of her wishes. She also explained that when her children fought that she carried a heavy feeling inside. After inviting them to speak nicely to one another and avoid the pitfalls of arguing, and after having her children demonstrate that they each carried the skills to engage better, this mother explained that she was no longer going to interfere when arguments took place. Instead, she told them that she would just simply keep track of the arguments and then assign rock duty on Saturday.

The family had purchased a home that had rock landscaping, which had become badly disheveled. A good portion of the rocks had become buried in the dirt and so rather than purchase more rock, this wise mother decided to have her children spend time unearthing all of the landscaping rock with hand tools and their bare hands. That first Saturday saw all of her children harvesting the rocks, putting them in buckets and pouring them out in an organized fashion on the backyard cement. The project was so big that it would take many hours to accomplish. The second Saturday also saw each of the children involved in rock duty. By the third Saturday, only two of the children were engaged with harvesting rocks and by the fourth Saturday – no children had earned the privilege, because the arguing had stopped. None of the children wanted rock duty.

Mother saw the opportunity to teach and asked what it was about the rock harvesting they liked the least. "Boring" was one of the replies, but from the smaller children came the reply that "the rocks were heavy to carry." Mother took the cue and talked to her children about how they felt when they quarreled with one another. With some coaxing, mother related their feelings to a heavier feeling that they would carry when they were filled with contention, kind of like the rocks were in the bucket. But then she asked them the feeling they had noticed in the home recently as a result of the diminished arguing. Each of her children were able to recognize a more relaxed atmosphere and better feelings they were experiencing inside.

Of course, this mother also asked which feeling they liked best. Without any exceptions, each child observed that they enjoyed the more peaceful feelings. This mother did an excellent job in tying her children's experiences with their emotions and demonstrated some real creativity in developing consequences that taught rather than punished.

OTHER GUIDELINES THAT MAY HELP

Aside from considering the questions above when trying to form a logical consequence, here are some other suggestions and counsel:

- Responding -vs- Reacting. (Reacting comes from unawareness, i.e., triggering of our own implicit memories, while Responding comes from high awareness of our own internal state, coupled with faith in our children's ability to learn)

  If we as parents still have unresolved issues about our own self-concept; if we haven't done the work to make these issues highly visible to our mental consciousness then we will be parents that will continue to react when our children trigger those unresolved issues. It is imperative that we dismiss the distortions of past experience and learning that interfere in any way with the truth about our standing, our worth, and our potential. For those parents that "overcome" these distortions, such are prepared to *respond* to their children's behaviors positively.

  Otherwise, unresolved pasts will have our unhealthy implicit memory interact with our relationship that may impair our ability to parent well. It does so because of self-concern, or being more driven to be attuned inwardly rather than being free to tune outwardly. It is your presence, your actively being so tethered to your child's experience that leads to healthy responding.

  As our child recognizes that healthy presence, he or she has the benefit of operating from a secure base. All children need a secure base from which to explore and practice life. If their base is filled with criticism, disappointment, emotional withdrawal and other forms of judgment it creates self-esteem issues, greater dependency rather than autonomy, and resentment. On the other hand, when returning to their base they experience respect, support and positive interactions, they will feel secure in themselves. Our added value of continually sending the message that we believe in them allows them to increase their belief in themselves.

- Use consequences as a means to provide new information. (Consequences are not about punishment, they are about teaching correct principles.)

- All consequences must fit the person not the behavior. (A two year old is not a sixteen year old – though the opposite may be true).

What in the world did the author just say? What he said was that we as parents have to understand who we are dealing with. To optimize our interaction we should be aware of brain development, task mastery (what years are associated with mastering which tasks), and a realistic understanding of our child's self-perception.

A tiny slap on a three-year old's hand can be surprisingly effective in the child not repeating an undesired behavior. To do the same to our teen would produce little – except laughter. The younger the child is the more immediate the consequence has to be in time to the unwanted behavior. Younger children would have a difficult time associating a consequence when it is delivered three days after the event. However, our older children will have no problem connecting a consequence that may come much later than the actual poor behavioral choice. For example, there may be an event your child wants to attend the following week – connecting that event (not allowing them to go) with the undesired behavior from the week before provides ample understanding to the older child.

Sometimes older children act younger developmentally than their chronological age. We would do better in providing consequences more suited to their younger emotional development.

Lastly, every child's personality is going to play a role in what consequences will fit them. One child may be motivated by intimacy, for example. If I explain to that child how his or her actions made me feel badly, that may be enough of a consequence because the child wants to have a close relationship. Another child may be motivated by fun. Taking away game time may be a more effective consequence than simply telling the child how I feel about what happened.

- Consequences do not have to hurt; they have to make a difference. (As long as the consequence led to increased learning without jeopardizing the child's self-concept then the consequence was adequate. Don't try and over think it.

- All behavior must be discussed and processed with the child. (This follows the law of associative memory). Repeated returning to principles strengthens the neural circuitry associated with that learning. It is impossible for a child to internalize principles (the process of creating value and self-motivation), with only speaking about a principle one time.

In addition, through the *power of observing* for our child what he or she is experiencing increases the associative memory. Lecturing to our children about right and wrong is an inferior way of having our children learn the connection between behavior and how they experience themselves and their relationships.

Behavior does not define the child and that is the message that they need to hear loud and clear. This truthful message helps shape their own perception and experiences. Many children turn their poor choices into who they are as a person – this is the development of shame. Our message assists with their perception as we are intentionally keeping separate their inherent worth from the poor choices exhibited.

- A recurrence of the behavior does not mean the consequence was not adequate. (Sometimes a child is simply testing your consistency and dedication)

We as parents recognize that impulsivity is directly related to immediate gratification. We become dismayed when our children can't seem to wait for anything or lose control when we tell them "no." One of the best ways to curb impulsivity is by providing experiences that will result in greater blessings or opportunities later, if they can forego the immediate desire to get something now.

Interestingly is that we as parents react similarly when the desired changes in our children's behavior don't come quickly enough. We too become impulsive. We throw the towel in, convincing ourselves that our new approach doesn't work. Remember, our family functioning has created long-term associations in how we interact with each other. Any attempt to change that "comfortable" environment is going to lead to resistance, sometimes even escalation. Our children know what buttons to push because they have been pushing them successfully for years. If suddenly you show that you are not affected by these button pushing attempts, your child does not know what to do, so he or she may escalate the behavior(s), in an attempt to get things back to normal.

There is a term in family systems therapy called "HOMEOSTASIS." This term refers to a family system that is used to a way of functioning, i.e., how they interact with each other, and how when change is presented within the system that some family members are resistant to the change. These members work really hard in getting back to the status quo or *homeostasis*, because they sense they may have greater control or comfort in the old way.

I have worked with many parents in developing the style and interventions discussed within this book and I am happy to say that those that stick with it are amazed at the decrease of contention and stress, and how their children begin to develop the confidence to take greater and greater responsibility for their lives in healthy ways. This was referred to previously in the section, "Learning and Responsibility – Who's is It," wherein was highlighted the understanding that this type of intentional parenting takes greater effort in the beginning, yet becomes less and less involved because the children experience themselves completely differently as the neurological and cellular systems adapt to implicit thoughts of worth, importance and capability.

Our decision to parent this way is not based on what is easiest. Easiest is to become frustrated, yell , nag, ground, take things away, and react in multiple other negative ways when we are not experiencing what we want to be experiencing with our children. Easy, is when through the right kind of focused interaction, our children begin to sense their worth, their capability, and their purpose and begin to act well in association of that which they firmly believe about themselves. That is when parenting becomes super easy, because we have assisted in developing a belief system and a physiology of a healthy implicit memory and we get to watch (observe) the transcendent miracles that occur on a daily basis as they "act" and are no longer being "acted upon" (2 Nephi 2:14).

When a parent that had at one time dealt with their children the *easiest* way and now have dealt with their children intentionally, such a parent will witness how much more exhausting it was to parent the *easiest* way. By parenting from a perspective of what will be most helpful to our children later in life, we no longer parent from the seat of our pants because we know that we are training a belief system that will allow our children to experience life and relationships in a good way. This is the reason why we have them for 18 years – it takes both time and consistency to produce these positive, staying outcomes. Internalization of a healthy implicit memory does not simply occur at a given age or a given moment. Parenting that develops healthy implicit memories occurs in the millions of small moments of healthy, kind and purposeful interactions.

The "ART" of effective parenting is directly tied to understanding human design. Parents, for example, usually spend too much time mentioning the negative behaviors and staying silent when the child chooses appropriate behaviors. The only signals being sent are therefore negative. If you would like to increase the appropriate behaviors then you better get in the habit of recognizing them and making mention of them to your child. Our children love positive strokes, because it is part of their human design to want to feel good about whom they are.

REINFORCE BEHAVIORS YOU WANT TO SEE

Reinforcement could include:

- Positive statements about desired behaviors
- Additional attention given to the child when desired behavior is demonstrated
- Just a simple "Thank you!"

We want to assist the child in *connecting* positive behaviors with positive feelings:

- When the child recognizes this *connection*, the reinforcement becomes internalized.

Now remember, I am dealing with behavior in a way where our children experience having the "law put in their *inward* parts, and writing it in their *hearts...*" (Jeremiah 31:33). These interactions we all have with our children can operate at different levels within them. Hopefully each of us would desire that the beliefs we are trying to instill become woven into the deepest aspects of their understanding and not just at surface levels. This parenting approach is dealing with the core level that creates changes neurologically, at the cellular level and within every receptacle utilized for motivation. Such interaction acts upon belief not just the desired behavioral change.

INTERNALIZATION vs. COMPLIANCE

Which of these *promote self-motivation*? Compliance is usually being directed from an external source. While children may comply due to wanting to avoid a negative consequence or receive a certain reward, parenting becomes exhausting when that is the only way we are interacting with our children to get them to do something or to stop doing something.

When we work toward observing well for our children and connecting their experience with their emotions, children come to value for themselves the positive results that come from choosing well. In observing for our children, *we miss opportunities* to change the negative processes they so instinctively use in order to get what they want. If these instinctive processes are not challenged, our children's implicit memory will be impacted negatively.

Many times it helps to ignore behaviors we do not like. You have to use discernment here, but typically, we can extinguish unwanted behavior by starving it (not feeding or rewarding it). Parents become so frustrated with their children when they have to ask them multiple times to do something. We want them to do it the first time we ask; correct? The problem is that we reward the unwanted behavior by coming back and reminding them, and it is not until we escalate into anger that our child responds.

That is our fault, not the child's. If we set the standard that he or she is expected to do what we are asking the very first time, then we starve or don't feed the unwanted behavior. In extinguishing the negative processes children use to get what they want, we must assist them in developing positive processes that lead to healthier implicit memories and social satisfaction. As our child experiences the greater benefits when choosing positive processes, those processes become internalized. This leads to self-motivation to engage in socially acceptable ways.

One day I was laying on a chaise lounge on our deck by the pool. The children were swimming and I was reading the newspaper. Normal sounds of laughter, splashing and some music were in the background. Suddenly, my youngest son, who was seven at the time, let out a scream that made me come off my stomach. My heart was pounding and my entire threat modulating system was activated. As I looked over toward my son, I noticed his older brother was below the surface of the water and was swimming away from the scene.

When I looked toward the son who had just screamed, I signaled him to come over to me. Immediately he was defending why he had screamed so loudly. I said, "Son, I just want you to come here so that we can talk." He continued to try and explain, but eventually with enough assurance he came over to me. I continued:

Dad: Son, I am sure that the reason you screamed was because you felt like you needed my immediate attention to assist you with your brother who was somehow antagonizing you – is that correct?"

Son: Yes dad. He is always picking on me!

Dad: Well, it doesn't appear that you like it and somehow you probably recognize that you are not as big as he is and so you need someone to be your muscle.

Son: Something like that.

Dad: Well hey, I am sure you probably want me to immediately get on him so that he will stop bothering you.

Son: Would you?

Dad: Before I do I want to first speak about my experience and then I am going to provide a way for you to enlist my immediate help – would you like that?

Son: Yes.

Dad: First of all I want you to know what your scream did to me. I shot out of my skin and I could feel my heart pounding. I don't like that feeling. So this is what you need to know. If you scream like that to enlist my help, you are not going to get it. However, if you would like me to help you, if you will just come over and talk to me about what you would like me to know, I will listen and I will help you immediately. What did you here me say?

Son: That if I yell you are not going to help me but if I come to you calmly you will listen and help.

Dad: Sounds like you got it.

It wasn't but two minutes later, when suddenly I heard my son begin to scream and then as quick as it started, it dropped off and became silent. As he looked over to me he saw that I was not responding to the initial signal. Instead, he walked over and began to explain what was going on and asked for help. In turn, I immediately threw his brother over the neighbor's wall. No, I am kidding – but I did immediately help him to express his thoughts and feelings with his brother, which appeared to have a positive effect.

One of the ways we help our children is by providing more and more resources for them. In the account I just shared, I provided my son with a choice that gave him access to what he needed. I then *ignored* his other way of trying to enlist that help. I gave him an expectation and he was able to learn very quickly how to extinguish the unwanted

292

behavior. As he chooses the desired behavior and I respond to it, I am supporting the behavior I desire and the behavior that will be more effective for him in many other situations.

Not rewarding the unwanted behaviors can be very effective in eliminating such behaviors. One parent weekend at the youth program, I previously spoke about; I had a mother who did not believe that ignoring unwanted behaviors would lead to a de-escalation of those behaviors. "You don't know my daughter," she replied. "She just won't stop until she gets what she wants; she is relentless."

I asked her to be her daughter and I would be her in a role play of this concept we were talking about. She did a wonderful job impersonating her daughter as she immediately set out attacking me, accusing me of not caring, of treating her sister better than herself, etc. I began to *observe* what I recognized she was experiencing, however she responded by not allowing me to speak, cutting me off and denying any thing I was saying to her:

Mom (playing her daughter Aubrey): You are never interested in me. You are always treating Samantha (this was the other daughter) like she could do no wrong. I am sick and tired of being blamed for everything. You owe me. When are you going to take me shopping?

Me (playing mom): Aubrey, it seems as if you are torn up inside because you sense...

Mom: Oh shut up. I don't want to hear you talk. You make me vomit when I hear your ugly voice.

Me: I am here to listen so that I can better understand how ......

Mom: What did I just say? I said shut the (bleep) up! You are so irritating. I hate you!

It was interesting to everyone watching this role play, myself included, as mom really got into this role. Her voice was getting louder; her tones were filled with venom. She really did an excellent job in having us see what she experienced on a regular basis.

In my position as mom, even though I was doing the best I could to connect with my daughter, she would have nothing to do with it. I was continually cut-off from expressing anything. Then suddenly I turned away from this mother, I turned so that she could not see my face. At first this caught her by surprise and she wasn't sure what to do. Then she continued being fouled mouth, becoming angrier and angrier. She became more aggressive. In her attempt to get in front of me, I would simply continue to turn away. Remember, mom said Aubrey was relentless. In attempting to stay in character, mom tried multiple times to get in front of me, but every attempt was met with more turning away. Finally mom stopped. She had exhausted herself. In some way in order to save face, mom said: "Aubrey wouldn't have given up this soon!"

The reality however was that no matter how mom tried to salvage the outcome of that role play, her behavior de-escalated – everyone saw it. She gave in because there was no rewarding response for the ugly behaviors she was exhibiting. I suggested to everyone there that Aubrey's behaviors were in part being fed by the distress on mother's face when these interactions took place. And that is exactly why so many children do what they do is because they see how it is affecting their parents. They usually sense a parent that is in distress and take advantage of that uncertainty.

So, the application may be this - the next time your little child throws a temper tantrum, simply turn around and don't look at them. That child's tantrum is no longer being fed by the distress on your face and now he or she is placed in a position to learn how to get your attention differently. When your child calms down, sit with them and provide other options on how to interact in order to get their needs met.

LIMIT SETTING

In the process of our children learning about the real world, it is our responsibility to provide *limits* that assist in the child practicing delayed gratification. A child that learns to not give into urges of immediate gratification experiences greater happiness than a child that is allowed to indulge consistently.

How much sugar does your child eat everyday? That sugar provides a huge reward in the dopamine cycle – that is why kids crave it. What is the outcome if there is no limit in place?

Recently, on a radio show I co-host, I was interviewing Dr. Art Devaney, a world renowned expert on nutrition and its effects on the brain. He provided an analogy of the effects of glucose on the nervous system. He said, "Imagine you are playing the piano, but while doing so you are spilling sugary items all over the keyboard. As you continue the interaction of pressing down on the keys to play music, you are simultaneously "gumming up" those keys, as you press the sugary foods down between each key where they begin to stick, so the music becomes recognizably distorted or even ineffective." He continued, "The level of glucose our children now ingest (the American diet) mixes with other sustaining substances, such as the fat in our brain. In the process, our nerves begin to be coated with a very sticky and gooey substance that is now interfering with optimal nerve conduction." In other words, the brain is trying to perform its duties, but begins to experience delays in synaptic firing, or even worse is unable to continue signals between cells at all. What does that look like? It looks like inattentiveness, spacyness, lost motivation and disinterest. It looks like disorganization, inability to complete tasks, moodiness and lack of personal responsibility. That's what it looks like when we are not placing reasonable limits around eating sugary foods. Of course I am speaking of the effects of glucose simply on the brain – its negative effects on the entire body are well documented.

How much texting does your teen do every day? The texts he or she receives back releases dopamine – that is why he or she indulges (6000 + texts each month). What is the outcome if there is no limit in place?

Children that become highly attached to their phones are doing just that, developing a relationship with their phone instead of a person. This sets in place a cascade of negative outcomes because we are not designed to be in a relationship with things, we are designed to be in a relationship with others.

What may look like as a link to the social world in large part turns out to hamper the very outcomes that come from being with others. Minimally, the impact of excessive texting is for the child to experience not so many nice things said about them. There is more negative communication that comes across in the form of texting than ever would in face-to-face interactions. The reason being is just that – people find it easier to be rude when they don't have to look at the person.

This excessive ugliness impacts the recipient's social confidence and such begin to struggle about self-concept. One of the greater impacts we see with youth that are excessive and consumed with their phones is greater isolation. Many young people turn the phone into the medium for connecting with others. The problem is that a sense of self-acceptance can only be activated by face-to-face interactions with others. It is in the non-verbal cueing taking place between two people where one can see themselves reflected back. A phone does not have eyes that are highly specialized to match emotional states. It is in the eye contact where one sees their worth, their beauty, and general acceptance. It is in the tone of voice where one is able to put meaning to words being directed toward them. It is in body posture, touch, gestures and other non-verbal cueing that tells us whether we are safe with someone else.

The phone has no capacity to provide these necessary collaborative types of communication, which act with our own internal states giving us a sense of identity, purpose and calmness. Whether this is true or not, I don't know, but I heard that some missionaries, when entering the Mission Training Center begin to develop anxiety or even depression as a result of losing contact with their phone. To assist these missionaries, they are provided a small block of wood (about the same size as a phone) that they place in their pocket providing a transition while they go from excessive use to no use.

Whether that is true or not - it would make perfect sense, as anxiety (denial) and depression are hallmark symptoms that humans experience due to loss of important relationships. Excessive phone users develop neural networks and continual releases of neurotransmitters that have them become attached to their phone. When, for whatever reason they lose that connection they literally grieve, just as we would do if we lose a loved one through divorce or death.

What is the outcome if there is no limit placed on dating? What is the outcome if there is no limit placed upon daily schedules? What is the outcome if there is no limit placed upon eating? What's the outcome if there is no limit placed upon spending? What's the outcome if there are no limits placed upon...... I think you are getting the picture.

Some children view limitations as restrictions of their freedom or as a form of parents trying to control them. It is important that we shape their perception so that they can begin to understand that limits are in place in order to maximize the best outcomes. Limit setting is often viewed as keeping behavior in check. *In its most positive light, limit setting is more about moving toward something positive* than about keeping the child from doing something negative.

Your children will understand when you invite them to get on their bike and ride five miles down a very busy street, ignoring any red lights or stop signs. The stop light and stop sign are forms of limitations that allow for positive outcomes.

When we analyze the roles we play, limit setting is coaching. It's being on the sidelines offering suggestions while the child plays the game.

The following *Guidelines for Effective Limit Setting* are adapted from the work of Foster Cline (Cline and Fay, 1990):

GIVE THE CHILD CHOICES, USUALLY TWO!

- In limit setting, when we provide the child with choices, we offer opportunities for them to practice decision-making skills.
- When we offer directives to set limits (i.e., when we just simply tell the child what to do), we are denying the child the opportunity to make decisions to change their behavior.
- By giving them choices, it promotes self-monitoring and behavioral choice that fits the youth's emotional growth

PROVIDE CHOICES THAT PROMOTE POSITIVE OUTCOMES

- These choices should be true choices as opposed to forced choices. Often the choices we provide result in a lose/lose situation.

    For example:

    a. "You can help set the table or be grounded," is a forced choice and does not necessarily move the child to a positive outcome.
    b. "You can help set the table or put away the groceries," is a true choice and provides the maximum opportunity

STATE CHOICE POSITIVELY

You can frame limit setting in a positive tone and put the responsibility for making the choice on the child. Examples of this may include:

    a. You're welcome to have _____ or _____.
    b. Would you rather _____ or _____?
    c. Yes, you may _____ or _____.

WIN/WIN EXAMPLES

    a. Mom, I'm hungry. [Limit Setting]: "You may have an apple or an orange"

b. This is an exciting weekend for me because of the snowboarding trip on Friday and the dance on Saturday. [Limit Setting]: "Son don't forget that mom and I will be going out this weekend, so you are going to have to choose. Would you rather go snowboarding or go to the dance? We will work around your choice."

c. I can't wait to get out this weekend and go four-wheeling with my perfect boyfriend. [Limit Setting]: "Honey, our conversation about how the bathroom is expected to look plays in your ability to have that time with dream-boy. So yes you may go four-wheeling or you may be cleaning the bathroom with him this weekend – it's up to you."

NOTE: When giving choices, remember, only give the choices when you are able to allow the child to experience the consequences of those choices.

When responding to their decisions, keep in mind that they are practicing and need feedback. When the choice works well for them, recognize it, comment on it, and applaud them. When the decision they make does not work out well, empathize with them. Empathic words focus on circumstances, the resulting feelings, and on natural consequences.

SOME EXAMPLES

In each of the following examples, take time to consider what may be some of the natural consequences resulting from the choices your children make. Remember, natural consequences are usually much more effective teachers. However, some natural consequences may be too extensive and too costly to bear. See if you can identify those situations that may be better suited to implementing logical consequences.

While I only give some idea of what a natural or logical consequence may look like, remember everything you have learned about *observing* and *encouraging* your children when handling the situations. Observing for our children in each of the scenarios will assist them in becoming empowered to see what has led to the unwanted behavior. Every skill spoken about in this book will assist in having these creative consequences become tender moments of teaching, learning and reinforcing positive belief systems.

Here are the scenarios:

1. Child does not leave T.V. to come and eat dinner with the family

Natural Consequence: Child goes to bed hungry. (Note to parents that do not like to see their children suffer – There has never been a reported death due to a child missing dinner)

Logical Consequence: The T.V. gets sold on Ebay.

2. Child doesn't do chores

Natural Consequence: The child deals with living under the conditions that result from lack of cleaning. These could include a smelly room, having to wear dirty clothes, being unable to find things because everything is so messy, embarrassment when a friend comes over and reacts negatively to your child's living conditions, etc.

Logical Consequence: Quarantine the bedroom and bathroom for two days, explaining that your child is not allowed access to either and may not use any other bathroom in the house. Watch how resourceful your children become at this point.

3. Child doesn't do homework

Natural Consequence: I like when a child has consequences that deal with real world institutions. I would wait and see how the school handles this situation. Most times, when the child has to become accountable to an institution rather than to parents, that institution can produce some pretty undesirable consequences. The benefit is that the parents are not the enemy because it is not the parents that are meting out the consequences.

Logical Consequence: Tying an activity that the child really finds enjoyable to the performance of homework. An example may be driving privileges.

4. Child is late from an outing with friends (i.e. curfew)

Natural Consequence: Child may not get enough sleep that night and be tired the next day

Logical Consequence: For every minute they were late they have to be in 15 minutes earlier than the established curfew next time they go out or you could simply say: If you are late, even one second late, you will not have car privileges for six months.

5. Child gets into a fight at school

Natural Consequence: The pain of any injury received as well as again dealing with the institution's consequences for fighting behavior.

Logical Consequence: If my child started the fight I would make tee-time reservations to play golf (usually a five hour activity) and upon arrival at the golf course surprise my son with our playing partners, i.e., the person he fought with and his dad. I believe after five hours of golf will provide a good environment for my son to get to know that peer, likely resulting in increased good feelings.

6. Child damages property in home

Natural Consequence: If it is something that belongs to him or is used by him on a regular basis (i.e. his bed, his closet clothes bar, his bedroom wall or window) then it stays that way until he fixes it.

Logical Consequence: If it affects the entire family, then he is responsible for its repair. He is not allowed to do anything else until the repair is complete.

7. Child runs away from home

Natural Consequence: It depends upon the age of the child. If in adolescence, then whatever those consequences that naturally come (i.e. sleeping on the ground, not having food, etc.) If a younger child I would not allow a natural consequence.

Logical Consequence: For a younger child, I would run away with them. At some point, your child is going to want to eat, I will respond by saying, "Honey, I didn't bring any money to get something to eat. What do you think we should do?" Likely your child will suggest that you both return home.

8. Child is caught looking on the computer at pornography

- Second time
- Third time

How would you handle it? Will your child come away feeling better about themselves?

On this last issue, I would love to hear from you. You may send an email to:

familyskillscenter@gmail.com

When you do, I will send you my thoughts on the matter. In addition, I will share your information with other parents.

CONCLUSION

The great human need is to:

1) Be understood; to know that others care about our internal experience
2) Feel like we are included; that we are loved and thought of in a positive way
3) Experience consistent feedback that has us know that we matter, that we are important, that we have something to offer to others; all of which informs our purpose
4) Know that our worth is inherent, that it remains constant, and that it is equal to every one else's
5) Sense our true capacity to accomplish and achieve, that through our faith and effort, we can meet the challenges and opportunities that will come to us
6) Have meaningful, healthy, reciprocal and supportive relationships
7) Learn about one's true identity by following the impressions that come through the Light that is in each of us.

If each of these needs is fully realized in our children, they will have developed wonderful, empowering personal beliefs. May we always remember that we have the largest influence in helping our children do so. Every interaction we are having with them is sending them a message (SIGNALING). Let us be intentional and purposeful in our parenting to send them those messages that will have them come to believe well of themselves.

The blessings of doing so will produce children who experience tremendous peace. The reason for the blessing of peace being the *natural* result is because these are the truths about our design and existence. These are the truths that Heavenly Father is trying to have us see in ourselves. If we will listen, each of us will have been taught of the Lord (Isaiah 54:13). As parents, Heavenly Father works through us in bringing to pass the implicit memory of these truthful beliefs in our children.

We stand in position and rank with apostles and prophets in carrying the burden of this great message to our children. We are on the front lines. We were called for this weighty assignment. God sustains us in our calling – never doubt that. Now go and do the greatest work we will ever be invited to do. Raise children of peace by influencing healthy and truthful belief systems. The Gospel of Jesus Christ provides the foundation to do so as it provides the TEMPL (ate) wherein we are constantly taught of our true nature, purpose and potential.

I look forward to your feedback as you apply the knowledge that is increasing in the earth (Daniel 12:4). Take the science and nature of human design and apply it. As has been experienced by Gods (Psalm 82:6), if you observe and watch your children well, you will see their increase in obedience (Abraham 4:18) and the development of personal beliefs that promote obedient behavior, not just during the time you have them, but throughout all eternity.

The journey of developing truthful belief systems, in any of us, not just our children, is just that – a journey. That journey is much more enjoyable and filled with patience when we can see promises "afar off" and become "persuaded of them" (Hebrews 11:13). When we are persuaded that the revelations concerning our potential is real, enduring to the end is observed as a daily activity that will one day lead to the fulfillment of the promises foretold. Living well day-by-day makes the journey more fulfilling.

As we work in partnership with the Almighty in this great endeavor of parenting, may we always remember that we cannot do it all – but we must be willing to do our part:

> "Therefore, dearly beloved....., let us *cheerfully* do all things that lie in our power; and then may we stand still, with the utmost assurance, to see the salvation of God, and for his arm to be revealed." (D&C 123:17)

Appendix A

NAVIGATING SCRIPTURAL REFERENCES

Before we begin the undertaking of learning, it is important that the reader be able to navigate some of the information that is found in parenthesis, located at the end of various sentences in support of a concept or principle being discussed. Most of these end of sentence parenthesis are in relation to scriptural references.

Some that will be reading this book will be unfamiliar with where to find the information being referenced, so the following is provided as a guide in doing so.

Latter Day Saints have as their Standard Works the following:

The Holy Bible

The Book of Mormon

The Doctrine and Covenants (Abbreviated as D&C)

The Pearl of Great Price

If the reader does not have access to these books in their own home and do not want to go and purchase them, you may also go to lds.org to find the references. On the home page you can click on "Scriptures" and then click on the main Standard Work from which the reference is drawn.

The Bible, Book of Mormon and Pearl of Great Price are formatted similarly in that each book is usually named after the author of the book. So if the Old Testament is referenced you would find the book, (i.e., Daniel 12:4) by clicking on Old Testament, then clicking on Daniel, followed by clicking on Chapter 12 and then reading verse 4.

If the reference is unfamiliar to you, then likely you will find the reference in the Doctrine and Covenants (D&C), Book of Mormon or Pearl of Great Price. For example, while Moses and Abraham are both prophets found in the Old Testament, there is no book named after them found there. References from Moses or Abraham are found in the Pearl of Great Price. On the website you would click on "Scriptures" then click on "Pearl of Great Price" and then click on Moses or Abraham (depending upon the reference), clicking on the chapter and then reading the verse(s) indicated.

The Book of Mormon is referenced throughout the text, so please make yourself familiar with the books contained therein by clicking on "Scriptures" and then clicking on "Book of Mormon." The list of authors is shown and you can navigate from there as you have done with the Bible and the Pearl of Great Price.

The remaining Standard Work is the Doctrine and Covenants (D&C). This book is divided by sections (i.e., D&C 88:40). After clicking on "Scriptures," click on "Doctrine and Covenants." Below you will find the word "Sections." Click on that and then click on the corresponding numbered section and then read the verse(s) that are indicated.

This book will mean more to you if you will take time to read the corresponding scriptural reference when it appears. Doing so will create greater understanding and appreciation for the information being presented.

Also at times I reference Latter Day Saint leaders. Each reference contains the information from which quotes were drawn. Many of the quotes come from General Conference talks. Again, turning to lds.org and on the home page, click on "Teachings" and then click on "General Conference." On the presenting page look to the left column and you will find "All Conferences." Click on it and you will arrive at an archive section. If the reference you are searching says for example: (The Greatest Challenge, October General Conference, 1990), click on "1990" and then click on "October." There you find the talk in its entirety under the title provided in the reference, in this case, "The Greatest Challenge." You may find that reading the talk will provide even more resources in pursuit to becoming the best parent you can become.

Appendix B

KINGS AND QUEENS

As has been clearly stated several times throughout the text of this manuscript, our children develop a sense of their identity in large measure by the way they perceive we view them. If they detect that we are annoyed with them or don't believe in them, then their identity formation will be less than stellar. On the other hand, if we can view them in terms of capability and inclusiveness, then they will thrive and become resilient in the face of life's challenges.

There is a scene recorded in the scriptures where Jesus is standing before Pilate and is asked by the Roman Procurator, "Art thou a king then?" In answer to that simple question, Jesus replies, "To this end was I born, and for this cause came I into the world, that I should bear witness unto the truth" (John 18:37). Jesus is speaking in terms of His own identity. He is aware of the truth of who He is. His life and ministry bear all of the markings of being a righteous, valiant King.

But what if you and I were standing before Pilate and he asked us the same question? What would be our reply? If we have been paying attention to the scriptures our answer should be the same (Revelation 1:6; 2:26; 5:10; D&C 76:56).

Let me elaborate a bit more on what I am trying to help parents understand by looking at some other events spoken of in the scriptural account. There are repeated accounts found throughout the scriptural record, where ministering angels are sent to converse with men on earth. It is common to find in these events an experience or reaction of the mortals being visited. We tap into this reaction because of the words that come from the heavenly visitor, "Fear not..." (Luke 1:13; Luke 1:30; Luke 2:10; Matthew 28:5). What is it about the appearance of the ministering angel that causes humans to have a fear response?

I would like to suggest that the angels appear in their true identity, which would include the glory of their being. I believe it is their glorious appearance that has mortal men sit-up and take notice – a stark realization of the difference in contrast of our viewing other humans. At times, this glory may even cause mortals to fall to their knees, signifying the desire to worship the beauty and majesty of the special visitor.

> And I John saw these things, and heard them. And when I had heard and seen, I fell down to worship before the feet of the angel which shewed me these things.

Then saith he unto me, See thou do it not: for I am thy fellowservant, and of thy brethren the prophets, and of them which keep the sayings of this book: worship God. (Revelation 22:8-9)

This particular visitor identified himself as a fellowservant and prophet with John. Whether he was a prophet that had previously fulfilled his ministry or was a prophet that had not yet been born and fulfilled his ministry (Jeremiah 1:5), is not made clear. What is clear is that the true form and identity of each of us is that we radiate with light and glory, which has the propensity to cause mortal eyes and understanding to be overcome with a desire to worship.

In support of this concept, there is this one account that has us understand that perhaps our true identity is veiled because of the mortal body.

Had you and I lived in the days of Jesus and we were His disciples, I think that we would have been impressed by the things we would have witnessed. His ability to heal all sorts of ailments and disabilities; to raise men from the dead, to discern people's thoughts and motives, to increase mere morsels of food into feasts for thousands; and His ability to simply speak and have earth's raging elements take notice and obey his words would have left an indelible mark on our hearts and minds.

Yet it was Isaiah that pointed out what most would experience when beholding the Mortal Messiah, as He would have "no form nor comeliness; and when we shall see him, there is no beauty that we should desire him" (Isaiah 53:2). While dressed in his mortal veil, we would have experienced this Jesus in many of the same ways we experience others of the human race, ordinary, and perhaps nothing really spectacular when viewing Him.

Yet in the midst of the human population that had experienced Him, there were three that had the opportunity to see Him in His true identity, a moment which would have each bear a testimony of this sacred experience in which the mortal veil had been drawn back. Matthew records:

> And after six days Jesus taketh Peter, James, and John his brother, and bringeth them up into an high mountain apart,
>
> And was transfigured before them: and his face did shine as the sun, and his raiment was white as the light.
>
> And, behold, there appeared unto them Moses and Elias talking with him.

> Then answered Peter, and said unto Jesus, Lord, it is good for us to be here: if thou wilt, let us make here three tabernacles; one for thee, and one for Moses, and one for Elias.
>
> While he yet spake, behold, a bright cloud overshadowed them: and behold a voice out of the cloud, which said, This is my beloved Son, in whom I am well pleased; hear ye him.
>
> And when the disciples heard it, they fell on their face, and were sore afraid. (Matthew 17:1-6)

Peter, James and John had beheld the glory of the Savior. They witnessed that His glory was greater than that of the sun which caused his whole being to shine with radiance. They each saw Him for a moment in His true identity. As with other special manifestations and appearances previously spoken of, the reaction of these three are the same, they fell on their faces being overcome by fear. How had these apostles been affected by this experience? I would like to suggest at least one way – they never looked on Him again simply as an ordinary being. Later, we hear of Peter's fervent testimony concerning Jesus, said he:

> For we have not followed cunningly devised fables, when we made known unto you the power and coming of our Lord Jesus Christ, but were eyewitnesses of his majesty.
>
> For he received from God the Father honour and glory, when there came such a voice to him from the excellent glory, This is my beloved Son, in whom I am well pleased.
>
> And this voice which came from heaven we heard, when we were with him in the holy mount.

I provide the foregoing to have us consider how we are going to view our children –

1. through the limitations brought on by mortal veiling
2. or in their true identity and purpose of their being born?

All of our children are the sons and daughters of a Heavenly King. If they enter into the covenant or are born under the covenant, they become princes and princesses, heirs to the same kingdoms promised to Abraham, Isaac and Jacob (Abraham 1:2-4; Genesis 17:3-7; Abraham 2:8-11).

The promises are that through the power of the Melchizedek Priesthood, faithful covenant keepers will receive grace to grace, including receiving the coronation ceremony or endowment, wherein they will be washed and anointed to become Kings and Queens, rulers and lords in their respective spheres (Revelations 1:6; 5:10). Such divine outcomes should have each of us view our children for who they really are and what they can become. In the revelations to us, the Lord states of those that remain true to their covenants:

> They are they who received the testimony of Jesus, and believed on his name and were baptized after the manner of his burial, being buried in the water in his name, and this according to the commandment which he has given—

> That by keeping the commandments they might be washed and cleansed from all their sins, and receive the Holy Spirit by the laying on of the hands of him who is ordained and sealed unto this power;

> And who overcome by faith, and are sealed by the Holy Spirit of promise, which the Father sheds forth upon all those who are just and true.

> They are they who are the church of the Firstborn.

> They are they into whose hands the Father has given all things—

> They are they who are priests and kings, who have received of his fulness, and of his glory;

> And are priests of the Most High, after the order of Melchizedek, which was after the order of Enoch, which was after the order of the Only Begotten Son.

> Wherefore, as it is written, they are gods, even the sons of God—

> Wherefore, all things are theirs, whether life or death, or things present, or things to come, all are theirs and they are Christ's, and Christ is God's. (D&C 76:51-59)

When we develop the capacity to see our children as they may become, our interactions with them will naturally improve. More importantly, when we consider their potential and the calling that has been given to us to influence their belief in who they really are, it humbles us knowing the weight of responsibility we have been entrusted with.

Our children's ability to fulfill the measure of their creation is dependent upon what they believe. Our children need to hear, both through action and word that they are valued, that they are beautiful, that they are worthwhile, and capable. If they come to believe these things then they will have the capacity to see beyond themselves and attune to others. Service, willingly given, is a marker of a healthy, personal belief system.

If our children are older and have struggled, we need to understand that change is a built-in process that emerges when individuals change their attitudes, their thoughts, behaviors and beliefs. Bad habits can be forsaken, repentance is possible and natures can change.

One of the ways these changes occur is in the environment we establish that gives them the opportunity to live as they should. This whole book has provided the backdrop to what that environment should look like. As we develop the capacity to see our children for who they can become, our interactions with them will align with such vision. May we as parents have the courage to try and try to interact with them in a manner that speaks of their glorious nature. May we, through humility, seek the guidance from our Father in Heaven as we fulfill our calling as parents. If we shall approach our children in this regard then the promise shall be fulfilled, which states:

> And that same sociality which exists among us here will exist among us there, only it will be coupled with eternal glory, which glory we do not now enjoy. (D&C 130:2)

One aspect of us not enjoying the glory now, is likely associated with the mortal veil that covers each of our glorious states. May we look beyond the mortal veil and see our children as the Kings and Queens they were born to become!

Appendix C

DEFENDING THE FAMILY

The world events unfolding in the coming months is not about terrorism, or plagues, or the overthrow of world leaders; or the latest technology that impinges upon our freedom. It is not about global resources shrinking; or high ranking officials making legal of that thing which societies have carefully guarded for years, recognizing that certain societal behavior, if allowed, weakens nations, communities and individuals. No, the design of forces combining are doing so for the purpose of destroying the family (Ephesians 6:12; Alma 43:9, 45-47).

The Book of Mormon prophets speak directly about similar forces they faced in their day. The combined forces of evil did all in their power to bring down institutions that promulgated the value and importance of families. Their attacks were masqueraded in terms of sophistry to allure the support of society against those that stood for families (Alma 48:10).

In order to properly prepare for the ongoing and impending action, President Gordon B. Hinckley prophetically instructed:

> "A better tomorrow begins with the training of a better generation. This places upon parents the responsibility to do a *more effective* work in the rearing of children. The home is the cradle of virtue, the place where character is formed and habits are established...." (In Opposition to Evil, Ensign Magazine, First Presidency Message, September 2004)

The doctrine that families are meant to have an eternal bond and destiny is a doctrine that has generally been lost to the world. The purpose here is not to defend this doctrine, but to simply assume its merits in having us see why the battle is for the family.

The family provides the entryway into mortality, and does so because of the inherent differences found in male and female characteristics. The characteristics go far beyond the biological differences. The nature and disposition of both male and female qualities work together in a complimentary manner, providing a wholeness that is evidenced throughout the universe.

The blessings that flow to us because of the family is part of Heavenly Father's plan in fulfilling His desire to bring to pass the immortality and eternal life of His children (Moses 1:39). It is in the family where principles are taught, where character is formed, where learning takes place. It is where vital data is transmitted that produces belief that one has a destiny. If this process breaks down in the family it will have serious side effects to society at large.

May we, that are reading this book, recognize that we can still righteously influence generations to come by our willingness to uphold the family in its intended creation. Let us not absorb the sophistry of our day which will bring calamity upon individuals and families who adhere to its subtlety. Instead, let us see things as they really are and as they really will be. Elder Bruce D. Porter reminded us of the tremendous blessings of developing an eternal family, said he:

> We gain happiness and salvation not by blindly pursuing our own self and our own will. We gain salvation by submitting our will, indeed our very selves, to the will of God. We must lose ourselves to find ourselves.
>
> The family by its very nature is an institution based upon righteous self-denial and sacrifice. It is not an individualistic or self-centered organization, but a highly cooperative and other-centered institution. Successful families require that men and women make substantial and long-term sacrifices of their time, money, and personal fulfillment in order to dedicate their efforts to rearing the next generation. Selfishness in any form or degree weakens the bonds that hold families together. The rise of selfishness in our society is the fundamental underlying trend that undermines families and makes successful marriages so difficult. Many today find it irrational to devote so much time and energy to the welfare of the next generation, but if this commitment is not deeply rooted in society, civilization will decline and perish, while children grow up in a moral wasteland, confused, unguided, and unloved.
>
> Moreover, the sacrifices that fathers and mothers make for their children ultimately will result in the greatest possible happiness for those making the sacrifices. In all of human experience, there are no joys more tender, no love more sweet, no fulfillment higher than that found in the family. Those who honor the calling of righteous parenthood will find their souls refined, their hearts purified, and their minds enlightened by the most important lessons of life. They will rise to far greater heights of happiness than those who engage in the narrow and ultimately unsatisfying pursuit of self. (Defending the Family, Ensign, June 2011)

May each of us keep this truthful perspective and fulfill our role as righteous parents, by teaching our children to believe in their eternal destiny.

Made in the USA
San Bernardino, CA
28 September 2018